Technology, Gender, and Power in Africa

Patricia Stamp

INTERNATIONAL DEVELOPMENT RESEARCH CENTRE
Ottawa • Cairo • Dakar • Johannesburg • Montevideo • Nairobi
New Delhi • Singapore

First edition 1989

© International Development Research Centre 1989
PO Box 8500, Ottawa, Ont., Canada K1G 3H9

Reprinted 1990, 1993

Stamp, P.

IDRC-TS63e

Technology, gender, and power in Africa.   Ottawa, Ont., IDRC, 1990.   x + 185 p.
(Technical study / IDRC)

/Women's role/, /technology transfer/, /social change/, /Africa/ — /women's rights/,
/decision making/, /self-help/, /economics/, /research needs/, /organization of research/,
/references/.

UDC: 396:001.92(6)   ISBN: 0-88936-538-5

Technical Editor: W.M. Carman

A microfiche edition is available.

Abstract / Résumé / Resumen

Abstract — This book demonstrates that the study of gender relations and the power of women is central to an evaluation of development efforts in Africa. The interactive relationship between technology transfer and gender factors is explored using case studies and examples from the development literature on agriculture, health, and nutrition, as well as from feminist scholarship on Africa. Faulty approaches to the topic and biases at all levels of policy-making have led to ineffective or even harmful projects. Insights about the significance of gender factors do not easily cross the boundaries between different fields of inquiry. Part I presents the different conceptual frameworks within which the topic has been considered. The fields of African studies, women's studies, and development studies are critiqued, and useful approaches are identified. The invisibility of gender in development studies and aid practice is explored at length. Part II examines the research findings of African women to identify the factors that either render women powerless and disadvantaged or create the conditions for their authoritative participation in development. Part III identifies issues and interrelations that have not been addressed in previous research and suggests promising ways to frame future research on women and technology in Africa. The social, economic, and technical empowerment of women at the community level is seen as vital to effective development efforts.

Résumé — L'auteure montre que l'étude des rapports des sexes et le pouvoir de la femme sont au coeur de l'évaluation des efforts de développement en Afrique. Elle explore l'interaction du transfert technologique et des facteurs liés au sexe à l'aide d'études de cas et d'exemples tirés de la littérature du développement en agriculture, santé et nutrition et de l'ensemble de connaissances sur le féminisme en Afrique. De fausses approches du sujet et les préjugés dont sont empreintes les politiques à tous les niveaux ont entraîné la réalisation de projets inefficaces, voire nocifs. Les idées sur la signification des facteurs liés au sexe ne franchissent pas facilement les frontières entre les disciplines. Dans la partie I, l'auteure présente les différentes perspectives dans lesquelles le sujet a été étudié. Elle fait la critique des perspectives études africaines, études des femmes et études sur le développement et indique des perspectives utiles. L'auteure s'étend longuement sur le fait que le rôle des sexes soit passé sous silence dans les études sur le développement et dans l'aide au développement. Dans la partie II, elle se penche sur les résultats de la recherche sur la femme africaine pour déterminer les facteurs qui la rendent impuissante et la défavorisent ou créent les conditions favorables à sa participation autoritaire au développement. Dans la partie III, l'auteure s'arrête sur les questions et les interrelations qui n'ont pas encore été étudiées et suggère des perspectives intéressantes dans lesquelles placer les futures études sur la femme et la technologie en Afrique. L'auteure estime que l'acquisition d'un pouvoir social, économique et technique par la femme au niveau communautaire est essentielle à l'efficacité des efforts de développement.

Resumen — Este libro demuestra que el estudio de las relaciones entre los sexos y el poder de las mujeres es fundamental para evaluar los esfuerzos que se hacen con el fin de desarrollar a Africa. En sus páginas se explora la interacción entre la transferencia tecnológica y los factores relacionados con ambos sexos utilizando estudios y ejemplos extraídos de la bibliografía del desarrollo sobre agricultura, salud y nutrición, así como del conocimiento feminista sobre Africa. Enfoques erróneos sobre el tema y prejuicios en todos los niveles de formulación de políticas han conducido a proyectos inefectivos o incluso dañinos. Los conocimientos acerca de la importancia de factores relacionados con el hecho de pertenecer al sexo masculino o femenino no se transmiten fácilmente entre diferentes campos de estudio. En la Parte I se presentan los diferentes marcos concetuales de trabajo dentro de los cuales se ha considerado el tópico. Se hace una evaluación crítica de los campos de estudios sobre Africa, las mujeres y el desarrollo y se identifican enfoques provenchosos. Se explora extensamente el papel invisible que ha desempeñado el sexo en los estudios sobre el desarrollo y en las prácticas de prestación de ayuda. En la Parte II se examinan los resultados de la investigación realizada sobre las mujeres africanas con el fin de identificar los factores que las despojan del poder y las dejan en situación de desventaja o bien crean las condiciones para que participen con pleno derecho en el proceso de desarrollo. En la Parte III se identifican cuestiones e interrelaciones no tratadas en investigaciones anteriores y se sugieren maneras promisorias para enmarcar investigaciones futuras sobre las mujeres y la tecnología en Africa. La concesión de autoridad a las mujeres en los niveles social, económico y técnico de la comunidad se considera como vital para que sean efectivos los esfuerzos en la esfera del desarrollo.

Contents

Foreword

It is only in recent years that researchers have started to examine the relationship between technology and gender. This report was originally prepared for a meeting entitled "Gender, Technology, and Development: A Diagnosis of Available Literature," which was held in New York, 26–27 February 1989. Jointly sponsored by the Rockefeller Foundation and the Health Sciences Division of the International Development Research Centre (IDRC), the meeting brought together a small group of developing- and industrialized-country researchers and specialists to discuss the gaps in the literature on the connections between health, agriculture, gender, and development.

One of the key findings of this meeting was that, for most women in the developing world, technology has failed. Attention was focused on health-related technologies aimed at nutrition, control of reproduction, and improvement of child care, and on agriculture-related technologies including mechanization, higher yielding seed varieties, fertilizers, pesticides, herbicides, food processing, plant breeding, and genetic engineering. It was recognized that most of the technologies that have been developed have not served effectively. Frequently, they are not being used, are being used sporadically, or are being used incorrectly. For the most part, these technologies have been developed on the basis of Western models and Western notions of what people in developing countries want and need. Technologies are not neutral — they are value-laden from beginning to end.

This book explores the relationship between technology, power, and gender. It provides an extensive review of the literature and makes many thoughtful suggestions for more effective and appropriate technology development and use. This book will undoubtedly be a valuable teaching and research tool for scholars, planners, and students involved in development.

Eva M. Rathgeber
Coordinator, Women in Development Unit
International Development Research Centre

Preface

This book emerged from a joint project of the International Development Research Centre (IDRC) and the Rockefeller Foundation. In 1986, the two organizations commissioned a number of studies on gender, technology, and development in the Third World: this publication, in its first version, was one of them. The study was to focus on the ways in which different types of community organizations in Africa, both indigenous and externally imposed, influence the introduction and sustained use of agriculture-, health-, and nutrition-related technologies. The report of the study was to cover the following four areas: existing conceptual approaches to the subject, major research findings highlighting areas of consensus and disagreement, issues and interrelations that have not been addressed in previous research, and promising ways to approach the topic for future research.

The work expanded considerably during substantial revisions in 1987 and 1988, developing certain lines of inquiry and including more references. While adhering to the original structure shaped by the four areas outlined above, this book has a wider focus, covering everything from technology transfer to a wider array of questions about the women in development (WID) enterprise. It is hoped, therefore, that this publication will be of use not only to those specializing in technology transfer but also to a more general audience of scholars and practitioners concerned with gender and development and, indeed, with Third World political economy.

Acknowledgments

I owe special thanks to several people at IDRC. Richard Wilson, Director of the Health Sciences Division, and Eva Rathgeber, Coordinator of the Women in Development Unit, supported and encouraged me at different stages of the endeavour. Margo Hawley, Reference Specialist in the IDRC Library, entered the literature search with enthusiasm, imagination, and efficiency, ensuring me access to a wide variety of material. In Toronto, my Research Assistant, Vuyiswa Keyi, provided valuable assistance in tracking down sources and in shaping the questions to be asked of the literature. My deepest appreciation goes to my husband, Stephen Katz, for his perceptive suggestions, tactical assistance, and his support of the intensive electronic cottage industry that writing of this kind has become.

Introduction

Technology, according to Achebe (1983), is "an attitude of mind, not an assemblage of artefacts." The experience of Third World societies with Western technology over the past 25 years has proven the wisdom of this statement. The massive transfer of technology, both as artefact and as information, has often been accompanied by misuse, misallocation, or misunderstanding in the recipient countries. In particular, it has generated negative consequences for women, children, and communities — nowhere more so than in Africa.

Whose fault is this? The issue has been debated in an endless series of publications and conferences written or sponsored by donor agencies, academics, and nongovernmental organizations. To answer the question and to get beyond blaming either the givers or receivers of the technology, we must take Achebe's (1983) idea a step further and understand technology as a social construct and a social practice — the product of a particular society's history. At the same time, we must recognize that new technology, arising from the political and economic needs of a particular era of development in a particular society, generates new forces of production and new social relations. In other words, technological artefacts are the raw material created out of historical experience, which, in turn, recreates society.

In the Western world, because technological advance and economic development have gone hand in hand, we do not see the historical and cultural specificity of our artefacts, instead viewing them as neutral objects, the inevitable products of progress "stacked conveniently for ease of lifting" (Achebe 1983). We may now be starting to question the effects of certain technologies — from computers to pesticides — on our society and environment; on the whole, however, we still see technology as a physical rather than social presence. Those who do argue that technology is a social construct, such as environmental groups, are not easily heard, given this dominant perception of technology.

For this reason, it is difficult for us to understand the problems of technology transfer in the Third World. Third World leaders and experts themselves, recruited to our vision of technology as a socially neutral force, have also been stymied. Critics within Third World countries rarely find a politically legitimized means of challenging this vision. Therefore, an inquiry into the problems of technology transfer must pay careful attention to the conceptual frameworks that shape the understanding of relations between the developed and the developing worlds. In particular, the way in which these frameworks define the problems of the Third World must be critically examined.

Fortunately for Third World development and our understanding, gender has become an issue. The feminist imperative has forced the search for answers to two key questions regarding technology transfer. First, it must be asked if the outcome envisaged is really development. Unless women and — by intimate but not previously self-evident implication — children are unequivocally served, society itself has not been served. 'Appropriate technology' initiatives, for example, have often been inappropriate for women. The great achievement of feminism in the past 15 years has been an emerging moral and scientific commitment to the truth that women are half of humanity and that gender relations are as fundamental a shaping force in society as are economic relations or political structure. Indeed, there is no political economy that is gender neutral, as those who are willing to look discover. In development discourse, women are no longer entirely invisible, even if they still get far from equal time.

The second question is closely related to the first. Because of the push to evaluate technology transfer in the light of gender questions, it must be asked if Third World social reality has adequately been taken into account in technology-transfer schemes and studies. It is no longer possible to view technology as artefact or to avoid the difficult task of examining our underlying assumptions about Third World societies. The scientific accuracy of each development study, or the degree to which it is value laden, can be tested by asking whether gender has been properly accounted for.

It is with these questions that this book is preoccupied. Implicit in the mandate of the study is an understanding that technological change is a social process. We cannot investigate this process, however, without considering the dialectical relationship previously discussed. Each element of technological innovation that has been introduced, whether transferred from the Western technology complex or designed for the perceived needs of Third World communities, carries with it assumptions regarding the proper social organization for its use. Community structures, from family to women's organizations, therefore, have not been inert recipients of the technological freight; rather, they have either actively reconfigured themselves to the requirements of the technology, or they have rejected or redirected the intended use of the technology. Only where the technology transfer has been designed on the basis of real needs, as perceived by the recipients, and on fully understood social relations has the technology clearly achieved its purpose.

In Africa, agriculture, health, and nutrition are largely the responsibility of women. Therefore, successful technology transfers in these fields are those that empower women, strengthening rather than weakening their community involvement and their decision-making authority in the village and the family. All too often the reverse has been true, with profoundly negative consequences. The new technology has not had its desired effect and, moreover, African women have found themselves with increased workloads, a more subordinate position within the family, attenuated communal life with other women, and lost rights to resources. These circumstances compromise women's abilities to fulfill their traditional production, health, and nutrition responsibilities, not to mention their new, development-linked responsibilities. Yet previous studies have tended to focus on technology adoption to the exclusion of questions of "technological maintenance and operational control" (Bryceson 1985:8). From such a perspective, it has been possible for many studies to construe the village and family as obstacles to technological change rather than as active participants in its acceptance, modification, or rejection. Furthermore, this approach has rendered invisible the effects of technology on social relations.

It is for this reason that planning efforts supported by development agencies have so often failed. Mohammadi (1984:80), of the Economic and Social Commission for Asia and the Pacific, asserts that "in every respect, attempts to sensitise planners and reorient national planning processes to increase women's participation have not yielded significant results; whereas, training women for participation in local-level decision making and planning has had surprisingly quick and strong impact." Nowhere is such participation more important than in technology-transfer issues: women, who are the primary producers and 'caregivers' in African communities, are the key users of the technology that has the most direct impact on the economic well-being, health, and nutrition of African families.

This book will thus pay particular attention to the dialectical nature of technology transfer, a process that can either disequip or empower village women to engage in genuine development. It will go beyond preoccupation with the moment of transfer to consider the complex ways in which new technology and society interact. Furthermore, the study will assert that the problems new technologies are designed to solve are themselves frequently a social construct. Africa is not naturally hungry, drought stricken, short of fuel, and diseased. As Doyal (1979:100–101) says with regard to disease, "contrary to common belief, [the] diseases of underdevelopment are not necessarily bound up with tropical conditions in the geographic or climatic sense. Cholera, plague, leprosy, smallpox, typhoid, TB [tuberculosis] and many intestinal parasites have all thrived in western Europe in the past." Contemporary health problems "must be seen not as a 'natural' and unavoidable part of life in the third world"; rather, they should be viewed as a consequence of specific historical developments. By shifting the technology-related problems of agriculture, health, and nutrition from the realm of the natural to the realm of historical and sociological analysis, we may engender a more scientific and optimistic approach to their solution.

The literature on women and development in Africa makes it abundantly clear that an understanding of national and international political economy is necessary to explain the processes working to disadvantage women and undermine development. The link between international markets, commodity production, and male control of cash crops, for example, with its concomitant negative effects on the economic and political participation of women, has been documented in numerous studies. The two chapters in Part I chart the development of the relevant fields of knowledge within the different loci of research and action and point to the different constructions of the problem of technology, gender, and development. An important dimension of this overview, treated in Chapter 1, is a review of the development of feminist inquiry as a new field challenging conventional social science assumptions and a consideration of the relationship between this new field and African studies. In Chapter 2, the continuing invisibility of gender in a number of the research/action loci is explored; next, the special problems and opportunities of health and nutrition research are surveyed; and, finally, the sources of challenge to conservative views regarding development, particularly challenges from African women (often supported by progressive elements in multilateral and bilateral agencies), are identified.

Part II, which surveys research findings, focuses primarily on the local community, where the subtle interaction of technology and gender can be explored. Bryceson (1985:8) comments that, in most of the existing literature on women and technology, "male domination in its cultural and institutional sense, is treated as an historical given fact. Having identified the extent and incidence of the edge that men have over women in the acquisition and control of technology, the analyses rarely offer an in-depth dissection of its nature." A major reason for the problem Bryceson (1985) identifies is the lack of historical and cultural specificity in much of the women and technology literature. Such specificity can be found, however, in the work of a small group of social scientists, including anthropologists and historians, who have done much to explain gender relations in different African societies. Chapter 3 explores the issues regarding technology, gender and development around which a consensus has emerged in the women-in-development (WID) and women-and-technology literature. Chapter 4 explores analyses of African gender relations that can provide a context for considering the issues presented in Chapter 3. The first part of Chapter 4 is an analysis of gender relations in Africa by way of a case study on women's self help groups in Kenya. In the course of this analysis, an argument is made for a particular approach to the subject of gender relations in Africa: feminist political economy (the term is introduced and explained in Chapter 1). Synopses of two studies by African feminist scholars in the second part of Chapter 4 substantiate the case for this approach.

A major purpose of this book is to show how the combined insights of WID research and feminist political economy might become the basis for future research on technology transfer. A boundary problem exists not only between areas of scholarship that do not adequately interact but also between policy networks, which frequently have been unable to take mutual advantage of each other's insights. According to Patricia Kutzner of the World Hunger Education Service (WHES) (personal communication, 1986), the inability of the food policy network to draw resources from the women's studies network is a case in point. Part III, therefore, addresses new issues and interrelationships that might direct future research and overcome the limitations of past approaches. Chapters 5 and 6 set forth the issues and relationships, giving examples to demonstrate the efficacy of the approach being suggested, and exploring the conceptual problems identified in the literature. Chapter 7 outlines five tasks, each using a different method, as possible concrete ways to frame the topic for future research.

This study has several necessary parameters. One is geographic: Africa north of the Sahara is excluded from the review. Although there is no sharp boundary between Black and Arab Africa, and many arguments can be made for historical and cultural continuity between the two, it is an accepted convention in African studies to treat "Black Africa" as a distinctive geographical and cultural region. For all its diversity, "Black Africa" shares common historical themes and environmental opportunities and constraints. African societies have developed common responses to these opportunities and constraints, as their ancestral people, divided into four major linguistic groups, populated the continent during several thousand years of successful migration and settlement. Later, during the mercantile and colonial eras, they shared the experience of serious human losses and blows to their economic and political integrity at the hands of the Europeans. Central to the nature of African society before colonialism was a prominent role for women in economic production, and a concomitant socioeconomic and ideological position that, while subordinate to that of men, appears to have been considerably more favourable than that of women in other regions of the world. Since then, women have seen a loss of their traditional autonomy and authority. One of the fundamental tasks of development in Africa today is to discover ways in which women may regain their decision-making powers and control over resources.

A second parameter is linguistic: English-speaking Africa is the basis for this study, both to limit the material reviewed and because of less proficiency in French than I would care to admit. I would argue, however, that although different colonial and postcolonial strategies have led to some different directions for Francophone and Anglophone Africa, and although the French intellectual tradition has led to some different theories and emphases in research, the language of colonialism did and does not make for substantial differences in the experiences recorded here. Examples are taken from many countries to illustrate both the problems and the fruitful lines of inquiry to be found in the literature. Case studies are derived from two countries in particular: Kenya and Nigeria. There are large bodies of scholarship on each country, produced by both foreign and indigenous researchers. Each has significant work on gender relations and women's position. Both countries exemplify the problems and opportunities for women inherent in contemporary African gender relations and both countries have examples of pastoral and agricultural societies facing the dilemmas of development. There are several important differences, however. One is the much greater degree of urbanization and the extensive involvement of women in trade in Nigeria. A further difference is the substantial presence of Islam in Nigeria; Kenya has a much smaller proportion of Muslims, religious affiliation being largely Christian. A third difference pertains to research on women and gender, an abundance of medical studies have been conducted in Nigeria; there is a relative paucity of such studies in Kenya. However, numerous sociological and anthropological studies, including some excellent theoretical work, have been conducted in Kenya; Nigeria's record in the social sciences is less exciting.

A third parameter excludes consideration of women's participation in the developed technology represented by factory production. Particularly in South Africa and Swaziland, women are being drawn into the type of light industrial wage labour that has been so well documented in Southeast Asia. Shifts over the past 20 years in the international division of labour have increasingly shunted production in such sectors as electronics and textiles to countries that can provide multinational companies with cheap — usually young, female — labour. Africa is not immune from this trend, and the implications for African women are potentially profound, as they have been elsewhere.

Exploration of these implications is, however, beyond the scope of this study. This publication, focusing on agriculture-, health-, and nutrition-related technologies, draws attention to the predominantly rural character of African societies. Whereas rapidly expanding cities have received much attention and industrialization is an important topic of analysis, the majority of Africans have seldom, if ever, encountered advanced industrial production. For women, in particular, problems must be identified and solutions sought at the local level. The wider technical issues that could be explored in the significant literature on urbanization, industrialization, and women and labour in Africa must, therefore, be left to another author.

The final parameter is a more haphazard one: the quantity of literature on

5

technology and development on the one hand and on women and development on the other hand is so huge that no literature review can encompass, let alone comment meaningfully upon, the entire body of work. This study does, however, present an account of the writing that to the best of my knowledge accurately represents the different schools of thought, approaches, and contents comprising the literature. The reader will notice that there is no categorization of the literature by African and non-African authorship. As the review reveals, Africans contribute to each of the conceptual frameworks; ethnicity and race do not form any basis for classification. There is no "African approach" — although there are African concerns about Western domination of African thought.

It is not the intention of this study to denigrate all technology transfer. Indeed, there are many cases of technology being adopted successfully, and to their great benefit, by women and communities — from safety pins and sewing machines to wells, mills, and cattle dips. The mandate of the IDRC/Rockefeller Foundation project, however, was to address the problem of understanding technology and gender in Africa, not to celebrate technological wonders for the Third World. Consequently, a major portion of this book is directed at how and why technology transfer fails and what might be done to make it succeed.

Part I

Conceptual Frameworks

1   The Fields of Knowledge

The problem regarding technology and gender in Africa is not a lack of knowledge, but the fact that the knowledge is fragmented. Understanding is structured by different conceptual frameworks derived from the different concerns and orientations of investigators in different professions, organizations, and fields. Furthermore, in much of the literature on Africa, technology is treated, if at all, incidentally or descriptively, as an artefact rather than as an active social force. Only by surveying the general conceptual frameworks can we uncover the assumptions underlying different explanations of technology, gender, and development. In the following review, it becomes evident that in many explanations a relationship between gender and technology has not been conceptualized at all.

Another dimension of the fragmentation of knowledge is the existence of different loci of research and action regarding Third World development in general and technology transfer in particular. Knowledge generated within each locus is not always easily shared or even sought by the other loci, although researchers and policymakers move between the loci as individuals, bringing insights and information from one to the other. The loci may be classified into five groups: academic research, multilateral agencies, bilateral research and development agencies, nongovernmental organizations (NGOs), and African governmental institutions.

For the purpose of this study, academic research may be classified as either Western or African and Third World research.

There are four types of multilateral agencies. First, there are the United Nations agencies such as the International Labour Organisation (ILO); the Food and Agriculture Organization of the United Nations (FAO); the World Health Organization (WHO); the International Research and Training Institute for the Advancement of Women (INSTRAW); the Economic Commission for Africa (ECA); the United Nations Institute for Training and Research (UNITAR); the United Nations Children's Fund (UNICEF); the United Nations Development Programme (UNDP); and the United Nations Educational, Scientific and Cultural Organisation (Unesco). Second, there are the financial agencies such as the International Bank for Reconstruction and Development (IBRD, the World Bank) and the International Monetary Fund (IMF). Third, there are the African regional organizations such as the Organization of African Unity (OAU) and the African Training and Research Centre for Women (ATRCW). Last, there are the other multilateral agencies that do not fall into any of the above categories such as the International Fund for Agricultural Development (IFAD) and the Commonwealth Secretariat.

The bilateral research and development agencies include organizations such as IDRC; the Canadian International Development Agency (CIDA); United States Agency for International Development (USAID); Swedish International Development Agency (SIDA); Danish International Development Agency (DANIDA); Research Centre for Cooperation with Developing Countries (RCCDC, Yugoslavia); and Centre for Development Research (CDR, Denmark).

Nongovernmental organizations may be broadly classified as either Western organizations or Third World and African organizations. Western organizations include foundations, church organizations, and special-purpose agencies such as the Equity Policy Center, International Planned Parenthood Federation, and Centre for Development and Population Activities (CDPA); umbrella organizations such as the Canadian Council for International Cooperation (CCIC) and WHES; and research institutions such as Isis International (for a useful survey of NGOs and development agencies, governmental and international, see Isis International 1983). Third World and African organizations include the Association of African Women for Research and Development (AAWORD); Development Alternatives with Women for a New Era (DAWN group); and country organizations such as Women in Nigeria (WIN), Maendelao ya Wanawake (Kenya), Women's Action Group, Zimbabwe (WAG), Women's Research and Documentation Project, Tanzania (WRDP), and Babikar Badri Association for Women Studies, Sudan.

African governmental institutions include ministries responsible for rural development, women's affairs, etc. (e.g., Zimbabwe's Ministry of Community Development and Women's Affairs) and government agencies, such as the Kenya Women's Bureau.

None of these loci can be characterized by a single conceptual framework. Nevertheless, each locus participates in a particular set of visions regarding the nature of technology-transfer problems that must be seen in the context of broad developments in social science knowledge over the past 20 years.

The most familiar classification of approaches is the spectrum of assumptions regarding the causes of underdevelopment (the condition that creates technology transfer as a problem for Africa). At one end of the spectrum are many African governments, Western governments, and institutions such as the IMF and the World Bank, who believe that Africa's problem is a lack of modernism in all its aspects, that integration into the world economy is the route to development, and that any policies or societal structures that prevent such wholesale integration are obstacles to progress. In other words, the problem of technology is constructed as the problem of overcoming the obstacles to its adoption. At the other end of the spectrum are those who believe that such wholesale integration has created a dangerous dependency that is itself the source of the problem, in that it serves the international capitalist order and not the developing Third World society.[1] In other words, the problem of technology is constructed as the problem of limiting its negative impact and rendering it responsive to social needs. This view is espoused

---

[1]Dependency and underdevelopment theories have a complex history, stretching from the pioneering work of Frank (1967) and Baran (1968), through the African contextual applications of Amin (1972), Leys (1975), and Rodney (1972), to the nutrition activism of George (1977, 1979) and Lappé (1978, 1980). In the past 10 years, there have been variations on dependency theory such as the dependent development of Evans (1979); other scholars, such as Taylor (1979), have challenged the theory for its economism, arguing instead for a 'modes of production' approach. Some of the arguments of this important area of scholarly debate are dealt with in the following pages.

by some African governments, leftist political economists, and an increasing number of Third World feminists.

Less familiar is the spectrum of assumptions regarding the nature of the gender problem in the Third World. Feminism, which has provided much of the energy for the critique of development planning in the last 15 years, is itself a problematic issue. The media image of the Western feminist movement has often been negative, portraying women as grasping individualists, concerned only for their own well-being and not for their family, menfolk, or society. African and other Third World women have often distanced themselves from Western feminist goals as they perceive them.

Setting aside the popular prejudices against and stereotypes of feminism, it is possible to categorize feminist thinking to determine what is and what is not relevant to an understanding of African gender relations and the problems of development. Resistance to feminist theory and research by planners, policymakers, and many Third World women stems from the confusion of radical feminism, which is ideologically based and polemical in its approach, with other forms of feminism, which have a more thorough grounding in social science analysis. It is radical feminism, with its assertion that the oppression of women is biologically based and supersedes all other forms of oppression, that has been selected by the media and popular prejudice to represent all feminism. The argument that all women have been oppressed by all men throughout time and across all cultures is pessimistic, politically unpalatable, and scientifically unsound; it has created an easy target for a sexist backlash against more reasoned feminist positions.

The more reasonable feminist approach has been to describe and theorize the precise ways in which women were and are oppressed in most human societies. The aim has been to generate models for change based on more egalitarian experiences of the past, and on the democratic principles of the present. The following review surveys the emergence of women's studies as a field of inquiry in the past 20 years. On the one hand, the review charts the diverse experiences that led to the different theoretical frameworks in Western feminism; on the other hand, it charts the emergence of feminist concerns within the field of African studies — itself a developing area of social science. The review reveals that radical thinking about women is not necessarily left wing (i.e., concerned with issues of social justice and redistribution of resources); conversely, radical political economy is not necessarily feminist (i.e., concerned with issues of gender equality and women's rights). Furthermore, radicalism of both kinds can be guilty of ethnocentrism and can share mistaken assumptions about non-Western societies with mainstream development thinking.

For the purpose of theoretical clarity and for the benefit of researchers and policymakers seeking to make sense of gender issues and to develop tools for structuring empirical evidence, I propose that we should identify a new perspective that has emerged to explain African gender relations. *Feminist political economy* is the term I give to the small but rigorous body of writing embodying this new perspective. Although it is based in certain Western scholarly traditions, the perspective avoids the ethnocentric biases and conceptual errors of those traditions. Central to the development of this framework is the work of certain Third World feminist theorists.

Women's studies and Africa: a history

In North America, both women's studies and African studies have a common origin in the popular movements of the 1960s and early 1970s. The ideological impetus provided by the civil rights and antiwar movements in the United States fueled the inquiry into both women's oppression and neocolonialism in the Third World. African studies itself was generated by a desire for a nonracist understanding of African civilization. The new opportunities for women scholars at this time, combined with the powerful ideology of the women's movement, blew the doors of academia open and led to the questioning of the very premises of Western social science, not to mention its methodologies and conclusions.

The first spate of feminist writing in the early 1970s was popular, enthusiastic, and from the gut; some of it was wildly radical. On the one hand, women took the skills and knowledge gained during their liberal education in the 1960s and used them to critique that education and its sacred texts (Millett 1970; Slocum 1975). On the other hand, they took the radical political activism of the 1960s and turned it in a new direction. The sexism of antiwar activism in particular ("women make coffee, not revolutions") triggered the women's movement and its supporting literature — from *Ms.* magazine to the *S.C.U.M. (Society for Cutting Up Men) Manifesto* (Solanas 1968) and *Sisterhood is Powerful* (Morgan 1970) . It is important to mention this nonacademic movement because out of it flowed the energy and directions for the different feminist schools of thought that matured in the late 1970s and 1980s.

The second stream of feminist writing emerged immediately out of the first: this was the academic movement toward women's studies. Established scholars and graduate students conventionally trained in different disciplines turned to feminist inquiry. Those of us who initiated the first women's studies courses in the early 1970s had to comb the literature for useful texts. A course on African women had to rely on the rare nonsexist anthropological studies such as Cohen (1969), a collection of French articles hastily put into paperback (Paulme 1971), and the now-classic survey by of Boserup (1970). The shortage of materials forced us to do our own research (Van Allen 1972; Stamp 1975–1976) and to anthologize our own texts and special journal issues (CAAS 1972; Bay and Hafkin 1975; Hafkin and Bay 1976). Some of this work began to critique mainstream social science, but most of the work of the early 1970s was within the liberal tradition of "adding women on" rather than presenting coherent challenges to the social science corpus. It was vital work, however, providing the critical mass of evidence necessary for new theories of gender relations.

As for the relations between the activist and academic feminists, the two groups were having different life experiences on the whole and, thus, formed two distinct feminist political cultures. Third World scholars in particular were not centrally involved in the issues and struggles of the activists. It was only when North American activist attention turned outward to the Third World in the late 1970s (the Women's Decade having much to do with this change), that "established" women's studies scholars were forced to face the other feminisms (for criticisms, see Davies 1983; Morgan 1984).

In African studies, the 1960s and early 1970s were also a time of liberal scholarship. The sociology of development, or modernization theory, following the tenets of Rostow (1971), perceived society as on a linear path between the 'traditional' and the 'modern.' This concept saw indigenous economic, social, and ideological practices as obstacles to progress, which was constructed as a cumulative process of expansion. Microlevel studies focused noncritically on the problems of the family and of urban life, often isolating them from larger political and economic processes (e.g., Hanna and Hanna 1971).

This work had little to say about women, except that they occupied the sphere of the 'traditional': it was only in this context that they were considered legitimate subjects of analysis. Out of this liberal tradition, however, arose a radical critique of developmentalism. In Africa, the critique led to a new political economy that endeavoured to generate more accurate and powerful analyses of past and present conditions. African political economy began in the early 1970s, when several scholars, inspired by the Latin American school of underdevelopment theory (e.g., Frank 1967), began to recast Africa's problems in the historical context of colonialism and the international capitalist economic order (see Amin 1972; Rodney 1972). It was not long before underdevelopment theory was also criticized. Although it opened up the possibility of analyzing the economic exploitation of the African 'periphery' by the colonial and postcolonial 'metropolitan centres,' it perpetuated a static and ahistorical view of Africa's internal relations. In particular, the approach was not adequate for understanding the class relations that developed in African countries in the colonial and postcolonial eras. By the mid-1970s, dependency debates were in full swing (for a summary of these debates, see Kaplinsky et al. 1980).

Scholars now turned to Anglophone and French Marxist theory in their quest for a more rigourous understanding of African political economy. Neo-Marxism, a development of the 1960s in Europe, had overturned the "vulgar Marxism" that dominated the era between the 1930s and the 1960s. "Vulgar Marxism," with its reductionist focus on the class struggle of advanced capitalism, had been of little use in the analysis of African societies, where a very different form of capitalism had developed. The French structural Marxism of the 1960s, translated into English in the 1970s, was a particularly useful tool for the new political economists of Africa. The provocative theories of Althusser (1971, 1977; Althusser and Balibar 1970), Poulantzas (1973, 1978), and Laclau (1977) challenged Africanists to develop more sophisticated analyses of the complex relations between the economic, political, and ideological aspects of society. The aim of much of the work produced during this time was to create theories about the nature of African political economy that relied less on Western models than earlier studies, both Marxist and non-Marxist, had done.

There were two closely related lines of inquiry within the new school of thought; together, they succeeded in generating a more accurate understanding of African political economy, past and present. One school explored the nature of the colonial and postcolonial state as it related to emerging capitalist classes (see Leys 1975; Mamdani 1976; Shivji 1976; Saul 1979; Kitching 1980; Stamp 1981). The debates on the state were carried out largely by political scientists. Another related line of inquiry explored the concept of "mode of production" in the African context and sought to develop an understanding of the ways in which precapitalist modes of production were articulated with capitalism in the colonial era (e.g., Mamdani 1976; Taylor 1979; Katz 1980). Anthropologists and historians were the most preoccupied with mode-of-production theories. The work of these scholars has yielded a rough consensus regarding the nature of society before colonialism. Africa is now considered to have been characterized by two modes of production: a tributary mode of production underpinning the trade-based kingdoms of the continent and a communal mode of production characteristic of Africa's numerous small-scale, kin-based societies (Amin 1972; Terray 1972; Coquery-Vidrovitch 1977; Crummey and Stewart 1981).[2]

Theories regarding Africa's contemporary mode of production have been more contentious. Many argued for the notion of "articulated modes of production," where elements of precapitalist modes are articulated with the dominant, capitalist mode of production that characterizes Africa today. Although there has been sound criticism of the notion of articulated modes of production (see CAAS 1985), there is general acceptance of the idea that precapitalist elements are retained in a dominated and distorted form in the service of capital accumulation. One such transformed and distorted element is ethnic identity; the theory thus rescues the concept of "tribe" from the realm of timeless, primordial conflict (another retained element is the sex-gender system; see Chapter 4). A wealth of studies on the peasantry also relies on the theoretical insights of this line of inquiry (e.g., Bernstein 1977).

Analyses of the state and of modes of production combine to produce a theoretical understanding of contemporary African class relations. In Africa's nascent class structure, there is neither a strong bourgeoisie nor a strong working class. The two main opposing classes of capitalism in Africa are thus not bourgeoisie and proletariat as in the Western model, but a dependent bourgeoisie and the peasantry.[3] In the field of politics, however, Africa's diverse and vibrant petty bourgeoisies have had a voice and impact out of proportion to their numbers. These classes began to form early in the colonial era around the new occupations created by the colonial government and economy. Made up of African traders, civil servants, professionals, and white-collar workers, the colonial petty bourgeoisies soon became politically active and economically significant. It was from among their ranks that the new indigenous bourgeoisies emerged after independence. Today, the petty bourgeoisies challenge the economic dominance of these new ruling classes, as they challenged the colonial bourgeoisies of the past.

The *Review of African Political Economy* (ROAPE), founded in England in 1974, was a crucial forum for the different Africanist debates discussed above. In it, for the first time, appeared a coherent analysis of African development problems based on an historical analysis of indigenous political and economic processes, as well as on an understanding of Africa's relations with the West through the mercantile, colonial, and postcolonial eras. Women, however, were largely invisible in this political economy school of thought (e.g., Lawrence 1986). With a few socialist feminist exceptions (Conti 1979; Sacks 1979; Bryceson 1980), work on women was left to liberal scholars, or relegated to anthropology or sociology

---

[2]There is a debate regarding appropriate terminology for precapitalist modes of production. For example, Sacks (1979) terms the latter "kin corporate mode of production"; Meillassoux (1972) labels it "domestic mode of production." For its simplicity, I prefer, as does Mamdani (1975), "communal mode of production."

[3]Some political scientists who worked within the political economy tradition have rethought the emphasis on capitalism and are returning to investigation of earlier concerns, such as clientilism and the problems of theorizing the personal rule that characterizes many African societies (see Sandbrook 1985).

readers on women and to 'women's panels' at conferences, where it was largely ignored.

It was these liberal scholars, who had been steadily conducting empirical field research throughout the 1970s, that saw the value of the new political economy. Their work described both the complexity of African gender relations and the declining position of women in recent years. Although their studies were not theoretically grounded in historical materialist method, they appropriated some of the insights of political economy in their attempts to explain the oppression of women. In particular, the concrete circumstances of African life observed by these scholars prompted them to challenge the assumptions underlying developmentalism's traditional–modern model of progress (see Elliott 1977; Staudt 1978; Buvinic et al. 1983; Lewis 1984; Afshar 1985).

The feminist scholars working on Africa in the 1970s and early 1980s also drew on insights from the theoretical debates on gender, production, and reproduction (in both the biological and social sense) that burgeoned in the West during this time. Of particular relevance were the questions, what is patriarchy? and is patriarchy a valid unifying concept for understanding women's oppression? These questions were argued vociferously in the West (see Barrett 1980; Duley and Edwards 1986). These debates, however, did not capture the attention of Africanists. The largely empirical thrust of research in Africa did not yield coherent theoretical frameworks, as in the West, and the understanding of the position of women and of gender relations, in general, remained rather fragmented. By the 1980s, however, two opposing positions on African gender relations had emerged in the literature. Some scholars talked about an egalitarian past for African women and charted women's "lost political institutions" and the decline of their autonomy and power from colonial times on (Van Allen 1976; Okeyo 1980; Muntemba 1982a; Stamp 1986). Others took an opposing position, promulgating a more negative approach to the past and a more optimistic vision of the present and future. They, too, saw colonialism and class structures as oppressive of women, but argued that women had always been oppressed in Africa. Such studies promoted the prospect of women being released from their traditional bondage once neocolonial and class oppression were overthrown (Urdang 1979; Cutrufelli 1983). Meanwhile, Third World scholars, including African women, were beginning to make their voice heard, particularly with regard to their dissatisfaction with Western "intellectual colonialism." Western feminists were seen as being as guilty as mainstream academics in this regard (AAWORD 1982, 1983).

Feminist theories: a classification

From our current perspective, we need to consider how to organize this great outpouring of ideas in a way that is useful for exploring African gender relations. Specifically, we should investigate how to put the new African political economy to work for feminist scholarship. Conversely, the work done in Africa and elsewhere in the Third World has been a test for the theories and assumptions of Western feminist theory, and we should consider the ways in which Third World feminist scholarship has contributed to the theoretical field.

The most useful rallying point for this dual exercise is the work of an imaginative, synthesizing American feminist theorist, Alison Jaggar. Jaggar (1977)

14

developed a "classification of feminist theories," which she has expounded in an undergraduate textbook with Paula Rothenberg (Jaggar and Rothenberg 1984) and in a major theoretical work (Jaggar 1983). Although the boundaries between her "feminist frameworks" are to some degree arbitrary and unfixed (as she admits), the classification is grounded in a clear understanding of the historical context of each school of thought. First, she analyzes the conservative, sexist traditions in scholarship, from Freudianism to the sociobiology of Wilson (1975), that feminists have challenged. Conservatism, which reaches back as far as Aristotle in social thought, has argued that a sexual division of labour and gender inequality are natural, whether God given, in our genes, or psychologically inherent. Jaggar (1977, 1983; Jaggar and Rothenberg 1984) then surveys four feminist frameworks: liberal feminism, radical feminism, traditional Marxism, and socialist feminism. The following discussion builds on Jaggar's frameworks, pointing out their limitations and opportunities for the cross-cultural study of women.

Liberal feminism

Liberal feminism has its roots in the social contract theories of the 16th and 17th centuries, with their ideals of liberty and equality based on man's rationality and the premise of a sharp demarcation between public and private spheres. Taking Wollstonecraft (1792) as its starting point, liberal feminism looks to Mill and Taylor (1851) for its inspiration. Arguing from the principles of the social contract and the rights of the individual, this feminism adds women on, basing its call for equal opportunity and equal rights upon the claim that "women, too, are rational" and, hence, worthy of being the beneficiaries of the social contract. In this framework, inequalities of wealth and power are not questioned: there is no critique of the structures of oppression that created sexist ideologies and inegalitarian laws and practices. The primary object of any study in liberalism is the individual; groups are construed as collectivities of individuals, and the notion of contradiction within a wider societal structure is usually absent.

Liberal feminism flowered during the First Wave of feminism in the late 19th and early 20th centuries, and was revitalized by the activism of the 1960s. It continues today as a significant force for legal reform and women's political participation, and its reformist vision inspires the struggles of many Third World feminist politicians, jurists, and academics. This is the feminism that motivated the United Nations Decade for Women and, because it did not challenge underlying assumptions regarding the structural causes of gender relations, it has proved an acceptable basis for reform in many Third World countries. The document that emerged from the end-of-decade United Nations conference in Nairobi, Kenya, *Forward-Looking Strategies*, exemplifies this point in its call upon governments to "identify the impact that unemployment has on women; provide employment equity programmes; provide equal access to all jobs and training for women; improve the conditions and structure of the formal and informal labour markets; recognize and encourage the small business initiatives of women; provide and encourage the establishment of child-care facilities; and encourage, through education and public information, the sharing of responsibilities for child and domestic care between women and men" (O'Neil 1986:20). It is under this umbrella that the major proportion of WID research (including the work on women and technology) has been carried out.

15

Radical feminism

Radical feminism exploded into being as a reaction against the sexism of the 1960s radical movements. Fundamentally ideological in its impetus, radical feminism does not offer a coherent theory. Rather, it is eclectic, borrowing concepts and language from several traditions. Notably, radical feminism uses Marxist language, applied analogically to women's oppression (Firestone 1970). Herein lies the great confusion created by radical feminism: a theory explaining women as an "oppressed class" appears Marxist but, in a rigorous sense, is not Marxist. Furthermore, it allows for an ahistorical approach to women's oppression. The premise that patriarchy is universal, preceding and superseding all other forms of oppression, obscures the cultural diversity and historical specificity of human societies. In addition, like conservatism, radical feminism reduces gender relations to a natural division based in biology. Yet the notion of global patriarchy has a powerful appeal to feminists and continues to compete for scholarly allegiance. As such, it impedes feminist progress in understanding and acting upon the oppression of women, particularly in the Third World.[4] It is in this realm that Western feminism stands accused of ethnocentrism. The moment of truth occurred in 1980 when African women walked out of the Copenhagen mid-decade conference because the Western feminists presumed to lecture them on clitoridectomy as a "barbaric patriarchal custom."

Radical feminism has made an invaluable contribution, however, precisely because of its ideological power. Because it is a direct response to women's experience in Western society, its critique of, and action on, Western sexism is highly relevant. Particularly important is its work on sexual violence and pornography (e.g., Brownmiller 1976). It has also led the crusade against sex tourism in Asia. Above all, it contributed the insight that "the personal is political," thereby creating the political space within which gender relations could become a legitimate subject of analysis. The legitimation of sexuality as an issue has led to several important cross-cultural studies on the subject that go beyond the limitations of radical feminism (see Ortner and Whitehead 1981; Caplan 1987).

Traditional Marxism

Traditional Marxism has, since Engels' (1884) important treatise on the family, private property, and the state, rejected the idea of a biological basis to gender differences. Scholars interested in social revolution (e.g., in Mozambique or Cuba) sought to apply Marxist theory to an understanding of women's oppression. Not interested in either Western feminist struggles or the liberal Third World scholarship on women, they argued that women's oppression is a function of class oppression, which supersedes all other forms of oppression (Urdang 1979[5]). Such an approach is fatally flawed in its reductionism: gender relations are reduced to relations of production. Critics of the application of "vulgar Marxism" to gender

---

[4]Coward (1983) engages in an exceptional critique of the use of the concept over the past century. Her study, which is an 'excavation' of the discourse on patriarchy, suggests that the patriarchy debates have deflected us from clear understandings of the family and of gender relations.

[5]In this and more recent studies, Urdang has performed a valuable service in describing colonial and independence government policy toward women in Portuguese-speaking Africa. She has also given vivid, insider accounts of the struggle of women in these societies (e.g., Urdang 1985).

relations have argued that Marxist theory is "sex blind" and incapable of theorizing the autonomy of gender relations in human society (Hartmann 1981). The contribution of this framework, however, is its insistence on a shift from a focus on the individual, which characterizes both liberal and radical feminism as well as conservatism, to a focus on the structures of oppression: state, family, and class. Furthermore, theoretical Marxism provides the underpinning for the fourth framework, socialist feminism. We should note that few feminist scholars now work from a strictly traditional Marxist understanding of gender relations.

Socialist feminism

Socialist feminism has proved to be the most theoretically fruitful of the feminist frameworks. Its value lies in its synthesizing approach. According to Jaggar (1983), socialist feminism combines the rigorous, historical, materialist method of Marx and Engels with the radical feminist insights that "the personal is political" and that gender oppression cuts across class lines. Through this synthesis, Marxist concepts are expanded to take account of the specificity of gender relations, and the biological reductionism of radical feminism is transcended.

> Socialist feminists have their own view of the problem of women's oppression. As they see it, a contemporary individual's life experience is shaped by her sex and gender assignment from birth to death. Equally, however, they believe that an individual's experiences are shaped by her class, race, and nationality. The problem for socialist feminism, then, is to develop a theoretical account of these different types of oppression and the relation between them with a view to ending them all.... In answering the questions that it sets itself, socialist feminism...seeks the underlying reasons for women's subordination in human praxis, in the way that people in each society organize to produce and distribute the basic necessities of life. Socialist feminists, like traditional Marxists, believe that politics cannot be separated from economics. Consequently, their project is to construct a political economy of women's subordination.
>
> (Jaggar 1983:134)

Unlike traditional Marxism, however, socialist feminism does not commit itself to the position that economic oppression is more fundamental than gender oppression; neither does it give priority to gender oppression, as does radical feminism. The framework draws widely from cross-cultural and historical studies, which provide the empirical raw material for a rigorous theorization of gender relations. It is no accident that anthropologists and historians are at the cutting edge of theoretical inquiry within the framework. Of particular value are studies that explore the complex articulation of gender relations and relations of production in precapitalist societies (e.g., Etienne 1980; Leacock 1981).

It should be noted that although Jaggar's (1983) terminology is widely accepted, some confusion remains in that certain scholars identified as socialist feminists according to their theoretical orientation claim to be Marxist feminists. Indeed, the boundary between more orthodox Marxist analysis and socialist feminism is porous. Beyond a certain point of utility, preoccupation with precise designations can obscure more than it clarifies.

17

Studies of gender relations in contemporary Third World societies pose a more significant challenge to Jaggar's (1983) system of classification. In the non-Western context, the separation of liberal and socialist feminist studies constrains rather than illuminates our understanding. The reason for this is that liberal feminist scholarship has a profoundly different political context than Western liberal feminism. The starting point is the oppression by international economic and political forces of the entire region where they conduct their research. Whereas much work on the Third World, including many WID studies, perpetuates liberalism's blindness to inequalities of wealth and power, a significant number of liberal scholars in the Third World transcend the framework's limitations because the subject matter demands a more critical stance. Such scholars are more inclined to identify and challenge the structures of oppression and inequity than are Western liberal feminists. The Third World liberal scholars do this not on the basis of a theoretical understanding grounded in historical materialism, but on the basis of their subtle and detailed empirical knowledge of Third World gender oppression and their understanding that this oppression is rooted in wider exploitative structures and practices. Even if they do not adopt the entire theoretical approach of underdevelopment theory or another radical analysis, they cannot avoid adopting the critical attitudes of such theory. In other words, "the evidence of their own eyes" demands that they challenge liberal assumptions. The fact that Third World liberal scholars make their challenge on empirical grounds does not devalue the political importance of their assertions.

Thus, although one can, in the African context, clearly identify studies that use a historical, materialist method on the one hand, and that perpetuate classical liberal assumptions on the other hand, there is a body of literature, consisting of both scholarly case studies and WID texts, that falls neatly into neither camp. Whether overtly inspired by Marxist analysis or not, many works take account of class relations, the importance of relations of production, and the complex relation between the economic and social realms. In particular, they recognize that there are inherent contradictions in gender relations — a notion often missing from Western liberal texts. Furthermore, these studies are not satisfied with simplistic universal explanations laying all problems at the door of an ahistorical condition known as "patriarchy." In these detailed empirical studies, a complexity of gender relations and of women's positions is encountered that belies the simplistic sex-class division of radical feminism. I therefore suggest that the concept of liberal feminism must be refined and a distinction must be made between critical liberal analyses and those that operate from the uncritical, individualist perspective of Western liberal thinking. In this book, therefore, I refer to liberal texts in two ways:

- to critique the application of Western liberal theory and ideology to the study of African society and

- to identify those critical liberal studies that challenge the hegemony of Western thought.

Today, in assessing feminist scholarship on gender relations in Africa, it is appropriate to designate a framework that encompasses both socialist feminist writing and the critical liberal scholarship just described. It is to this body of literature that I assign the term "feminist political economy."

Feminist political economy and the study of African women

Feminist political economy specifies the pluralistic framework within which the most rigorous attempts at theorizing African gender relations have been made. The theoretical core of feminist political economy is the work that has sought to demonstrate the centrality of gender relations to relations of production in both precapitalist and capitalist societies (e.g., Sacks 1979; Leacock 1981; Amadiume 1987). It also includes, however, those studies that, through the rigour of their analyses of non-Western societies, have corrected some of the biases and limitations of Western feminist thinking, including some socialist feminism. The materialist method has encountered some serious theoretical problems in its attempts to explain precapitalist and capitalist societies in the Third World (as the previous discussion of Africanist political economy reveals). The problem lies partly in the inappropriateness of Western class categories and Western economic conceptions.[6] These categories are fundamentally rooted in the West's historical experience of the development of capitalism.

Feminists have contributed to the development of more appropriate theories to explain Third World class relations and have performed the vital task of rendering visible the substantial economic contribution of women in the Third World. Nevertheless, they have rarely broken free of received Western truths about the nature of society (including gender relations) and truths grounded in assumptions held across the political spectrum of Western feminism and across the spectrum from Marxism to developmentalism. In particular, the fact that the economic realm is given priority over other aspects of human life may have more to do with Western experience than with appropriate theories of causality in the non-Western world, especially with regard to the precapitalist past. Analyses that recognize the complex interaction of economic, political, and ideological aspects of society, rather than seeing economic aspects as determinant in all instances, may be more appropriate. For example, the ideology of kinship and the practice of kin relations in precolonial Africa, far from being the mere superstructure of production relations, are central to the shaping of production relations. Economic work and fulfillment of kin obligations were inseparable both conceptually and in practice.

Another conceptual problem shared by much feminist thinking as well as by nonfeminist approaches to the Third World is the acceptance of a public/private dichotomy, whereby men inhabit a 'public,' more social sphere, while women are confined to a 'private' sphere that is closer to nature (see Rosaldo and Lamphère 1974; Sanday 1981). Thorough, gender-sensitive case studies have provided evidence that challenges the reality of this dichotomy in Africa's past and present.

Another common mistake is the assumption that "family" and "household" carry the same meaning and structure as they do in the West. Again, the evidence from many African societies challenges the notion of an undifferentiated "household" unit, devoid of internal contradictions or divisions. Instead, women and men within households are often revealed to have different, competing interests with regard to

---

[6]There is also a vigorous debate under way as to the appropriateness of traditional Marxist analysis for understanding contemporary Western society. Laclau and Mouffe (1985) argue that it is not, and propose a "radical democratic politics" as the appropriate socialist strategy for the present. Wood (1986) argues vociferously against this position, charging that Laclau, Mouffe, and others have abandoned socialism in a "retreat from class."

family and community resources. A branch of Western feminism has explored the concept of the family at length (see Tilly and Scott 1978; Barrett and McIntosh 1982; Thorne and Yalom 1982; Briskin 1985; Dickinson and Russell 1986). Some studies have even raised questions about cross-cultural notions of the family (see Collier et al. 1982). Up to now, however, the issue has not been substantively addressed by feminist scholars studying the Third World. As a result of the lack of subtlety in conceptualizing family and household, these writers frequently resort to a reductionist argument attributing women's problems within the family to "male domination," a vague, ahistorical notion without much explanatory power. (See chapter 6 for a discussion of these and other conceptual problems facing feminist inquiry in the Third World.)

What certain liberal studies contribute to feminist political economy is not a theory of gender. As I have already indicated, the premises of liberal feminism limit its ability to conceptualize structures of oppression. Rather, in the richness of their empirical detail, these studies provide the basis for challenging Western epistemological assumptions regarding the universality of many features of economics, politics, and gender relations. A study that demonstrates this point is Ladipo's (1981) comparison of two women's cooperatives in Nigeria (see pp. 100–103). Through her careful exploration of the reasons for the failure of one and the success of the other, she makes a valuable contribution to the elucidation of African women's organization for collective production, showing how traditional practices are an important means by which women combat both gender oppression and economic exploitation in the present. Her analysis thus draws on a subtle understanding of the relation between gender and production, even though there is no overt theorizing of this relation. Furthermore, Ladipo's account has more to say about gender ideology than a number of more theoretical studies because of her sensitivity to the local voice. It is studies such as these that become the testing ground for feminist theories developed in other historical contexts.

What I am calling for here is a reconsideration of both the political and theoretical value of empirical research. Studies such as Ladipo's (1981) are valuable precisely because of their commitment to "description from the inside." Empirical research tends to be devalued by theorists, who are prone to dismiss it with the often undeserved epithet of "empiricism." Theorists of course have a very important point when they argue that preoccupation with the empirical often disguises, under its cloak of neutral description of 'reality,' a host of hidden values and biases. But theory that does not constantly test itself against "the real world" also opens itself to bias. Theoretical work without sound empirical referents is assuming common concrete experiences about which we can make general propositions and to which we can apply common concepts. Ideas about public and private and about the family are examples of the common concepts we believe we can work with. What the literature review in this book reveals, however, is that common experience is precisely what we cannot afford to assume. Not only are we ignorant of the differences in concepts of family, politics, and economy in the Third World, we are also unaware that such differences exist. Our ignorance leads us to universalize our own Western categories and concepts. The concrete realities as constructed and lived by Third World people thus disappear from our view (and often, as a result, from their own).

In the context of this intellectual hegemony, empirical studies that rescue detailed knowledge about Third World societies are vital. Foucault (1983:217) says that "the little question, What happens? although flat and empirical, once it is scrutinized is seen...to [attempt] a critical investigation into the thematics of power." Studies of gender relations in Africa that carefully ask "the little question, What happens?" thus form the critical core of knowledge within which we can develop our theoretical inquiries, free of the assumptions of our own construction of reality.

The generation of Africa-centred knowledge of gender and society is aided by an important new avenue of inquiry that is currently stimulating new thinking in social science: discourse analysis. Feminist political economy studies in Africa have not up to now explicitly confronted discourse theory. With regard to their exposure of inaccurate Western conceptions of African political economy and in their exploration of discourses amongst women and between women and men in African societies, however, feminist political economy studies create the basis upon which discourse analysis can be developed. I see such theorizing as the next step for feminist political economy (for studies that move in this direction, see Mbilinyi 1985a; Stamp 1987; Mackenzie 1988).

"Discourse" is used in many different ways in contemporary social science. Cousins and Hussain (1984:77–78) provide a useful classification of its uses, which will serve to focus the term's designation in this study. First, its use in the analysis of speech and language to elucidate social dynamics constitutes a branch of sociolinguistics. Second, it is used to explore the relationship between language and human subjectivity. Third, a more philosophical use of "discourse" explores the epistemological problem of the relationship between knowledge and reality. Fourth, it is used in the development of Marxist theories of ideology, where discourse is viewed as "a particular level of social relations" that has "particular mechanisms and effects." These mechanisms and effects consist of both discursive and nondiscursive practices and are intimately connected to the processes of power.[7]

The study draws primarily on the fourth use of discourse, although it is also concerned with the broader epistemological issues (for a detailed discussion of the utility of discourse theory, see pp. 129–133 and 146–158). For the Third World, a starting point for this approach is Said's (1979) ground-breaking study on 'Orientalism.' His analysis of the idea of the "Orient" as a Western construct and hegemonic practice focused on West and East Asia, but is also relevant for the Third World in general. Only by understanding the discourses created over the past several hundred years to explain the non-Western world can one understand "the enormously systematic discipline by which European culture was able to manage — and even produce — [the Third World] politically, sociologically, militarily, ideologically, scientifically and imaginatively...." (Said 1979:3).

Mueller (1987:1), in her study of WID discourse, explains why we should engage in discourse analysis:

---

[7]One lineage for this thinking on ideology can be traced from Marx through Gramsci (1971; his notes were written in the 1930s) to Althusser (1971; Althusser and Balibar 1970), to Poulantzas (1973). The other lineage is the work of Foucault (1973, 1979, 1980b), who, in turn, draws on several traditions (Marxism, structuralism, linguistics, and the philosophy of Nietzsche and others). Over the past 10 years, the two lineages have converged in a number of studies (e.g., Poulantzas 1978; Laclau and Mouffe 1985). Scholars such as Coward (1983) (see also Coward and Ellis 1977) have commenced the theoretical synthesis of materialism, discourse, and feminist analysis. This and related thinking is sometimes designated as "poststructuralism." Weedon (1987) makes an important case for the utility of the approach for questions of gender, class, and race.

21

> Much of what members of the North American intelligentsia know about the women who live in Third World countries is made available to us through official modes of knowledge. Few of us have the opportunity to travel to meet and talk with even a handful of women from other countries. Our knowledge is not of a directly experienced world. We are largely dependent for our understandings on texts which have been written in North America...[as part of] Women in Development knowledge, produced in the social organization of Development to bring women to the attention of Development agency policy-makers and planners.

Mueller (1987) argues that WID discourse, far from liberating women in the Third World, emerges from the development effort that fosters the international capitalist order and, in turn, contributes to the maintenance of that oppressive order. I am suggesting here that Western feminist scholarship must also be scrutinized for its contribution to the West's hegemonic discourse about the Third World. It is important to stress that this approach does not retreat to a liberal position, which leaves underlying structural causes of inequality unexamined. Rather, it is an attempt to stand back and evaluate the historical context in which both liberalism and Marxism emerged and to render political economy analysis more accountable to the realities of Third World gender relations, past and present.

In sum, I am arguing for a materialism that, on the one hand, sheds ethnocentrism and economism and, on the other hand, develops socialist feminism's commitment to historicize gender relations. Another aspect of the project of socialist feminism that is advanced here is the attention to ideology as a vital component of gender theory. The aim in introducing the concept of feminist political economy is, thus, to identify a field of inquiry that presents the opportunity for the development of a coherent framework, both in terms of specific theoretical points regarding non-Western gender relations and in terms of the necessary empirical basis for developing those points.

I endeavour to show in Chapters 4–7 that the concept of feminist political economy, as a revision of Jaggar's (1977, 1983) classic formulation, is a more expansive category of feminist analysis: one that builds upon the insights of socialist feminism to generate unbiased analyses of African gender relations. Jaggar called for socially responsible feminist theory. Indeed, Jaggar and Rothenberg (1984) responded to criticism from women of colour regarding the exclusion of race as a category of analysis from the first edition. Thus, the second edition included "feminism and women of colour," not as a new framework, but as "a distinctive perspective on social reality." The variation on Jaggar's frameworks proposed here is an attempt to act on that responsibility, which, in the Third World context, is twofold: first, to uncover the ways in which Western knowledge has silenced the local knowledges of gender relations; and second, to rectify those silences.

The feminist political economy framework was inaugurated with Rubin's (1975) germinal work on "the traffic in women." The work was valuable not only for its theoretical insights but also for its contribution to feminist methodology: Rubin (1975) showed how nonfeminist theories could be recruited to a feminist analysis. She took the sexist ideas of Freud (on the psychoanalytic theory of femininity) and of anthropologist Lévi-Strauss (on kinship systems and women-exchange) and developed them into a theory of "the political economy of sex." Central to her thesis, and to work building on it (e.g., Collier and Rosaldo 1981; Mackenzie 1986; Stamp 1986), is a concept of relations between women and men that are grounded in biological gender but are expressed at the level of society in concrete, historically specific ways. The "sex-gender system" in any society (to use Rubin's [1975] useful term) is closely linked to relations of production but is separate from them and not reducible to them.

Gender relations are not simply an aspect of mode of production, although certain types of gender relations are associated with certain modes of production and certain forces of production (technology and work organization). For example, the bridewealth sex-gender system of Africa is linked to the communal mode of production that characterized precapitalist society and to its hoe technology (Stamp 1986). Similarly, the dowry sex-gender system can be associated with the plough technology and tributary mode of production that characterized Asia. With regard to contemporary political economy, studies that document the differential impact of capitalism on men and women are beginning to appear (e.g., RFR/DRF 1982; CWS/cf 1986; Robertson and Berger 1986). Some of this work is developing a rigorous approach to the relationship between sex-gender systems and production. Many of these studies are by African women. Amadiume (1987), for example, is a particularly rich Nigerian case study that challenges the orthodoxies of anthropology while exploring the way in which Igbo sex-gender relations have been undermined in the colonial and contemporary eras (other African studies include Okeyo 1980; Muntemba 1982a; Mbilinyi 1984; Afonja 1986a,b; Obbo 1986).

The relevance of the feminist political economy approach takes on concreteness and immediacy in the context of current efforts to reinsert women into the heart of African studies, both in new fieldwork and in an interpretive reading of older, sexist texts (e.g., Clark 1980). Examples of the phenomena that may now begin to be adequately theorized are polygyny, and, as suggested above, dowry and bridewealth. Regarding the latter, the approach allows for an analysis of the custom in terms of a contractual relation that, in previous times, signaled the social and economic worth of women and provided the basis for a measure of power (Stamp 1986). However, this custom has now become articulated with capitalist relations of production. Bridewealth, formerly not a 'price,' has become a capitalist transaction of putting a price on the heads of daughters (Parkin 1972). The contract is thus now a commodity transaction and, as such, is oppressive of, rather than empowering for, women. In Zimbabwe, feminists have made the legal abolition of *lobola* (bridewealth) a priority (for an example of this concern and for a succinct analysis of the commodification of *lobola*, see Kazembe and Mol 1986).

Feminist political economy thus rescues history; as well, it has implications for action. The restoration of African women's centrality and relative autonomy in most precolonial, precapitalist societies counters the negative image that has been given to many African women and engenders optimism for the future. The achievement of women in the past maps out the possibilities for overcoming the oppression that developed in the capitalist era. Furthermore, certain recent achievements by women can be understood in a new light: as ideological and economic resistance to oppression rather than simply "coping with change" (see Chapter 4 for an exposition of this argument in the context of a case study on Kenyan women).

The following questions are central to the current work of feminist political economy scholars engaged in African studies.

Is the general assumption that women have been universally oppressed accurate? Under what conditions have women held relative power and autonomy, and what factors are responsible for undermining these conditions? African societies and native North American societies are seen to have provided considerable power, authority, and autonomy to women (Van Allen 1972, 1976; Sacks 1979; Etienne 1980; Okeyo 1980; Leacock 1981). Colonialism and its attendant underdeveloped capitalism are seen as primary agents of the decline in the power and autonomy of women, as the example demonstrates. In a special issue on African women, the *Review of African Political Economy* (ROAPE 1984) has rectified its earlier indifference to gender relations with a collection of incisive feminist political economy articles which affirm the value of this approach. A substantial portion of its 1986 biennial conference in Liverpool was devoted to women's struggles in Africa.

To what degree has the power terminology of Western society, and the use of unitary concepts such as "position" and "role" distorted our understanding of gender relations? The work of Schlegel (1977), Sacks (1979), Leacock (1981), Mackenzie (1986, 1988), and others attests to the multifaceted nature of power, decision-making, and authority in precapitalist societies and undermines the concept of a simplistic dominance/submission dichotomy. For example, Sacks (1979) argues that African women had more authority and autonomy as sisters than they did as wives. We cannot, therefore, talk of a single high or low position for African women. Role and position, furthermore, are essentialist categories, excluding a dynamic view of change. The focus on "roles" is a serious limitation of such potentially influential publications as the USAID-sponsored *Gender Roles in Development Projects: A Case Book* (Overholt et al. 1985) for example.

To what degree have cross-cultural studies been stunted by the separation of women from the central core of social science analysis and by the relegation of family relations to the realm of "women's role?" The focus on "women's role" often implies that women are more central to gender relations than men, a stance that supports the discredited public/private dichotomy, whereby men occupy the realm of "public affairs" and women occupy the "private" realm of the home and family. African studies show that the extended family is the public realm, continuous with wider levels of political organization, and that women are economically and politically central to it (see Mbilinyi 1984). There is a particular danger in the implication that women are more central to gender relations than men. Because they are the chief occupants of what is seen as the sphere of "the traditional," the separation of women from the core of society constructs them as an anomaly for development, less likely than men to become modern participants in politics or the economy. Women become "the problem."

Increasingly, questions such as these are informing the critiques and analyses of the most fruitful investigations on gender and technology — those studies that can be included in the nascent feminist political economy. The concerns embodied in these investigations, however, are neither dominant in the thinking about technology and gender, nor have they been used in concrete development research and planning. The following chapter discusses the continuing invisibility of gender in many of the research/action loci. Chapter 3, in summarizing the findings of the WID literature, reveals the need to develop a more systematic and powerful framework of analysis.

2 Conceptualizing Technology, Gender, and Development

The conceptual approaches dominant within each technology-transfer research/action locus may be considered in terms of the broad frameworks of knowledge outlined in Chapter 1. It is also possible to identify frames of reference characteristic of the different disciplines involved, from medicine and nutrition to economics and geography to sociology and anthropology. In the case of some loci, the conceptual approaches are relatively impervious to new ideas; other loci, however, are receptive to both researchers and ideas from other loci.

The most marked phenomenon of the massive WID initiative of the past 11 years has been the constant movement of feminist scholars between academia and policy-oriented research and action. Scarcely had these scholars launched women's studies as a field of research and completed their first fieldwork on gender relations, when they were summoned in the mid-1970s to provide critiques of existing development policies and generate guidelines for new directions in development. Kathleen Staudt, Achola Pala Okeyo, Nici Nelson, Deborah Fahy Bryceson, Edna Bay, Marjorie Mbilinyi, Claire Robertson, Shimwaayi Muntemba, and Carol MacCormack are just a few of the Africanist scholars who have made substantial contributions both to the theoretical understanding of gender relations in Africa and to development efforts. When governments, aid agencies, and nongovernmental organizations recognized the fundamental error in ignoring women, it was the energy and flexibility of such scholars that fueled the gender revolution within these institutions. For these feminist scholars, there was no time to build an ivory tower, and their work, both in academic journals and for development agencies, reveals their grounding in the concrete concerns and urgent priorities of African societies.

For their part, many agencies proved willing to support seminars, research, and projects inspired by the concerns of African and Western scholars. The conference on rural development and women in Africa held in Dakar, Senegal, in 1981 and cosponsored by ILO and AAWORD was an important example of such collaboration (ILO 1984). In 1986, IDRC sponsored a research methodology seminar focusing on gender issues for 31 African research officers; the host institution was the Eastern and Southern African Management Institute in Arusha, Tanzania. The support of the United Nations Fund for Population Activities (UNFPA) and CIDA for a special issue of *Development: Seeds of Change* (SID 1984) is an example of support for research and critique, as is the funding provided by CIDA and the Women's Bureau of the Secretary of State, Government of Canada, to publish the special issue of *Canadian Woman Studies/les Cahiers de la femme*, on Forum '85, the conference of nongovernmental women's organizations held in Nairobi, Kenya, in July 1985 (see CWS/cf 1986).

Commitment to WID is becoming institutionalized in agencies in several different ways. CDR in Denmark lists "women in the third world" as one of its three main research areas. IDRC has established a WID unit; this unit serves as a resource group for IDRC, sharing information and advising on issues related to the integration of women in development, as well as carrying out its own projects. CIDA has developed a WID policy framework whereby all project proposals must include an analysis of their impact on women to be accepted (CIDA 1987:42–43). The Commonwealth Secretariat (1984) developed a briefing strategy for delegates to national and international development meetings so that they can "integrate women's issues into international development dialogue."

Both conceptually and practically, we cannot separate Africa from the rest of the world when considering gender, technology, and development. Scholars not only have circulated between development organizations and academia but also have interacted widely around the world. The current, major method of presenting research findings is in books organized thematically and including case studies from each region. These books, and the conferences that often inspired them, have provided exciting cross-cultural comparisons and generated important general conclusions on the impact of development efforts upon women. They have also, through their documentation of the wide variety of sex-gender systems and the concomitant different articulations with the development process, highlighted the importance of cultural and historical specificity in approaches to development. Three major texts on gender, technology, and development written in the past 8 years attest to the value of this approach, in spite of the limitations inherent in their use of a liberal feminist framework: Dauber and Cain (1981), D'Onofrio-Flores and Pfafflin (1982), and Ahmed (1985).

The continuing invisibility of gender

Despite the outpouring of information and analysis on gender and development over the past 10 years and the formal commitment to WID initiatives, sizable portions of mainstream academia and the research and action loci remain impervious to the challenge to their unexamined assumptions. This intransigence is all the more striking in the light of the cross-fertilization of ideas and flexibility of approach previously discussed. The phenomenon can only be explained by the continued adherence of many scholars and practitioners to a conservative framework of thought regarding women and gender issues. As stated in Chapter 1, such a framework is based on the notion that gender inequality and a sexual division of labour are natural rather than socially constructed. Ingrained in this thinking is a dichotomy between a 'public' male sphere and a 'private' female sphere. Hence, the question of revising the concept of the 'public' realm of politics and economy in the light of historically created gender relations does not arise. That the public/private dichotomy is based on specific Western economic and social practices is an invisible question within this framework.

Compartmentalization of "the women problem" is the chief means by which gender issues are excluded from socioeconomic study and planning. A telling example of this practice is a new book that is being used as a reference source by World Bank planners: *Strategies for African Development* (Berg and Whitaker 1986). This book includes a good chapter on women in development (Guyer 1986) that charts many of the problems of the subject, including a critique of agency programs in donor countries and a perceptive analysis of the reasons for the invisibility of women. However, this 603-page book indexes the topic "women" in only one other chapter, that on education, where inequalities for women in education are briefly mentioned and decried. Nowhere else is gender taken into account: indeed, the chapter on technology, entitled "Manpower, technology, and employment in Africa" (King 1986) is notable for its neglect of the issues so dramatically documented in a host of studies over the past 10 years. Instead, technology is treated as a problem in training for its use, construed in terms of gainful employment, whether in the formal or informal sector, in the factory, or on the farm (King 1986:431–442).

In this text, therefore, it is possible for Guyer (1986:406) correctly to identify "current indigenous practices and small scale intensive enterprises" as a potential development asset, while Hyden (1986:55–63) argues exactly the opposite: he derogates the "economy of affection," which he sees as characterizing African societies.

> The economy of affection denotes networks of support, communications, and interaction among structurally defined groups connected by blood, kin community or other affinities such as religion.... The economy of affection is the articulation of principles associated with "peasant" or "household" economics....
>
> (Hyden 1986:58)

Hyden argues that these networks and principles are detrimental to development, and suggests ways in which the "uncaptured peasantry" may be captured by the internationally integrated national economy.

The World Bank has contributed to the ghettoization of the gender issue. Although the organization has identified the problem (IBRD 1979), its major policy documents on Africa perpetuate the invisibility of women in major economic policy initiatives. The practice is deeply problematic given that these initiatives help shape the financial programs and development plans of African governments. In 1981, the influential *Accelerated Development in sub-Saharan Africa: an Agenda for Action* (the so-called Berg Report; IBRD 1981) included no text or tables referring to women or gender. In the chapter entitled "Basic constraints," underdeveloped human resources are identified as one of the "internal 'structural' problems" that are "obstacles to growth" (IBRD 1981:9–16); nowhere does it mention women as one of these "underdeveloped human resources." Even in discussing agriculture, health, and population, the document neglects the necessity of including women in planning for development. The chapter on human resources (pp. 81–90) is deficient in the same respect. Technology is not treated as a distinct problem, rather, it is an aspect of labour problems.

A recent policy document on Africa, *Financing Adjustment with Growth in sub-Saharan Africa, 1986–90* (IBRD 1986), takes the same approach. Focusing primarily on the structural reforms perceived as a necessary response to economic crisis and required by the IMF, the document criticizes African policies that "discriminate against agriculture and favor the urban sector" (IBRD 1986:18). However, the policies regarding agricultural development favoured by this document are those geared toward a further integration of the agricultural sector into the world economy, with no consideration of the well-documented problems for women — and, indeed, for families and the environment itself — of intensified cash crop production. Further, the recommended incentives for farmers (IBRD

1986:20) take no account of their differential impact upon men and women and, hence, given women's importance in agriculture, the likelihood of their failure. Once again, the social dimensions of technology transfer are not treated as a discrete issue for consideration. The report simply states "Most observers agree that the technology shelf in sub-Saharan Africa is nearly bare. Most farmers make little use of fertilizer, and hand-hoe cultivation is still the most common."[1] From such an analysis, the report is content merely to propose the development of research capacity as the solution (IBRD 1986:32).

In contradiction to its approval of the fact that "the thrust of structural adjustment in Africa has been toward a greater role for prices, markets, and the private sector in promoting development," the World Bank argues for stronger involvement of governments, which should make a concerted attack on the "constraints on growth." In particular,

> On issues such as family planning, resource conservation, and agricultural research, governments must commit themselves to change and promote a social consensus in its favor. Consensus must spring from a clearer understanding of the link between these long-term factors and prospects for a better quality of life.
>
> (IBRD 1986:25)

This report raises grave questions about the propriety of a multilateral agency issuing directives bearing upon internal political processes, particularly in that the World Bank is dictating the policies for which governments are required to mobilize support. This is a fundamentally undemocratic action. Apart from this impropriety, there are other serious limitations to the document. Nowhere does the report address the importance of including women as participants in such a consensus. Moreover, there is a serious question as to whether a consensus can be generated around the change that the World Bank envisages as self-evidently desirable, when policies geared toward such change have, at best, neglected and, at worst, seriously disadvantaged women. Finally, the World Bank assumes that development initiatives flowing from the top down can be successful: the role of ordinary people is simply to accede passively to a consensus on government policy. Most of the research on women and development, including that on technology transfer, has shown the poverty of this approach. An evaluation of the ability of the measures to achieve their stated, long-term, macroeconomic goals, a highly controversial issue, is beyond the scope of this study. Kutzner (1986b) provides a useful review of structural adjustment policy and summarizes the critical responses of NGOs and UNICEF to the policy (also see Mosley 1986). Elson (1987) made an important contribution to the feminist critique of structural adjustment policy at a conference convened by the Institute for African Alternatives (IFAA).

The World Bank approach has set a bad example for African governments: during the United Nations Decade for Women, women and gender issues continued

---

[1]In contrast to this opinion, numerous studies have shown that the hand hoe, labour-intensive as it is, is the most appropriate piece of technology for retaining women's control over food production. Once farming is mechanized, women lose control of the crop and subsistence crops give way to cash crops. See the synopsis of Muntemba's Zambian study in Chapter 4 for a sobering account of the consequences for national production of introducing mechanization to the family farm. There is no straightforward relationship between agricultural productivity and labour-saving technology in Africa. Families eat if their female members wield the hoe: it would not be extreme to suggest that, to the extent that Africa can still feed itself, it is the hand hoe that feeds it. The neglected connection between food self-sufficiency in Africa and women's agricultural production is also explored in Chapter 3.

to be prominent in their absence from concrete African governmental planning. For example, Kenya's *Development Plan, 1984–1988* (Kenya 1983), while it discussed briefly the employment problems of women (p. 9) and called for "special policy measures" to tackle them, suggested no concrete guidelines for such a policy. Furthermore, the interrelation of gender issues with development problems in health, nutrition, and agriculture was not even raised.

At the international level in Africa, radical critique of development theory and policy has filtered into collective responses to agency and donor programs. The Organization of African Unity (OAU) has taken issue with the vision of development promulgated by the World Bank and IMF. In its *Lagos Plan of Action for the Economic Development of Africa, 1980–2000* (OAU 1980), OAU emphasized the negative effects of world economic trends upon African development and urged that African countries collectively generate their own strategy for development; in vigorously implementing this strategy, they should "cultivate the virtue of self-reliance." In this worthwhile vision of self-reliant development, however, women, once again, remained largely invisible. AAWORD (1985:2) commented on the OAU plan:

> It is worthy to note that a chapter was dedicated to women and in it the role our Association among other women's groups can play in the creation of equal opportunities for women has been recognized. In the debate that followed the dissemination of this document, we have both appreciated the attention given to the issue and criticized its compartmentalization as a chapter. In other words, we argue that women's absence as well as presence in major concerns such as agricultural development, industrialization and the development and transfer of technology, educational and health programmes should be included within the major analysis and not as an aside. Presently we continue to argue that emerging development theories and strategies are faulty and incomplete to the extent that they fail to include gender as one of the major analytical categories.

OAU did sponsor some WID activities in the years following the Lagos Plan of Action and took a formal stance of encouraging the development of women-focused national and governmental organizations in Africa (see OAU 1982). The efforts were half-hearted, however.

The "stubborn obliviousness," as Henn (1983:1043) calls it, to the overwhelming evidence on the importance of gender relations and the vital economic role of women in African society is not the only reason for the invisibility of women in the realm of technology and development. By the nature of the specialized fields that bear on development policy, there is a structural separation between research efforts in different areas involving technology transfer. The otherwise excellent research that has been done by IDRC exemplifies this problem. In the area of agricultural research, for example, an "inventory methodology" is used, whereby research is classified according to each commodity. The IDRC workshop on resource allocation to agricultural research held in Singapore in 1981 (Daniels and Nestel 1981), which was structured by this methodology, affirmed the utility of the methodology, given its widespread use and its value as a comparative tool. Nevertheless, the workshop admitted the limitations of the "inventory" approach:

> All of the country studies classified research activities on a commodity basis. There was considerable support for such a classification on the grounds that it was easy to prepare and of immediate use. It was recognized, however, that a

> commodity classification may not be useful in readily identifying research
> activities directed to planning and development objectives that have a strong
> socioeconomic element, such as farming systems, integrated rural
> development, and transmigration programs.
>
> (Daniels and Nestel 1981:12)

In other words, commodity-by-commodity study makes it difficult to address the larger question of technology transfer as it relates to gender issues, among other "socioeconomic elements."

Other research efforts have made a more sustained effort to bring together discussion of technical and social issues. The training workshop on rural water supply in developing countries held in Malawi in 1980 (IDRC 1981), for example, presented a section on technology that included technical findings and research on training; social factors were addressed in a section on operation and maintenance. Bringing together studies of the social and technical aspects of a development problem, however, does not guarantee that the studies will influence each other. Even in the case of this workshop, which comes close to the heart of the development problem for women (the procurement of water), most of the technical and training studies drew little from social analysis. The workshop proceedings, therefore, reveal a dramatic anomaly: while one paper highlighted the importance of including women in water development projects in Kenya (Getechah 1981), another paper on training for water development in Kenya (Shikwe 1981) neither mentioned the primary responsibility of women for water procurement nor made any suggestions for the training of women in this field. A conclusion drawn by Sue Ellen Charlton from her experience in a USAID workshop on women in international development is probably relevant in the case of the water supply workshop as well as in most seminars on technology and development. She found that "although there was ignorance of technical areas among most social science students...many students from professional fields such as nutrition and agronomy were ignorant of the basic political, social, and cultural realities of development" (Charlton 1984:xiii).

I have dealt at length with the boundary problem, whereby the analysis of gender is either ghettoized or not integrated into technical subjects, because this is probably the most serious problem facing both further fruitful research on development and the generation of adequate development policy. I address this point further in Part III (Chapters 5–7).

Gender, health, and nutrition: conceptual approaches

Health and nutrition are areas conducive to the specialist compartmentalization previously discussed. Sometimes, this is a result of the structural requirements of specialist knowledge, but, more often, it is caused by unexamined assumptions on the appropriateness of Western medical practices and nutrition inventories. Indigenous practices and eating habits well adapted to the social and physical environment are often given little attention by specialists. In particular, the expert knowledge of African women has tended to be ignored (some notable exceptions regarding traditional medicine include studies on the value of indigenous midwifery; e.g., Gumede's [1978] study of Zulu obstetric medicine). Yet neither the general WID literature nor the more specialized women and technology literature has much to say about health technology, its impact on women, or women's influence upon the absorption of such technology. The feminist political economy scholarship has also neglected this area. The critique of health technology transfer in the Third World, therefore, falls to a disparate assortment of interdisciplinary journals and political economy studies.

Research on health and nutrition in Africa, presented in a number of medical journals, is characterized by a large number of statistical surveys and an abundance of data (e.g., Ogunmekan 1977). Given that the involvement of women in health and nutrition, as mothers and as primary "caregivers," is more self-evident than their contribution to production, the health and nutrition literature targets them in a way that the economic literature does not. However, it focuses on women as individuals and as passive recipients of health and nutrition programs, rather than as active agents shaping the absorption of programs by the community. For example, Oleru and Kolawole (1983) examined a random sample of 500 pediatric case notes and interviewed 200 mothers attending a pediatric emergency unit in Lagos, Nigeria. In this study, inquiry was limited to the impact of housing, water supply, sewage disposal, and the educational status of mothers on child health; the study neglected dynamic and community-related aspects of maternal decision-making.

Another example demonstrating the problems inherent in the health and nutrition literature is a study on the accessibility of rural general hospitals in Nigeria (Okafor 1984). The study defines accessibility narrowly, in terms of barriers. The measure of these barriers included "distance travelled, travel mode, travel cost and treatment cost" (Okafor 1984:663). Inaccessibility is seen as a "syndrome of deprivation," to be corrected by better allocative decisions by local authorities.

The focus on the delivery of better rural health care in this study is laudable; its conclusions are of limited value, however, because of the neglect of gender factors affecting accessibility. An example of such a factor, which any Nigerian study should take into account, is the Muslim practice of secluding women: precisely the people responsible for health care within the family (see Callaway 1984). Within a frame of reference that treats the issue in terms of individual women who are passive recipients of care, the only practical policy recommendation possible is to raise the educational level of all mothers: a simplistic solution indeed.

The boundary problem, whereby medical researchers are unable to draw upon the insights of social science research, is demonstrated in many studies. Rehan's (1984) investigation exemplifies the problem. Employing a widely used and somewhat criticized (see Wicker 1969) methodology known as a KAP (knowledge, attitude, and practice) survey, the study covered 500 fertile Hausa women of northern Nigeria "to test their understanding about family planning and reproductive biology." In identifying education as the predominant factor affecting family planning attitudes and excluding structural societal factors from its scope, the study once again is operating from a framework of the individual rather than the social. The author feels no responsibility to consider the numerous anthropological studies on Hausa women. As a consequence, a socially functional practice such as multiple marriage is characterized as "marital instability," a designation that is more an ethnocentric judgment than an accurate description of Hausa gender relations. (See Cohen's [1969] classic study for an insightful analysis of the social relations of gender involved in multiple marriages among the Hausa. Both alternating periods of single and married life, and numerous children, are a rational strategy on the part of Hausa women in the context of urban life.) Studies underpinned by such judgments are forced to such unscientific conclusions as the following assertion by Rehan (1984:843): "This population places great emphasis on a large number of children, either for reasons of self-pride or of fatalism."

Another example of the limitations of this methodology and of the boundary problem is a nutrition study of 250 low-income, pregnant women in Zaria, Nigeria, on their attitudes and infant feeding practices (Cherian 1981). This substantial survey concludes that 66% of the women surveyed used commercial milk formulas for no particular reason. The fact that fathers purchase formulas, mentioned by some respondents, does not suggest to the researcher that complex aspects of marital decision-making patterns might, indeed, provide a "particular reason." The researcher also ignored the role of advertising in promoting commercial solutions to infant care, a role highlighted by the international boycott against Nestle's Corporation for its aggressive marketing of infant formula in the Third World. The analysis of dominant health discourses, a growing field of inquiry, is highly relevant to the topic of child nutrition. The conceptual framework of their study, with its focus on the individual, however, precludes questions about such discourse.

Some studies do refer to community decision-making and social factors; however, there is little attempt to investigate in depth the nature of community. For example, a comparative article on primary health care in Nigeria, Sri Lanka, and Tanzania (Orubuloye and Oyenye 1982) stressed the importance of community participation as a component of the Nigerian Basic Health Services Scheme (BHSS) and criticized national and state governments on the grounds that "little attempt has been made to carry the people along with the programme" (p. 679). The authors' notion of such participation is restricted to financial contribution and acquiescence to government programs. They applaud "communities and their leaders [who] generously donated land and cooperated with the officials responsible for the implementation of the scheme" (Orubuloye and Oyenye 1982:679). In referring to a lack of community participation as a constraint, the article makes no attempt to consider the possible deficiencies of BHSS in terms of lack of community input to the program. Here, the approach is the same as in studies focusing on the individual, with the community rather than the individual being treated as an essential category and a passive recipient of top-down directives. Once again, the dynamic and complex nature of social relations is ignored.

Certain journals dealing with health and nutrition have attempted to synthesize medical and nutritional analysis with social science approaches. *Social Science and Medicine* and the *International Journal of Health Services* have sought to bridge the gap between the two. In 1981, the editor of the former journal called for "more scope for the social scientist." Cautioning that the current "curative enthusiasm" (e.g., regarding oral rehydration packages and education aimed at health specialists) should be "coupled with preventive action and more emphasis...on better water supplies and sanitation," he listed the issues, topics, or programs of concern to developing countries that require an interdisciplinary partnership in research and policy-making.

Breast feeding and supplementary feeding; diarrhoeal disease and water and sanitation; disabilities and handicaps; logistics and drug and vaccine delivery; refugee health; monitoring, evaluation and indicators; appropriate technology; and Primary Health Care, which also embraces the above. These issues are of great current concern and form the basis of projects or programmes into which bilateral and multilateral assistance is being channelled in large amounts. However, there seems to have been little involvement of social scientists as reflected either by their activity in the field, or by their recent publications.

(Bennett 1981:233)

An example of the more sophisticated analysis possible as a result of such a synthesis is Igun's (1982) study of child-feeding habits in Maiduguri, Nigeria. In a survey of 250 low-income women, similar to Cherian's (1981) study, Igun (1982:769) was able to attribute the adoption of bottle feeding by these women to Western industrial culture and, in particular, to "mass media advertisement and the example of elite mothers whose visibly displayed adoption of bottle-feeding elevates it to the status of a fashion in the eyes of" lower income mothers. Once the problem is identified in this way, in terms of social context, solutions may be devised that directly address the cultural dislocation.

Some studies on community involvement in health care have been concerned with the dialectical relation between health plans that are introduced and local culture, including the indigenous medical system. Two studies in Kenya exemplify this approach. Feuerstein (1976) argues for a "comprehensive community approach" to rural health problems and, in particular, for the inclusion of women in decision-making, to improve their own health and, hence, their contribution to social change, and to equip them to fulfill their health-care responsibilities more effectively. Were's (1977) study surveyed 400 village women to determine their attitudes toward equal rights for men and women; it discovered that women consider their participation in the community to be hampered by their more limited opportunities in comparison to those of men. The women argued that better education would improve their community involvement and enhance family health. An excellent symposium on health needs of the world's poor women, sponsored by the Equity Policy Centre in 1980 (see Blair 1981), explored every aspect of women's contribution to health care and presented exemplary case studies. It appears, however, that such an approach has neither worked its way into the general medical scholarly framework nor have its conclusions been adopted to any great degree.

Nutrition is another area requiring a synthesis of social and technical analysis. In many studies, Western concepts of appropriate diet are applied uncritically. An important study prepared for the Institute for Development Studies in Sussex points out the hazards of this approach. Gordon's (1984) report concretely summarizes both the problems of ethnocentrism in nutrition education and the need for a detailed local understanding to uncover its negative impact. Beginning with the assertion that "nutritionists are often less willing and able to research the underlying basic causes of malnutrition to do with social and economic factors and processes," she records her field experience under the heading "Eat More Eggs and Oranges":

Equipped with a BSc Nutrition (London) and great enthusiasm, my career began with the Ministry of Health, Zaria, Northern Nigeria in 1966.... My inherited tasks were to run a nutrition rehabilitation unit, to teach mothers at clinics, and to train local auxiliaries. These were the universal nutritional messages at this time: start to give supplementary foods at the age of three months; make a soft "pap" with water and cereal flour; add mashed or pounded protein-rich foods to the pap, for example egg; [and] give young children plenty of vegetables, mashed fruits and juices, for example, orange juice. We energetically spread these messages to as many mothers as possible. The year passed with little feedback from our clients and no formal evaluation. In common with many nutrition educators, we did not know whether our activities were useful or not.

(Gordon 1984:38)

On evaluating the results of a study she conducted in 1969 to measure the results of such nutritional training, she found that "nutritional status measurements suggested that nutritional education was having a negative impact on nutrition." She concluded,

The costs of earlier supplementary feeding may outweigh the benefits in a poor, insanitary environment. Watery, contaminated paps will cause earlier diarrhoea.... Pap is less nutritious than breastmilk even if an egg is added. The local weaning food...is a soft millet dough, *saab*, with dark green slippery leaves and fermented locust beans, *dawadawa*. This is easy to swallow, tasty and given between the ages of seven and 12 months. It is more nutritious and safer than the pap and egg because it is fermented, preserved with ash salts, and contains less water and animal proteins. The local weaning practices probably worked better in this situation than imported, "optimal" practices. Many nutrition educators "blame the victim" and aim to change the practices of individual mothers. Advice does not deal with real problems or match the resources and opportunities of the mother. This type of education increases guilt and anxiety but does not enable parents to change their situation. Nutrition education rarely involves dialogue and the information controlled by "experts" changes every few years. As indicated above, in cases it may be dangerously inappropriate. Participatory research is needed to understand what prevents parents from feeding their children as they would like.... Personal experience has taught me that many nutritional messages which seem logical in scientific isolation are absurd in practice.

(Gordon 1984:39–42)

This study also challenges the developmentalist adherence to the notion of a traditional/modern dichotomy, whereby traditional beliefs and practices are assumed to be obstacles to progress. Even though there is no doubt that all food preferences are not necessarily nutritionally sound (as our own society all too well demonstrates and as structural anthropology such as the work of Mary Douglas explains), more care must be taken to uncover the indigenous logic of dietary practice and to expose contemporary distortions of previously sound nutritional habits. Studies such as Ojofeitimi and Tanimowo's (1980) research on nutritional beliefs among pregnant Nigerian women, where they argue that traditional beliefs are the principal obstacle to good diet, exemplify the lack of such care. By contrast, Kimati's (1986) assessment of malnutrition in Tanzania is more enlightened. The UNICEF food scientist demonstrates that 70% of Tanzania's children under 5 years are well nourished precisely because of local nutritional knowledge. Kimati's (1986) study is a rare one, however. (The study and Kimati's indictment of nutrition experts' devaluation of traditional nutrition knowledge are discussed further in Chapter 6).

In a wider context, there is a body of political economy literature that challenges the method of transferring medical technology and enterprise from the West to the Third World, seeing it as a part of the functioning of the "capitalist political-economic world-system" and as an aspect of a "worldwide cultural hegemony." Elling (1981:21) summarizes this conceptual approach to the problem:

34

A number of world health problems which have been discretely considered in the past are viewed...as interwoven with each other.... Thus, climactic explanations ("tropical medicine"), and even poverty when conceived in cultural terms or as a structural problem resident entirely within a single nation, are seen as inadequate for understanding any or all of the problems... [These are] poor general health levels in peripheral and semi-peripheral nations, especially rising infant mortality rates in countries such as Brazil; commerciogenic malnutrition; dumping and exploitative sale of drugs, pesticides and other threatening approaches to population control; export of hazardous and polluting industry to peripheral and semi-peripheral nations; similar export of human experimentation; the sale of irrelevant, high medical technology to countries lacking basic public health measures; the "brain drain" and medical imperialism.

The approach also discounts

moralistic inveighing, complaints about inadequate information and its transfer, discussions of bureaucratic bumbling or inter-agency politics and professional rivalries, various forms of victim-blaming, and other explanations and corrective approaches which ignore class structures and the control, distribution and expropriation of resources in nations and the world-system.

(Elling 1981:21)

As long ago as 1974, the Director General of WHO, Dr Halfdan Mahler, pithily described the situation that the organization was required to address in terms of this political economy critique:

The general picture in the world is of an incredibly expensive health industry catering not for the promotion of health but for the unlimited application of disease technology to a certain ungenerous proportion of potential beneficiaries and, perhaps, not doing that too well either.

(Mahler 1974:1–2)

In this framework, which includes two important texts (Navarro 1981; Doyal 1979) (also see ROAPE 1986), medical technology is removed from the realm of the material and placed within the sphere of the social. The transfer of medical technology is seen as a profoundly political act having far-reaching economic, social, and physical consequences. Furthermore, Africa's health problems are given a historical context. Doyal (1979:101–102), for example, discusses the effects of colonialist expansion upon health and, conversely, the contribution of European disease transmission to colonial domination:

From the sixteenth century onwards, European expansion unleashed a series of catastrophic epidemics in every corner of the globe.... The intention here is not to apportion moral blame, but to make clear the objective significance of this process in the particular context of capitalist development. although the spread of infection was often unintentional, it clearly reinforced the genocidal policies carried out in many white settler territories, as well as weakening resistance to imperialist domination elsewhere. Epidemics also helped to destroy the economic and social foundations of indigenous communities and the resulting disintegration and impoverishment greatly facilitated the establishment of colonial hegemony.

With respect to African nutrition, Doyal (1979:102–103) is also precise regarding the historical dimensions of the problem:

The health of the indigenous populations has also been seriously affected by the wars which accompanied imperialist expansion. We can see this very

35

clearly if we look at the experience of East Africa during the late nineteenth and early twentieth centuries, when it was torn by resistance struggles and also by the fighting between rival imperialist powers. In the case of Tanganyika in particular, early military intervention was required to deal with a growing resistance struggle.... Villages were burnt and harvests destroyed.... The repeated devastation of farmland over a thirty-year period had enduring structural consequences. It not only undermined the economies of some of Tanganyika's major peoples, but crucially reduced the capacity of the countryside to feed the remaining population. Thus much of the malnutrition and disease which came to characterise rural Tanganyika in the twentieth century was in a very real sense a product of early colonial repression.

It is on the basis of such analysis, for the present as well as the past, that Doyal asserts that none of the specific dietary deficiencies causing chronic diseases, "serious as they are, should obscure the fact that malnutrition in the third world today is primarily due to a general lack of basic sustenance. People simply do not get enough food ever to be healthy. Hence it would be more accurate to describe the problem as one of *under*-nutrition, rather than malnutrition" (Doyal 1979:98). The distinction is an important one: "malnutrition" carries the connotation of incorrect diet that is the fault of individuals, whereas "undernutrition" compels thought about the structural causes of poor diet.

Such concrete historical analysis, and clarification of the underlying assumptions regarding health problems in the Third World, is a corrective to the fallacy that Africans are primordially disease-ridden and backward and that disease is a purely "natural" category. Once this approach is accepted, then the focus on removing "traditional obstacles" to health modernization (the tradition/modernity dichotomy once again) ceases to be a viable solution for health policymakers. Instead, it becomes self-evident that solutions can only be found in policy oriented toward social and political processes and designed to build upon local initiatives and expertise.

As is characteristic of the political economy school in general, the literature on the political economy of health does not focus consistently on gender relations as a necessary part of the analysis. Any reference to Third World women generally renders them passive recipients of negative health policies, as in the case of experiments using them as subjects for testing birth-control substances banned as unsafe in the West (Doyal 1979:283). Again, the active agency of women in health care and the impact of health technology upon their ability to carry out their customary responsibilities is passed over.

The absence of analysis of gender relations within this and other frameworks leaves a serious gap in the understanding of an area of health that is an increasingly urgent concern: venereal disease. Van Onselen (1976) conducted a rare study in Southern Rhodesia (now Zimbabwe) that explored in depth the political and economic factors contributing to the promiscuity among urban African populations that is so uncharacteristic of indigenous African societies. Both men and women were proletarianized in the colonial era: males as migrant workers in industry and females as prostitutes, who, out of economic necessity, migrated to the compounds to serve the men. On the one hand, the care given by the prostitutes to miners subsidized the industry by relieving it of responsibility for employee health care; on the other hand, the phenomenon contributed to the massive spread of venereal disease.

Syphilis derived from conditions of the compound.... The mass of workers came to the mines without their women, and from the very earliest days of the industry prostitutes were a feature of compound life: throughout this period they actually lived inside the compounds themselves. Since their services did much to attract and stabilise labour, mine management and state alike were unwilling to eliminate it, in spite of its direct contribution to the spread of a deadly disease throughout the black work force.

(Van Onselen 1976:49)

The study is exhaustive in its analysis of the breakdown of traditional sexual relations and the establishment of the damaging patterns that still characterize African cities. In the light of the present AIDS (acquired immune deficiency syndrome) epidemic, such an understanding of the relations of sexuality in all their complexity is the most urgent health task facing Africa. For example, the most recent information from East Africa reveals that major paths of AIDS dissemination are through long-distance truck drivers and a large group of Nairobi prostitutes visiting their homes in Tanzania (R. Wilson, personal communication, 1986; *Globe and Mail*, 23 May 1987).

In sum, the health literature that takes account of social factors falls into two of the conceptual frameworks discussed earlier and shares the limitations of each. The liberal medical and nutritional scholarship characterized by some of the publications in such journals as *Social Science and Medicine* focuses on the individual, or on communities as aggregates of individuals, as the locus of health-care problems. Within this framework, it is difficult to generate a dynamic understanding either of gender relations as they interact with technology transfer or of the collective agency of communities as a primary influence on health-technology absorption.

Political economy critiques of international health systems provide a dynamic understanding of the dialectical relation between health technology and Third World communities; however, this understanding is marred by an economic reductionism that grants no autonomy to gender relations as a powerful shaping force in society. In spite of its limitations, the approach creates the space for analyzing the role of gender relations, in that it starts from the premise that structure and process (particularly historical process) are important and that contradictions exist within and between societies. Given the boundary problem in the sharing of knowledge, however, we can question whether the insights of such thinkers as Doyal and Elling and, indeed, many WHO officials are influencing the methodologies of current health and nutrition researchers.

Women and gender issues in research/action loci

It is important not to cast aid agencies as monolithic institutions. Different branches of the organizations have differing levels of commitment to the issue of gender, and different feminist frameworks may inform researchers within these branches. It is a reasonable generalization, however, that WID offices stand in some degree of isolation from the rest of the institution; once again, women and gender issues being considered as an aside. Furthermore, organizations customarily disassociate themselves formally from the conclusions reached in commissioned studies. Actual organizational policy may thus often be less progressive than the course of action suggested in the research published by the organization.

USAID is a case in point. In response to 1973 Congressional action, USAID established a Women in Development Office. According to a policy paper issued in 1982, summarized by the director of the Office in her introduction to *Gender Roles in Development Projects* (Overholt et al. 1985),

> One of the premises of A.I.D.'s [USAID's] women in development policy is that gender roles constitute a key variable in the socioeconomic condition of any country — one that can be decisive in the success or failure of development plans. Additionally, the policy paper stated that it is critical now for A.I.D. to move beyond its initial activities, taking an active role and providing leadership to ensure that women have access to the opportunities and benefits of economic development. The paper also clearly stated that the responsibility for implementing A.I.D.'s women in development policy rests with all of A.I.D.'s offices and programs at all levels of decision-making.
>
> (Tinsley 1985:xi)

One of the many studies commissioned to contribute to this initiative is Isely's (1984) excellent literature review on rural development strategies regarding health and nutrition and their impact on fertility. Isely (1984) charts four approaches to rural development, paying particular attention to the importance of community participation and improved local food production in development strategies. This study is valuable because of its focus on structure and process in the community, including the involvement of women, and its emphasis on the health of women and children as key indicators.

Yet, in spite of valuable research efforts, Staudt (1985a) showed that only 4.3% of regional bureau funding for USAID projects in Africa went to projects that were either specifically directed at women or had a component including women; in addition, only 4 of 45 agricultural projects designated women as beneficiaries. The pattern uncovered in USAID, where sufficient resources are allocated to mount a WID program but not to carry it out effectively, is also charted for the United Nations and other organizations. Between 1974 and 1980, a period that included half of the United Nations' Women's Decade, only 4% of projects involved the participation of women; of these, half had only a minor level of participation by women (UNDP 1982).

Guyer (1986:416) sums up the difficulties inherent in WID programs as follows:

> Women's offices seem to have intrinsically incompatible aspects to their mandates. Research in technical areas, from tax policy to crop rotations, requires integration into the rest of the technical community. Political action, on the other hand, such as advocacy of a women's perspective within the organization as a whole, lobbying for more funding for women's projects, or the maintenance of links to other women's groups, demands cross-disciplinary organization and a somewhat more confrontational collective stance. Working on project administration involves yet another kind of structure defined by authority and cooperation. Individuals may be able to do all of these at once, but an organization runs up against the limits to flexibility in level of expertise, loyalty, collective morale, and so on. This is all the more problematic when the issue itself is as controversial as that of "women," and adversaries are looking for ways to avoid dealing with it.

In the light of this well-documented experience, giving priority to increasing "the knowledge of gender issues among USAID personnel" (Tinsley 1985:xi) and, consequently, the publication of such books as *Gender Roles in Development Projects* (Overholt et al. 1985), would seem an admirable effort, but of little effect in overcoming the structural and political constraints within aid organizations. Certainly, a USAID research effort on the same subject 9 years earlier (Mickelwait et al. 1976) did not have an impact on the boundary problem.

Rogers (1980:48–58) provides a trenchant account of the problem and some wry commentary. She gives examples of her conversations with planners, such as the following visit with senior officials of a World Bank project (p. 55):

> "Meet Barbara Rogers, she's visiting this project and wants to know what we're doing for women. I warn you though, she's a feminist."
>
> Embarrassed silence.
>
> "Well, actually I don't think there's anything of much interest to you here. Perhaps UNICEF can show you something. We're a huge program, millions of dollars, a consortium of agencies, got a job to do, and we haven't got any time for special projects."

Recently, by the nature of their mandate, certain research/action loci have been able to take a less ambivalent position on gender and development. Some have been particularly concerned to draw in African scholars and practitioners and to encourage a stance critical of development theory and policy. ILO will be taken as one example, although other research/action loci have made similar contributions (see Flora 1982; Were 1985).[2] Because of its connection to labour movements and its overtly progressive raison d'être, ILO has been a leader in this regard. According to Dharam Ghai, the Chief of the Rural Employment Policies Branch of ILO, "with respect to rural women workers...the approach has been to focus on critical but neglected questions, to build up a knowledge base for launching of practical programmes and to encourage involvement of researchers and NGOs in grass-roots action with women's groups...." (ILO 1985:4). Among its significant contributions in the past 8 years have been an African and Asian Inter-regional Workshop on Strategies for Improving the Employment Conditions of Rural Women, held in Tanzania in 1984 and cosponsored by DANIDA (ILO 1985); a Tripartite African Regional Seminar on Rural Development and Women held in Senegal in 1981 (ILO 1984); and a conference on women and rural development held in Geneva in 1978 (ILO 1980). In addition, the organization has commissioned many studies (e.g., Feldman 1981). With regard to women and technology, specifically, ILO was responsible for commissioning an important recent overview (Ahmed 1985).

In the seminars particularly, an Africa-centred voice for feminist political economy is emerging. The 1985 workshop in Tanzania, attended predominantly by African women, including several outstanding scholars, is evidence of this. The workshop was the outcome of "a common concern among women researchers in Africa and Asia to move away from pure research identifying why rural development has not helped women to documenting initiatives which are working in some way to improve the economic and social conditions of poor rural women.... The participants, both women and men...were acutely aware of the processes that were pauperising and marginalising a large section of the rural population, particularly women..." (ILO 1985:1–2). The Workshop's critical summary of

---

[2]In 1982, the Dag Hammarskjöld Foundation funded a seminar entitled "Another Development with Women" (DHF/SIDA 1982). The seminar was particularly significant from the point of view of African women: it provided a forum for the promulgation by AAWORD of a policy of intellectual indigenization, both of research and of development action.

women's projects and programs demonstrates the participants' sharp judgment of existing approaches to rural development:

> The problems of adopting a "project approach to development" in general and women's projects in particular, are many. The "project approach" is often reformist in character and does not plan for or contribute to structural changes. It is generally top heavy in administration and has limited multiplier effect. In many instances, women's projects and programmes marginalise women's concerns instead of integrating them in mainstream development. They are often designed as hobbies — part-time activities to give women supplementary income and ignore women's main economic activities and their critical need for full-time employment and income to sustain themselves and their families. They generally maintain and replicate the existing sexual division of labour and do not give women skills and knowledge to adapt, change and advance with changes in technology and labour markets....

> [However] it was argued that the "project" approach was necessary because most national development plans and programmes are broken down in the form of projects and projects are one way of demonstrating what can be done to field level bureaucrats and implementers who may otherwise either lack the initiative to launch a programme or resist it. In addition, projects/programmes can provide poor women with opportunities to handle resources, manipulate power and make decisions — opportunities which many of them would not have in the absence of these projects. The importance of this experience in tackling the issues of underdevelopment and dependency was emphasized.
>
> (ILO 1985:6–7)

Behind this general statement is a sophisticated, historically detailed understanding of African gender relations, women's economic participation, and the realities of contemporary national and international political economy. It is from the insights of such collective pragmatic thinking by African scholar/practitioners that new directions for research and development planning may fruitfully emerge, as Chapters 3 and 4 suggest.

Obvious sources of impetus to indigenize research on women in Africa are the regional organizations that have been set up to promote women-related research. AAWORD, at seminars and through publications, has repeatedly stated that research on African women should be in the hands of African women.

> AAWORD arose partly as a reaction against the onslaught of WID researchers from outside, descending on African countries to extract information about African women, get their degrees and promotions on the basis of publications written for a non-African audience, and ultimately take the knowledge away with them. African researchers faced growing competition from foreign researchers who had an unfair advantage in that they had much greater access to research funds and publication possibilities.
>
> (Mbilinyi 1984:292)

Mbilinyi (1984) recognizes, however, that "the drive to decolonise African Women's Studies has necessarily developed in contradictory directions." Elite African women are able to monopolize research opportunities and funding, and many follow the conceptual approaches established by Western, liberal scholars. Another group takes a more critical stance and aligns itself with ordinary African women. The predominant view in AAWORD, which has led to the exclusion of all but racially defined African women, allows class inequality to remain invisible. In Mbilinyi's eyes, this tendency "represents a mirror image of colonial racism in South Africa." In several countries, groups of African feminists (e.g., Women's

Research and Documentation Project [WRDP], Tanzania, and Women's Action Group [WAG], Zimbabwe) are struggling to ensure that poor women are adequately researched and that their voice is heard. Women in Nigeria (WIN) is attempting to come to grips with class issues; as yet, however, there is no feminist research group with these concerns in Kenya. The difficulty for such groups is that their approach challenges the very structure of society upon which development assumptions are based.

The approach favoured by most African feminist researchers, therefore, is the liberal project of integrating of women into the existing structure of society. This is the direction of most of the work of the other regional organizations for research on women, e.g., ATRCW, which is part of ECA and is based in Addis Ababa, Ethiopia (see ATRCW 1985a,b) (ECA [1977] documents the origin and growth of ATRCW). Almost entirely funded by external donors, ATRCW follows the WID ideology of Western donor agencies. As Mbilinyi (1984:292) says, "the integration line is exceedingly powerful, and arose as a result of what were progressive demands for human equality directed towards women's lack of full equality internationally and in Africa." The liberal approach, whether promulgated by African feminists or Western researchers, however, does not fully explain the dialectical relationship between technology transfer and African family and community. For example, ATRCW is preoccupied with social indicators as a means of understanding women's situation (see ATRCW 1985a). Even though such a preoccupation is useful in ensuring the proper collection of necessary data, it excludes, by the way it constructs the research subject, dynamic and historically grounded questions about the relationship between changing sex-gender systems and the "situation of women." It also provides no space for considering the contribution of women's organizations to the maintenance and enhancement of the "situation of women."

The value of AAWORD's contribution, in particular, should not be discounted, however. It is providing political legitimation for indigenous research and is prompting a more careful attitude among Western researchers. As well, it is providing a conduit for agency initiatives that place priority on African involvement. For example, AAWORD advertised the Rockefeller Foundation's program to explore "long term implications of changing gender roles" through funding projects that "address the social, psychological, political and economic phenomena associated with the rapidly changing status of women" (AAWORD 1985:15).

Another research/action category that should be discussed is the large number of NGOs concerned with women in development. Because they are organizations with specialized purposes (e.g., family planning, education, religious association), their goals are more modest and their perception of development issues is often a more accurate representation of grass-roots concerns. Most NGOs are defined by altruistic aims and, frequently, these aims are compatible with concerns of feminist political economy. Usually short of financial resources, they have been unable to fund any large scale involvement of Western "experts," instead fostering human resources in the developing country. In many cases, these resources have been female. The NGOs' chief liability, lack of funding, is also their strength: they are not constrained by national policy directions, as are both bilateral and multilateral aid agencies.

The Centre for Development and Population Activities (CDPA n.d.), for example, has produced a manual on project planning and implementation designed to yield innovative, highly focused development efforts. It distinguishes between "vague objectives" ("to improve the status of women in Tokara Village") and "smart objectives" ("to provide 3,000 women from Tokara Village and neighboring communities with information on reproductive health and family planning by the end of one year"). WHES is another example of an organization that has provided a valuable service on limited resources. It provides seminars, publications, and consultancy to disseminate understanding on the causes of hunger and poverty, and acts as a networking centre. It has focused much attention on Africa and, particularly, women (see Kutzner 1982, 1986a,b; WHES 1985).

In recent years, particularly preceding the Nairobi Forum '85 (the NGO conference held concurrently with the United Nations End-of-Decade Conference), NGOs dealing with every aspect of the lives and struggle of women have proliferated throughout the Third World (for an excellent overview of these organizations and the experience of the conference, see CWS/cf 1986). Exemplary of Western organizations addressing themselves in a concrete way to issues of technology and gender is the Equity Policy Centre (see Blair 1981). Providing a vital communications service to the Third World is the Geneva-based Isis International; it was established as a nonprofit organization in 1974 in response to "demands from women in many countries for an organisation to facilitate global communication among women and to gather and distribute internationally materials and information produced by women and women's groups." By 1983, it had a network of 10 000 contacts in 130 countries and a resource library of 50 000 items from books to films; it also offered a wide variety of services, including training in communication and conference organization (Isis International 1983:221–222). Its resource guidebook (Isis International 1983), intended as an action tool for Third World feminists involved in WID efforts, addresses in a brief, common-sense way many of the issues raised in Chapter 3 and throughout the book, such as the invisibility of women's knowledge, the problems with the "income generation" approach, and the undermining of women's rights and economic control by development projects.

The United Nations Development Fund for Women (UNIFEM) is promulgating an important project on women and food technology. The project intends to disseminate food technologies for "high-priority foods." The technology transfer will be integrated with social and economic support for women in the form of credit, marketing, and other facilities. The aim is to "promote national self-sufficiency in food through support of the women food producers, processors, marketers" (Carr and Sandhu 1987; see a discussion of this study in Chapter 3, pp. 57–61, and their critique of the economic assumptions of such projects in Chapter 6, pp. 119–121).

In Canada, CCIC has been an umbrella organization for a wide range of Canadian and Third World organizations. CCIC performs a valuable service in bringing together grass-roots women leaders (see Gascon 1986). Commonly, it is the elite wives of male leaders who attend international conferences; there are severe financial, political, and logistical barriers to interaction among nonelite feminist leaders of the Third World. Organizations such as CCIC are attempting to address this problem.

In the Third World, the DAWN group is a project that began as an international feminist initiative in Bangalore, India, in 1984 (see DAWN 1986). Founded as an umbrella organization to improve links between women's organizations within the

Third World, DAWN was a vigorous presence at the '85 Nairobi Forum. The group, with which AAWORD and other regional associations have affiliated themselves, promises to provide a powerful Third World feminist voice. It is unlikely, however, that DAWN will have access to funds and resources on a scale comparable to Isis International and CCIC.

Chapters 3 and 4 explore the conceptualization of gender, technology, and development in academic scholarship and review the major research findings. Again, the feminist frameworks outlined in Chapter 1 provide guidelines for evaluating the explanatory value of different studies. Most academic studies on technology and gender are conceived within the liberal feminist framework. Because this approach focuses on the individual and lacks in-depth analysis of social process and structure, problems relating to technology transfer can only be described. Such studies cannot explain and, hence, provide guidelines for solving problems that emerge from the dialectical interaction between gender, community, and technology. Many of these studies are reviewed for the valuable data they provide and for their identification of problem areas needing research.

A consensus has emerged in the literature on a series of issues regarding technology transfer and gender in the community. Chapter 3 introduces and describes these issues. It is feminist political economy that explains sex-gender systems and processes of change. Such explanations are necessary for generating appropriate solutions. Chapter 4 develops a case study and presents synopses of two works by African scholars to demonstrate the value of this approach.

Part II

Technology Transfer:
Gender and Power in the
Village and Family

3   Technology, Gender, and Development in Africa: the Findings

Scholars researching women, technology, and development have identified a common set of problems throughout the Third World regarding technology-related development efforts. Africa shares these problems, although its particular sex-gender systems and historical experience create unique technology-transfer problems. As previously indicated, however, the studies of the problem, whether conceived globally or regionally, are richer in description than in explanation. It is feminist political economy that has explained African gender relations and social change in the village and family. Feminist political economy, however, has not yet addressed itself substantially to problems of technology transfer. A deeper understanding of technology, development, and gender, therefore, requires a synthesis of these two areas of inquiry.

This chapter deals with one of these areas, the women and technology literature and technology-related components of WID literature, drawing on case studies from Kenya, Nigeria, and elsewhere. Chapter 4 focuses on the findings of the other area, feminist political economy, using an extended Kenyan case study and synopses of research by two African scholars to demonstrate the explanatory power of the framework. Chapters 5 and 6 in Part III discuss the synthesis of the two areas as an interrelation that has not been addressed in previous research. Throughout these chapters, the goal is to elucidate the dialectical relationship between technology and local community. Inevitably, in this investigation, national and regional organizations must also be considered, given that state policy impinges directly upon choices made at the village level.

African women and technology

Writers on women and technology generally share with scholars working on WID the view that women are caught in a nexus of political and economic dependency (e.g., see Dauber and Cain 1981; Nelson 1981; Charlton 1984; ILO 1984; Afshar 1985; Ahmed 1985; Momsen and Townsend 1987; for succinct overviews of the social science literature on African women, see Strobel 1982; Robertson 1987). Concepts from dependency theory inform this writing to some degree, although the full implications of the dependency framework are usually not explored. In some studies, the dimensions of the analysis are undermined by a reductionist tendency, borrowed from radical feminism, to treat men as a unitary category responsible for the oppression of women. Furthermore, most of this work shares the major flaw of dependency theory: a static, ahistorical perception of dependent societies, in which nations and individuals are seen as passive recipients of exploitative, capitalist structures and practices. In the dependency framework, therefore, neither the complexities of indigenous political economy, including class formation, nor the agency of local communities can be adequately understood. Specifically, the influence of community organizations upon the introduction and sustained use of technology remains largely invisible in the literature. Even though many studies call for more community involvement, especially of women's groups, they rarely explore the historical basis upon which such involvement could be built.

Nevertheless, the dependency approach applied to women and technology sets a useful, descriptive context. Charlton's (1984:23–28) description of the powerlessness of women in development decisions exemplifies this utility. She sees women as being caught in a "triad of dependency," whereby

> In virtually every country in the world...women are dependent upon men in formal politics at the local, national, and international levels. Equally important in this conceptualization is the recognition that these three levels are increasingly interrelated. Events at the local level, whether in the private (family/kingroup) sphere or public sphere are more and more influenced by the institutions of the national state. Moreover, the expansion of multinational organizations means that virtually no country can be considered impermeable to influences that originate outside its border.... The choice by a village woman to breast-feed her infant is conditioned in part by forces over which she has no control: the availability of manufactured formulas, advertising and other sources of information (such as health workers), prices and cash income, and government policies regulating the operations of multinational corporations.... The conditions of a woman's life — even in remote villages — are influenced by institutions and events that are physically far removed from her.... Whatever their traditional condition, women in general have little or no formal, institutionalized power at the local, national, and international levels in comparison to men. Even when [women] do acquire public influence locally or nationally, that influence is often undermined by the limited autonomy of their nation-state.
>
> (Charlton 1984:24–25)

The powerlessness of women to choose is especially important with respect to technology transfers, which impinge so dramatically upon their lives. Many researchers (e.g., Cain 1981:5–6) agree that the people responsible for technology choices are usually those least affected by them; those most affected, who must adapt and live with the choices, have the least say about them. To make matters worse, this contradiction has scarcely been recognized, let alone addressed, in any quarter. Geographers, for example, have ignored the issue. The Women and Geography Study Group of the Institute of British Geographers has criticized the silence of their discipline regarding gender issues (Momsen and Townsend 1987). However, two feminist atlases have been compiled to address the gap in geography (Seager and Olson 1986; Sivard 1985).

Women's lack of choice and the invisibility of this powerlessness are significant in the context of Africa's dependence on women as food producers. Lewis (1984:170) summarizes this role (see also Monson and Kalb 1985):

> African women are usually the primary food producers in the countryside. Rural women typically work two to six hours per day longer than rural men. On the average in African societies, women put in 70 percent of all the time expended on food production, 100 percent of the time spent on food processing, 50 percent of that spent on food storage and animal husbandry, 60 percent of all the marketing, 90 percent of all beer brewing, 90 percent of

time spent obtaining water supply and 80 percent of time spent to obtain the fuel supply.

Agricultural technology has had the most profound negative impact upon the ability of women to maintain not only their responsibilities as food producers but also their position within the village and the family. Inherent in much of the early policy from which agricultural technology flowed were what Tinker (1981:52–53) described as "irrational stereotypes of appropriate roles for women." According to these stereotypes, which are reinforced by inappropriate definitions of economic activity, "women don't 'work,' or, if they do, they shouldn't. Thus a draft of [a USAID] agricultural policy paper done in 1977 could suggest that a measure of development would be reducing the number of women working in the fields" (Tinker 1981:52–53). WID organizations and WID branches in aid agencies have recently engaged in much rhetoric regarding the neglected economic contribution of women (e.g., see ILO/INSTRAW 1985); however, this rhetoric is at odds with assumptions that govern concrete aid policies regarding technology.

There are serious consequences to such thinking. The role of African women in production is ignored because it does not fit into existing economic models. Because women's choices regarding their economic activities have been so drastically curtailed, their allocation of labour time is considered irrational when measured using Western economic theory (this theory assumes that individuals allocate labour time as they allocate resources, according to marginal utility, i.e., according to rational choices that maximize return). As a consequence of being considered economically anomalous, women's farm labour has not been computed as a measurable economic activity. For example, the United States Department of Agriculture (USDA 1981), drawing conclusions from a study of African farming that only surveyed male labour, asserted that labour is the major scarce resource in African food production.

Henn (1983) points out the absurdity of this assertion, citing data for Tanzania and Cameroon that are probably fairly typical for Africa as a whole. Beti men in Cameroon and Haya men in Tanzania spent 220 and 450 h/year on food tasks, respectively; Beti and Haya women spent 1250 and over 1000 h/year producing food, respectively (an average of 4–5 h/day compared with the men's 1 or 2 h/day). In the light of this, "it is ludicrous to suggest that *all* labour will remain scarce in the food sector until the gap between urban wages and [economic return] on food production is closed" (Henn 1983:1047–1048). It is precisely on assertions such as the USDA's, however, that the World Bank policy on correcting rural–urban bias (cited in Chapter 2) is based (removal of food price controls to close the gap between urban and rural income is an important component of this policy). The focus on labour renders invisible the real scarcities in African food production: material and financial inputs to the major producers. The role of women as primary producers, unequal access to inputs, and the inequitable distribution of food crop income within the family remain unaddressed in conventional Western economic thinking. Almost all WID studies reveal, however, that any increase in farm income is appropriated by men and put to uses that do not benefit women and children. Women, meanwhile, are largely responsible for generating such increases, the production involved adding seriously to their workloads and reducing their ability to produce food for the family.

Given women's different experience of development opportunities, it is not surprising that they have different perceptions of development than men. Nelson

48

(1981:4–6) and many others describe the increasing gender conflict in the context of development processes and "attribute the situation to women's unequal share of the new options or society's resentment when one group of women...) has co-opted a large enough share to threaten the balance of power in gender relations." Nelson cites a study of Zambian nurses (Schuster 1981:77–97) to illustrate this point. The nurses were drawn into radically different gender relations as a result of their high-profile role as healers in a Western system of hospital nursing. This system did not account for social problems arising from conflicting indigenous and Western healing principles. Consequently, the nurses became scapegoats for hospital problems, as well as for disruptions in gender relations in Zambian society generally.

Agricultural development projects have created a principal arena for gender conflict. Dey (1981:109–122) discusses the deep rivalries that emerged between women and men in a Gambian wet rice scheme. The Chinese engineers who designed the project misunderstood the division of labour: Gambian women are traditionally responsible for wet rice cultivation; yet, women were left out of the project design. These and other studies "underscore with depressing predictability the ways in which the new economic opportunities have been controlled and co-opted by men. African men (as elsewhere) have moved into a more advantageous position vis-à-vis women in their respective communities over the past century" (Nelson 1981:5). Some studies (e.g., Stamp 1986:42) also point out, however, that such privileging of men within the sex-gender system contributes to the inequitable political economy that disadvantages both men and women as peasants.

The loss of traditional rights and power in the village and family is a constant theme of the WID literature on Africa. As Bryceson (1985:7–8) notes, however, there is surprisingly little material written specifically on the topic of women and technology, in contrast to the large amount of material on women and work (such as Nelson 1981; Bay 1982; Hay and Stichter 1984; Monson and Kalb 1985; Leacock and Safa 1986; Robertson and Berger 1986). This material tends to analyze the relationship between women and technology in a cursory fashion. Nevertheless, both the general literature on women and work and the specific studies on technology transfer describe clearly the complicity of new technology in the subversion of women's position. The following survey of key issues regarding technology and gender is gleaned from the few specific studies on women and technology and from a disparate variety of studies that touch on the subject (for a review of relevant literature, see Bryceson 1985:37–44).

Bryceson's (1985) lucid definition of technology serves to summarize the meaning usually given to the term in the women and technology literature. In its wider sense, technology is the

> objects, techniques, skills and processes which facilitate human activity in terms of: first reducing human energy expenditure, second, reducing labour time, third, improving spatial mobility and fourth, alleviating material uncertainty.... [These] objects, techniques and processes...have arisen from the application of human understanding and knowledge of matter and...serve to enhance human capabilities. "Human capabilities" denote not only an individual's physical and mental capacities but also the social freedom for pursuing one's capacities.
>
> (Bryceson 1985:8–9)

This definition is useful in that it takes a step away from the notion of technology as artefact toward an understanding of technology as a social construct (I would add to the definition of 'human capabilities' the community's capacity to fulfill its members social and physical needs). The definition delineates what technology is supposed to accomplish and optimally does accomplish, rather than what is actually achieved in the process of technology transfer from the Western world to Africa.

In exploring the realities of this process at the local level, whereby technology's purpose is subverted, I identify 10 issues in the literature around which a degree of consensus has emerged:

1. African governments and development agencies treat technology as a neutral, value-free tool, which renders the problems cited above invisible. Development will inevitably flow from a technological "fix" in this erroneous view.

2. African government policies generally show a sexist bias, whereby development planning and implementation are structured so as to ignore women's relationships with technology, even where insights about this relationship are available.

3. "Appropriate technology," a slogan in development literature and policy, is often inappropriate when gender issues are taken into account. Who decides what technology is "appropriate" and whose interests does it serve?

4. "Income generation" projects, popular with WID policymakers, are of questionable value or are even harmful to women. Projects that push women to make objects for sale trivialize their main work as food producers and reinforce the "home economics" stereotype of appropriate women's activities. Furthermore, market demand is rarely investigated before craft production is encouraged.

5. Development literature and policy often view women as "welfare" subjects (recipients of social service projects) rather than as active agents in development. This approach overlooks the centrality of women in the African economy. Furthermore, the "target-group" approach assumes that there are systematic links through which resources can be channeled to women: an erroneous assumption (although he does not make the point in connection with women, see Hyden 1986:63).

6. Women have unequal access to development resources, particularly sources of capital formation and credit.

7. Women commonly lose legal rights and political, economic, and social autonomy within the community. The loss of land rights is a particularly severe aspect of this problem.

8. Gender relations are disrupted, enhancing traditional tendencies to male domination and undermining the counterbalancing power of women within the family. Consequently, African women experience both a greater degree of subordination to their husbands as well as a loss of control to their husbands over their own labour. This often results in resistance by women to innovations they perceive, quite rightly, as contributing to their loss of power and economic control.

9. New agriculture and health technologies often intensify the labour of women. This is coupled with a loss of decision-making power in the realm of production, health, and nutrition.

10. Positive consequences for technology transfer and sustenance are evident when women are central decision-makers. The decision-making power of women depends on effective grass-roots women's organizations.

These 10 issues are inextricably intertwined in the experience of African women and African communities. The first five issues relate to the politics of aid, development ideology, gender bias in policy, and misguided conceptualizations of the problem. The next four issues bear intimately upon the relationship between new technology and changing political economy in Africa, both national and local. In particular, these issues pertain to the relationship between technology and sex-gender systems (a more detailed analysis of the transformation of gender relations, which are the background to these technology and development issues, is given in Chapter 4). The final issue remains largely in the realm of potential and should be the primary focus for future research and policy.

The politics of technology and gender

Issue 1. The technological fix

The inherent difficulties in perceiving technology as artefact have already been mentioned. Anderson (1985:59) succinctly summarizes the problem for women in development:

> The basic assumption persists that technical solutions can be found for any problem. Efforts to develop Science Policy Institutes in many developing countries, to negotiate systems for the equitable transfer of technical knowledge, to develop international journals for the publication and dissemination of discoveries — even the appropriate technology movement — all rest on the assumption that a technological "fix" may be found. If we can only get the technology "right," then the assumption is that progress and development in the Third World will be inevitable. Many advocates of women's involvement in development are now searching for the "right" technologies for women to assure their participation in and benefit from development. [Behind this is the belief] that science and technology, because based in nature, are separate from all normative and political influence and free from cultural or class bias. In fact, there is evidence to the contrary. Among scientists there is an increasing acknowledgement of the interactions of their discoveries and knowledge with their social experience.

Anderson (1985) stresses the importance of acknowledging the power of these hidden assumptions and of exploring the link between "access to and control of knowledge and the effective application of technologies in development." A major consequence of the view of technology as a neutral tool is that technology transfer efforts, with relatively few exceptions, have carried with them a Trojan Horse of Western economic ideology: development means increased productivity through large scale, capital-intensive enterprise (or at least through intensive commercialization of small-scale farming).

Thus, as Palmer (1978) and many others (e.g., Sharma 1973) have pointed out,

51

the high-yielding variety (HYV) technology of the Green Revolution, seen as a miraculous solution to Third World food problems, has had a serious impact. It has resulted not only in less equitable gender relations but also in growing class divisions as land becomes concentrated in the hands of those land owners with previous advantage (such as access to credit or membership in the dominant ethnic or religious group), who are able to maximize that advantage in the use of the new technology. All aspects of crop production are affected by the new seeds and their accompanying technology. Thus, even though there has been an overall increase in cereal yields, the burden of work has increased considerably and large categories of peasants are no longer able to produce food or have been forced to sell their land and become labourers. Women have been particularly hard hit by the new agricultural technology. Therefore, one can question whether it is accurate to measure increased productivity simply by the gross statistics on crop yields.

In recent years, the neglect of women in agricultural policy has been increasingly linked to the theme of environmental degradation. As Baxter's (1987a) collection of studies on women and the environment in the Sudan shows, a neglect of women's roles contributes to destructive policies. In turn, the resulting environmental impoverishment creates more hardship for women, whose work is most directly affected. The studies in the collection (Baxter 1987a), which is based on a workshop held in the Sudan, pursue this theme in analyses of energy, food production, water, and nutrition. In her introduction to the study, Baxter (1987b) gives an example with regard to water development schemes:

> Some parts of Sudan have bore holes installed with pumps, but these...have their difficulties: Long line-ups may consume as much time as the trip to other water sources; pumps often break down and may not function for months if spare parts and benzene cannot be found; or other, less safe, water sources may continue to be used during the rainy season because they are closer. In villages where water is brought to the houses by donkey, some families may not be able to afford the cost. Although the provision of bore holes seems a relatively simple solution to the water supply problem, nearly 75 percent of the country is not underlain with the water-bearing strata necessary for bore holes to function. Even when bore holes are present and working, they can create a "cone of depression" effect, pulling water away from nearby areas, causing wells to dry up and women using them to struggle harder to raise the water.

An important conclusion to be drawn from these studies and analyses such as Palmer's (1978, cited in Whitehead 1985:30–36; see also Palmer 1985) is that those technological changes having the most significant impact upon women are not usually aimed at women at all: large-scale development projects and their attendant technology rarely include policy regarding women in their initial planning stages. The problem does not lie chiefly with projects aimed at women (although these are indeed problematic); rather, as Whitehead (1985:32) points out, "for large numbers of rural women the most significant forms of technological change are more likely to be the indirect consequences of both planned and unplanned innovations in agriculture as a whole. In many cases, far-reaching effects on women's work derive from the powerful drive to commercialise the potentially profitable sectors of women's work."

In the context of Africa, the drive to commercialize has involved not only food land but also nonfarm productive activities that were also the province of women. The consequence for women has been not only a loss of income from production but also a dependency on sophisticated consumer goods, often imported or made from imports. This dependency creates debt problems for the country as well as placing severe financial strains on the budgets of women, who are traditionally responsible for consumer items. Commodities removed from the realm of local, small-scale production to factories include beer, cloth and clothing, bread, bricks, and cookware. Women were responsible for much of this production. "But urban-based planners and industrial ministries viewed production of pots, clothes-making, brick factories and modern bakeries as potential fields for government promotion of investment to spread modern technologies" (Seidman 1981:117). The industries did not involve much capital or skilled labour and, thus, were attractive. Seidman (1971:117) records that

> The rural industries division of Zambia's parastatal development corporation, INDECO, for example, proclaimed that it was introducing "modern" bakeries in small towns throughout the countryside. Little attention was paid to the fact that local bakers, many of them women, would no longer be able to sell their home-made produce in competition with these government sponsored concerns.

Tanzania, where a massive bread factory was built with Canadian funds, has a similar story.

New agricultural technology carries particular dangers for women, and may consequently harm the local economy. In Tanzania, for example, tractors introduced into settlement schemes allowed a dramatic expansion of the acreage cultivated; weeding, however, remained the task of women, and they were unable to keep up with the work. As a result, yields fell substantially below that anticipated by planners (Fortmann 1981).

Capital-intensive technology does not always have a negative impact on women. In western Cameroon, for example, corn mills bought by the Department of Education in the 1950s and loaned to villages continue to function today, benefiting both the women who run them and the communities they serve (O'Kelly 1973:108–121, cited in Wipper 1984:75–76). It is only when, by coincidence or design, women collectively appropriate capital-intensive technology, however, that such success stories can be told. In other words, the miracle of technology lies not in its physical attributes but in its enlightened application.

Issue 2. Sexist bias in policy

Although feminists are always hoping for something better, it is not surprising that sexist bias exists, given the cloistered, men's club environment of policy-making. Afshar (1987) has provided an evaluation of the impact of sexist ideologies on state policies in several African and Asian countries (for a good analysis of Kenyan policies toward rural women, see Feldman 1984). Mohammadi's (1984:4) generalizations regarding the national planning process generally hold true for Africa.

> With few exceptions, planning takes place in a small unit, dominated by economists, and in a large number of countries...by expatriates. These planners and their concepts of planning have little to do with the conditions of people in general. The decision making and policy formulation is dominated by the wishes of a small group in power, the process is influenced by powerful interest groups, more often than not, unaware or indifferent to a consideration

53

of women as participants in planning, policies, and national strategies. Not only women, but the ordinary male citizen is also only a number in the work force. Secondly, a realistic look at the levels of decision making and the sex composition of people who occupy them would show that women can hardly have much influence on policy and planning decisions as the majority occupy lower echelons and are mere workers. Inequality of access to training, education, employment and also traditions have limited the number of trained women who could participate in planning.

This is the setting within which notions of technology as a neutral tool, as previously discussed, are easily promulgated. It is also the setting, however, where positions far removed from the needs and roles of women can be taken. In many cases, these positions are assured of no challenge from men at the local level, relying as they do on current stereotypes and expectations of women. Particularly popular with governments (and many aid agencies) is the technological fix for women's overburdened workloads, which are seen as a major constraint upon development. A comment by a Tanzanian village leader gets to the heart of the matter (Wily 1981:58, cited in Henn 1983:1049): "RIDEP [the regional development agency] should help the women with water. Water is a big problem for women. We can sit here all day waiting for food because there is no woman at home. Always they are going to fetch water."

Similar assertions of male prerogative, supported by sexist bias, may be found in the more sophisticated guise of social science jargon. The following statement in a recent book on social services in Nigeria by a geography professor at the University of Benin (Onokerhoraye 1984:156) exemplifies an attitude and language that categorizes women as minors and a "problem" in a way that would be unacceptable in Canada today. As well, it presents a stereotypical and erroneous view of the past position and role of Nigerian women.

> Women — like children, the disabled and the aged — represent a special group of people in Nigeria as in many other parts of the developing world. Consequently, they require certain personal welfare services to enhance their contribution to contemporary Nigerian society. The need for special services for women in Nigeria arises from their traditional subordinate economic and social status compared with that of men. Although, traditionally, the conception of the status and role of women varied slightly from one part of Nigeria to another depending on the customs, religion or culture, a woman's role was largely restricted to the home where she was expected to rear children while the men were the breadwinners. Although women in some localities were involved in farming, fishing, trading and the fetching of firewood, their primary function was to rear children.

It is analyses such as these that inform contemporary Nigerian policy toward women, as the Women in Nigeria (WIN) organization has noted. In a recent policy recommendation document (WIN 1985:6–7), the organization complained that

> Men remain dominant, wield and disburse power. Despite the crucial and basic contributions of women to the economy of the nation, their indispensible labour is unacknowledged, unpaid-for and poorly taken into account in national development plans.... We hope [the policy recommendations of the WIN Document] will be received seriously and will not go the way of most recommendations which end up neglected, un-read, stacked up in file cabinets or on dusty floors....

Bryceson (1985:24–28) confirms these insights through an analysis of the relationship between the state, technology, and women. In it, she reviews policies affecting women's relationships to production technology, reproduction technology, scientific exploration, destruction technology. She agrees with a number of writers that both Western individualist ideology as well as traditional ethnic and religious notions maintain women in a state of social dependency.

Bias in national policy presents one set of problems; another set exists at the level of field administration, as Staudt's (1975–1976, 1978, 1985b) extensive research on agricultural policy implementation in Kenya reveals. In 1975, Staudt conducted a study in Kakamega District of western Kenya, in which she surveyed 212 small farms in terms of the impact of agricultural services. The services included visits from agricultural instructors, loans, and training, and were structured by an agricultural development policy that included among its objectives the provision of technology "on an equitable basis" (Staudt 1985b:xi). Staudt found that those farms jointly managed by a man, as opposed to female-managed farms of the same size, received a much higher level of service in the form of visits and training. Farms managed by women received no loans at all.

Staudt attributes this inequity to "prejudicial attitudes and ideological bias" (Staudt 1985b:37) institutionalized in a system where "men dominate administrative offices and political authority networks which provide contacts and information about valuable agricultural services" (Staudt 1985b:xi). The exclusion of women from cooperatives or the discrimination within cooperatives against women members was one of the most serious aspects of this dual ideological and institutional bias against women, hampering their ability to develop their farming practices or adopt improved technology. Cooperatives were important sources of soft loans for maize seed and fertilizer, tractor services, and high-grade cows. Kenya has an advanced artificial insemination program, and cross-breeding of European dairy cattle with hardy indigenous stock has been a major means of increasing milk yield. One high-grade cow may make a substantial difference to family nutrition. Staudt's findings regarding access to high-grade cows demonstrates the disadvantage of women in this respect:

> Given the high value of a grade cow and the committee selection process used to determine eligibility for the cow loan, the potential for discrimination was high, be it political, economic or gender-based. Not enough cows were available for the entire membership. Influence and contacts were thus essential for pressing or "reminding" committee members of an application. This is generally considered men's activity, particularly because it is largely men who sit on the committee.
>
> (Staudt 1985b:30)

Thus, even though most women belonged to organizational networks providing mutual aid and shared labour, they had no means of countering the bias that dominated local policy-making and implementation. According to Staudt's findings, sexist bias was the most important factor explaining the inability of women to take advantage of new knowledge and technology offered to households. Her interviews with agricultural instructors recorded negative comments about women farmers. They also revealed that the instructors were avoiding women on customary grounds, where speaking directly to women was considered incorrect. The preference of agricultural staff for speaking with men is articulated in the following comment by an interviewee: "In the African way, we speak to the man who is the head of the house and assume he will pass on the information to other household members. Being men, of course, it is easier for us to persuade men" (Staudt 1985b:37).

55

There is a disingenuous quality to the pleading of "customary propriety" by agricultural instructors. The political economy evidence in Chapter 4 reveals that "household," "head of household," and men's authority over women were not always as conceptually clear cut as they appear in today's stereotypes. As with the notion of "breadwinners," "head of household" as a characterization of men in traditional African families has a distinctly imported flavour. This is not to say that, in precolonial African society, authority and "family" were not coterminous. Relationships between fathers and sons, between brothers, between cowives and their husband, and between sisters and brothers made it very difficult to assign "head of household" status to one individual.

It is a Western vision of family and its spatial disposition that has informed a particularly crucial area of development technology: that of housing construction. In Tanzania, during the "villagization" campaign of the mid-1970s, men were encouraged to build Western-style houses in the new collective villages (Caplan 1981:106–107). A district official called the men in one village and gave them the following instructions:

> Let there be one house, and let that house be built according to the family that you have.... To build one small hut here, and another over there in a corner, that is not a good way to lay out a village.... We want everyone to have proper houses. So try to get corrugated iron for the roof, and cement floors. If you can't manage all at once, buy a little at a time. We don't want people living any more in houses which are full of snakes and mice.
>
> (Caplan 1981:106)

Among the many problems Caplan (1981) identifies in this speech, the most serious is the lack of recognition of the complexity of the African family, whereby women's autonomy is practically rooted in her right to her own dwelling. Complex and shifting family responsibilities cannot be encompassed within the four square walls of a Western-style house. No provision is made for the widow, the polygynous family, or the young couple. Caplan (1981) points out that the speech referred to the men as "You and your families." Yet,

> In Swahili, the term "family," in the sense of a bounded domestic group does not exist. Indeed, it has been necessary to take the English term and turn it into a Swahili form "*familia*." Such a linguistic usage contains a number of premises — that the unit in society is "a man and *his* family," and that this unit requires a house and an area of land. In other words, concepts foreign to this society, of closely bounded units in the form of households, possessing property in the form of a house and land, and headed by a male, are being introduced. If this becomes a reality, then women, along with old people, will have lost much of their autonomy.
>
> (Caplan 1981:107)

Along the same lines, a poignant illustration of the linguistic subversion of African sex-gender systems can be found in the dedication of a classic medical text, a text that was the bible for a generation of African health-care workers. Maurice King (1966) dedicated his *Medical Care in Developing Countries* "to the common man and his family in developing countries everywhere."

A final, concrete example of policy bias at the level of the village is a case from the Sahel involving a matter of not only resource development but also of survival itself. An American solar technician promoting the use of solar water pumps gave demonstrations to male village leaders only, claiming that women would not understand them. Given the gender division of labour, whereby men are rarely if ever involved in water procurement, the demonstration was thus received by members of the community who were in no position to use their new knowledge or to evaluate the appropriateness of the technology (Hoskyns and Weber 1985:6).

Issue 3. Appropriate technology

Once the negative impact of capital-intensive technology began to be recognized, a new approach was adopted by agencies and governments as the basis for development programs. The concept emerged in the 1970s with a growing concern about world poverty and a shift to a "basic-needs" strategy (see ILO 1977:145–149). According to usual definitions of the term, "appropriate technology" is the most effective and acceptable technology in any given social, economic, and ecological context. The notion of appropriate technology is, therefore, relative as well as subjective, i.e., susceptible to the judgement of the users (this is, of course, desirable; unfortunately, it is also susceptible to the subjective judgement of the providers).

Appropriate technology would appear to be an admirable concept, in that it treats technology as a social process. Indeed, its appeal is such that its celebration in an exhibition held in Nairobi during the Forum '85 Conference, *Tech & Tools: an Appropriate Technology Event for Women*, was one of the most popular features of the Forum. The objectives of the exhibition were "to increase women's access to, use of, and control of technologies in agriculture, food processing, health, energy, communications and income-generation" (ATAC 1985:1). Displayed at the exhibition, with accompanying brochures including blueprints for manufacture, were a number of devices (including a series promoted by UNICEF): e.g., the Umeme energy-efficient charcoal stove, the oil drum bread oven, and the bamboo-reinforced water tank for collecting rainwater from the roof. African educational institutions are enthusiastically endorsing the dissemination of appropriate technology and training for its use (e.g., see Osuala 1987).

There is no question that appropriate technology is an improvement over earlier approaches. However, evaluations of appropriate technology programs reveal that many projects do not achieve their objective of significantly improving women's lives. Furthermore, if a criterion of success is the spread of the technology beyond the original recipients, then the record is even bleaker. What has gone wrong? Once again, value judgments by development planners and a lack of account of social and economic impacts have undermined effectiveness of appropriate technology. As Bryceson (1985:11) says,

> There is a wide array of technological devices that could reduce women's labour intensive activities in transformation work [i.e., domestic labour] e.g. for food processing: grinders, graters, oil extractors, improved stoves, solar cookers, low cost refrigeration; for water supplies: pumps; for transport: handcarts, wheelbarrows, etc. Often these 'appropriate technologies' have met with less-than-hoped-for success because of limited dissemination, limited access or poor design.

Part of the problem is a lack of clarity as to what is appropriate. The thinking of Ventura-Dias (1985:194–196) is a case in point. In discussing the question of appropriate technology in the context of Kenya, she distinguishes between the concept of "improved" village technology and "appropriate technology." The former is a conservative notion, she argues, because it does not intend to introduce changes into the environment or into the social or cultural order. Instead, it should "provide a solution to a felt need, should depend predominantly on locally available skills and materials, should be affordable and culturally and socially acceptable to the community" (UNICEF 1980:7). An improved technology could also allow a traditional task to be performed better or enhance the use of existing technology.

Ventura-Dias (1985) argues, however, that such village technology cannot be considered appropriate because it does not reorganize production to increase either output or the competitiveness of the producer in the market. What is important is that appropriate technology be supportive of the ability of women to produce for the market and to obtain credit and technical assistance. The analysis of Ventura-Dias (1985) is intended as an advocacy of women's empowerment vis-à-vis technology and her argument has valuable points, including a critique of the limitations of the "project approach" and an insistence that production as opposed to consumption be highlighted (see also Hoskyns and Weber 1985:6). Her argument has problems, however.

The distinction of Ventura-Dias (1985) between a conservative "improved technology" concept and a more modern "appropriate technology" concept reveals the flaws in much of the thinking about appropriate technology. First, the economic bias of earlier approaches remains. It is assumed that noneconomic benefits (such as improved health) will flow inevitably from improved market position and from activities that further integrate village economies into the world market. Furthermore, the traditional–modern dichotomy is implicit in the denigration of customary technology management in the village.

Second, the error of discounting the importance of collective village involvement in the technology-transfer process also remains. As a result, women are once again passive, problematic recipients of "inappropriate" technology, a situation that can be fixed by providing them individually, within the Household Unit of Production (HUP), with the means of improving their lot. In this case, an improved lot is equated with an improved ability to produce for, and improved access to, the market. Ventura-Dias's (1985:157) basic premise is that "the problem of rural women in Kenya is...one of level of income and physical assets." According to her, it is through analysis of the "specific characteristics of the HUP [household unit of production] and its insertion in the market economy" that an understanding of appropriate technology transfer can be generated (Ventura-Dias 1985:196). Another flaw in this thinking, the assumption of a unitary, bounded category, "the household," was previously analyzed in the summary of Caplan's (1981) thoughts on the concept of "family" in Tanzania. "Family" is one of the problematic concepts requiring evaluation that is cited in Chapter 6.

The reasons for the failure of appropriate technology programs must be sought in factors other than women's low productivity and lack of access. Hoskyns and Weber (1985:6) give a clue to the problem:

> Introducing appropriate technologies is not new. Groups throughout the ages have shared or copied others' technologies when they found them appropriate. On the other hand, some groups living next to each other for centuries, in what appear to be similar situations, have rejected the others' tools, materials and techniques.

This statement implies that societies throughout history have had valid grounds — cultural or environmental — for rejecting available technologies. If we start from the reasonable assumption that women are refusing to accept or sustain appropriate technology on sound grounds, rather than out of "backwardness" or "ignorance," we can begin to see the problems with the appropriate technology movement. Who controls the technology would be the first issue to enter the mind of an African woman. In many projects, technology introduced for the benefit of women has been co-opted by men for their own use. For example, where women have been given carts to carry water and firewood, the carts have often been put to other uses by men (Hoskyns and Weber 1985:6).

There are other issues relating to technology acceptance. One is that the quality of the product may be compromised. Another is that traditional technological processes may be lost. A third is the question of propriety; for example, some equipment requires women to assume immodest body postures. A fourth is the effect of the technology upon work patterns; for example, solar pumps restrict water lifting to daylight hours. A fifth involves the expenditure of energy; certain water pumps are tiring to use, requiring foot pumping, an unfamiliar and awkward muscular activity. A final and particularly important issue is the fact that some technology requires a level of organization for specialized tasks that does not exist in the community. The collective maintenance of community property such as well pulleys is an example of this; governments rarely budget for such maintenance.

The experience of a Nigerian community with new technology in the form of a hydraulic palm-oil press demonstrates these issues and makes the point that "to be fully appropriate, a technology should ideally grow from within a society and reflect local choices" (Charlton 1984:86).

> For generations, the extraction of oil-palm fruits, a time and energy
> consuming task, has been done by women in some Nigerian communities.
> When a hydraulic oil press was to be introduced in one community, the
> village, a piece of land was allocated by the village head. When the oil press
> had been installed, 72 percent of the people used it, but after a year the figure
> dropped to 24 percent. Although they knew about the benefits, they withdrew
> from the use of the oil press for several reasons — the by-products of the
> pressing pit were lost, i.e., the fibre was used as a source of heat; the daily
> time schedule for using the oil press did not coincide with that of the women;
> the size of the mortar was designed for men and women could only use it with
> an increased labour force; during peak season, the women had to wait for the
> use of the press; all oil from it belonged to the men, and the women did not
> benefit from the increase of oil per unit of fruit processed.
> (Janelid 1975, cited in Charlton 1984:85–86)

Improved stoves are one of the most popular artefacts of the appropriate technology movement. Although valuable in many situations, they have also created a host of unforseen problems and have been accepted only slowly and unevenly. Many stoves are unsuited for local cuisine; do not fit the local cookware; require women to cook and serve food in the daylight at the expense of other tasks, as there is no longer firelight to see by; or, in many cases, require the purchase of expensive charcoal in places where gathering free fuel is still an alternative (only in areas where fuel is habitually purchased, such as in towns, is there large-scale reliance on such stoves). Solar stoves require women to cook in the heat of the day. Hoskyns and Weber (1985:8) identify the most common complaints by women about their new stoves.

[they have lost] smoke for chasing insects or waterproofing roofs,...a centre for conversation and a symbolic focus for the household. The three stones offer the benefit of flexibility of being moved due to the weather, etc., and of cooking with pots of various sizes. There are technical solutions to some of these losses, if women have carefully identified and project officials have listened to the real uses and benefits of traditional cooking fires.

Stove projects also fail because they do not take account of polygynous households. Replacing the traditional three-stone fireplace in each hut with a single stove for the "family" raises the question of where to locate the stove and how to allocate cooking time. Given that separate hearths structure polygynous marriages, the promotion of technology that undermines this practice is bound to fail or, worse, seriously disrupt the marriage institution.

The Kenyan poet Okot p'Bitek's diatribe against stoves from the *Song of Ocol* says much:

> I really hate the charcoal stove!
> Your hand is always dirty
> And anything you touch is blackened...
> I am terribly afraid
> Of the white man's stove
> And I do not like using it
> Because you stand up
> When you cook
> Who ever cooked standing up?
> You use the saucepan and the frying pan
> And other flat bottomed things
> Because the stoves are flat
> Like the face of a drum
> The earthen vegetable pot
> Cannot sit on it
> There are no stones
> On which to place
> The pot for making millet bread....

At the 1981 seminar on rural development and women in Africa held in Dakar, Senegal, criticism of appropriate technology was sharp.

> Appropriate for whom? Who exactly benefits from this "appropriate technology" and why is it now felt that Africa needs appropriate technology? Given the fact that the ideology behind what is appropriate for Africa as well as the original design and parts would be brought from external sources, what is the implication for the balance of payments?... What may seem cheap to an urban male official may be impossibly expensive to a poor rural woman given her very limited access to resources. This is particularly true when the work to be assisted does not yield any income.... The assumption that rural women do not accept or are slow to accept innovation is a false assumption generated by an ideology of disdain for rural people; and it is a concrete symptom of blaming the victim. Given the precarious nature and economic insecurity of the rural poor, women are cautious rather than backward. Once convinced of the usefulness of a given innovation, rural women not only accept it but have often adapted and improved the technique.
>
> (ILO 1984:22–23)

Carr (1981) gives a brief, useful overview of the "theory, practice, and policy" of technologies appropriate for women. In more recent work, Carr and Sandhu (1987) introduce another important question on appropriate technology: Even if technology is adopted successfully, does it achieve the planners' desired ends? If not, what does this say about the planners' goals? An important example is the misplaced assumption that appropriate technology will automatically release women's time for economically productive activity — farming or income-earning activities. The studies surveyed by Carr and Sandhu (1987) reveal, however, that women often spend their time improving the quality of family life (i.e., sewing and child care) rather than on food production or cash-generating activities. One reason for this is that women cannot take advantage of time saved because of a lack of access to land or credit. This point demonstrates the necessity of taking the complex socioeconomic approach when planning technology transfers. Another important consideration in appropriate technology planning is the possibility that the new technology may put many women out of a paid job, such as the sale of water or wood (Carr and Sandhu's [1987] findings are discussed further in Chapter 6, pp. 119–120).

Issue 4. Income generation

Like appropriate technology, income generation is a pet concept of WID policy. Resting on the same assumption underlying the appropriate technology initiative, that improved income is the answer to the exclusion of women from development, income-generation schemes encourage women to make articles for sale, providing them with the necessary technological know-how and, sometimes, equipment. For an indication of the popularity of income-generation schemes in Kenya, see the list of activities and organizational goals presented in the Mazingira Institute (1985) guide. As Ventura-Dias (1985:202–204) points out, however, a major reason for the popularity of the schemes in Kenya is that they do not challenge conventional ideology about the sexual division of labour. The productivity of women would be enhanced, without challenging the prerogatives of men in the sphere of commercial enterprise. Bryson (1981:44, cited in Ventura-Dias 1985:203) noted that "it is important to avoid presenting [income-generation schemes] as commercial programmes as that would defeat their purpose, i.e. "cash" crops are male crops and men would be more likely to take over such programmes."

Central to income-generation schemes, therefore, is the concept that they are "female" projects that are ancillary to the main business of the nation. This approach is not that different from the view that Western women work for "pin money" rather than for a serious wage. Skills training (e.g., sewing) can be viewed as an aspect of women's "domestic" role. The consequence for African women is that they are discouraged from viewing themselves as competent individuals making an economic contribution to national production. To make matters worse, the presence of a long-term, stable market for the articles they are prompted to make (e.g., by the World Bank, see IBRD 1979) and the existence of an adequate transportation and marketing infrastructure are rarely considered. The danger of assistance agencies giving grants to set up noncompetitive industries has been documented: the industry often fails once the grant runs out, reinforcing the prejudice that women are economically incompetent (Tinker 1981:78). Furthermore, inadequate coordination leads to contradictions in development policy, whereby the left hand may not know what the right hand is doing. In Burkina Faso, for example, the increased production of millet beer, encouraged by income-generating schemes subsidized by the government, was jeopardized by the new Heineken beer factory, also subsidized by the government (Tinker 1981:78).

The Zambian Association for Research and Development (ZARD) duplicates Kenya's experience with income-generation schemes. ZARD (1986:82–84) notes that government and local district councils have shifted from favouring home economics instruction for women to emphasizing training for income generation. One recently initiated project is the George Weaving Group in Lusaka, sponsored by the World Alliance of Young Women's Christian Associations (YWCA). For ZARD scholars, this new approach shares many of the flaws of the home economics approach. Even though many women have benefited from the scheme, the majority of poor women have other, more important basic needs. Once again, the priorities and needs of the women have not been researched. ZARD (1986) also points out that this approach assumes that women's most basic need is income. An arithmetic view of development, as previously above, seriously limits an understanding of the structural social processes that must be implicated if successful development is to occur.

Income-generation schemes do not account for the capital purchases necessary to pursue the acquired craft, such as a sewing machine. They also do not provide training in setting up a production unit or in obtaining credit. For the few who do manage to find work, whether part-time or full-time, long hours and subminimum wages are the norm. The increased burden these schemes place upon women remains unrecognized. Ironically, income-generating schemes, designed to reduce women's drudgery by generating cash with which to buy goods and services they formerly produced, have increased the drudgery by adding the income-generation labour to traditional subsistence tasks. The meagre earnings from craft production are rarely adequate to purchase expensive food and services (usually from men) in the marketplace (see Ventura-Dias 1985:202–205). Meanwhile, Zambian governmental policy has paid little attention to the main occupation of women: agricultural production.

WIN (1985b:47–48) confirms Zambia's experience with income-generating schemes in uncompromising language, providing a poignant description of the working conditions that follow logically from the promotion of such schemes.

> Employment in home-based industries has for women the "advantage" that they can earn some money while carrying on their household activities. This, however, is a dubious blessing, for the ability to cater to their children and family needs is outweighed by their lack of mobility and independence from men and the fact that they have to work in isolation from other women and thus are less able (compared to market women) to organize around the conditions of their work. Like market women, those employed in cottage industry provide for low cost, labor-intensive goods and services that are essential for the reproduction of the urban proletariat. Yet (as a survey conducted in Kano has indicated) often their earnings do not match the minimum wage and they are always by far inferior to those of men employed in comparative work in the "informal sector" (e.g. mechanics, leather workers, construction workers, etc.). Like the traders, women who work in cottage industry suffer from the absence of any form of social security and social services. But they suffer more from the dilapidated housing conditions and restricted space which are typical of Nigerian workers quarters, for they must spend all their time in the house and the little space available is further reduced by the presence of both their equipment (e.g., a sewing machine) and the materials and products they must store. Further, being home all day means that the double job is continually impinging on every minute of the day.

62

Issue 5. Women as 'welfare' subjects

Implicit in the previous four issues, as well as the issue of conceptualizing health problems treated extensively in Chapter 2, is the perception of women as a "welfare problem" to be targeted by development projects. The statement of Onokerhoraye (1984:156) that Nigerian women "represent a special group of people" epitomizes this problem. Income-generation schemes, as projects "giving women something to do," also participate in this view of women. The view is an outcome of the application of the liberal approach to development policy, whereby individuals, or groups seen merely as aggregates of individuals, become the objects of projects. Participants in the important 1984 workshop in Tanzania on resources, power, and women (ILO 1985), in criticizing the "project approach," identified income-generating projects as a major contributor to the categorization of women's issues as "welfare" issues. "The orientation of women's income generating projects should be changed from welfare to development. They should be based on women's main economic activities and should be economically viable and profitable" (ILO 1985:6–7). Tinker (1981:78–79) supports such a change of orientation:

> There is a tendency to overload women's projects with welfare concerns: health, education, family planning. These often take precedence, and sink the enterprise. As self-sufficiency is preferable to dependency, so economic activities should be given priority over welfare programs. Recognizing the economic role of women is the starting point.

Even though much of the WID effort over the past 10 years has had as an overt purpose the treatment of women as active agents rather than passive recipients of development, the aim has not materialized in a substantial shift away from the perspective. This is not surprising, given the lack of recognition within the liberal framework that a person's potential as an individual agent can only be actualized through collective action and, hence, that collective action is the necessary subject of research and policy.

Faulty perceptions of women are found throughout development activities. The discussion of bias in policy-making and policy implementation revealed both ideological and structural barriers to considering women differently. Staudt's (1985b) study clearly demonstrates this dual barrier. Regarding the ideological barrier, it is hard to consider women as other than objects when they are excluded, by reticence on the part of the extension workers and planners, from decision-making and receiving instruction in the new technology. Regarding the structural barrier, given that women are absent from the formal institutions that channel policy and information, there is an organizational construction of women as "other," standing apart from the development planning process. However, this conceptual marginality, so deeply a part of Western philosophical tradition, has not characterized African philosophy in the past.

Technology transfer and the decline of women's power

Unequal access to development resources (issue 6), loss of legal rights and political power (issue 7), disruption of gender relations (issue 8), and the intensification of women's labour (issue 9) all bear upon technology transfer and must all be seen in the context of the complex array of political and economic transformations that have occurred in Africa over the past 100 years. Each case study discussed here documents most or all of these issues, although they usually do not provide an analysis of the political economy context. It is important to note that, in talking about the decline of women's power, we are discussing the distortion of gender relations in such a way that men also suffer in the long run from the profound disruptions to family and community life, even though they appear to be the beneficiaries of the extra labour of women and the Western ideology of male dominance.

In examining the dialectical relationship between technology transfer and social process, a distinction must be made between large-scale projects designed to develop an entire community or region or to introduce economies of scale in production of agricultural commodities and projects or programmes designed to influence production and transformation work on an individual or household basis. Many of the factors impinging on the individual and household were reviewed in the survey of the five issues pertaining to the politics of technology and gender. As well, many of the social and economic phenomena documented by the researchers assessing large-scale development schemes are characteristic of small-scale technology transfer processes (as Staudt's [1985b] study of agricultural extension services in Western Kenya so clearly demonstrates). This section therefore focuses on large-scale projects to develop an understanding of the complexity of the issues pertaining to the decline of women's power. Two large-scale projects are considered, one in Kenya and one in Nigeria. Both have been thoroughly assessed in terms of the interrelationship between technology transfer, gender, and community.

The Mwea rice irrigation scheme (Kenya)

The Mwea rice irrigation scheme in Central Province, Kenya, introduced commercial rice cultivation to an area that did not traditionally produce rice. This scheme exemplifies the range of problems generated for women, gender relations, and the peasant economy in general (see Hanger and Morris 1973; Wisner 1982; for a synopsis of the Mwea scheme, see Lewis 1984:181–182; Agarwal 1985:102–105). Designed to fulfill both a social and an economic purpose (the settlement of landless peasants[1] and the production of a valuable cereal crop for the Kenyan market), the scheme has been touted as a development success story by some development policymakers. There are over 3000 titled tenants and their families working 1.6-ha family plots on a settlement where surface irrigation is provided. In 1982, the scheme was still showing a profit and incomes were, on the whole, higher than expected.

Robert Chambers, one of East Africa's foremost researchers on, and planners for, rural development has studied Mwea since its inception in the mid-1960s. He refers rather scathingly to the Mwea scheme as a showpiece of the "rural development tourism" circuit (Chambers 1983:16).

> Those concerned with rural development and with rural research become linked to networks of urban–rural contacts. They are then pointed to those

---

[1]Thousands of Kikuyu were dispossessed of their land by British settlers in the colonial era. See Muriuki (1974) for an excellent history of the Kikuyu and Brett (1974) for a succinct account of the process of dispossession.

rural places where it is known that something is being done — where money is being spent, staff are stationed, a project is in hand. Ministries, departments, district staff, and voluntary agencies all pay special attention to projects and channel visitors towards them. Contact and learning are then with tiny atypical islands of activity which attract repeated and mutually reinforcing attention. Project bias is most marked with the showpiece: the nicely groomed pet project or model village, specially staffed and supported, with well briefed members who know what to say.... Such projects provide a quick and simple reflex to solve the problem of what to do with visitors or senior staff on inspection. Once again, they direct attention away from the poorer people.

(Chambers 1983:16)

What of this showcase of development? Fortunately, the obsessive attention identified by Chambers (1983) has yielded a body of empirical material that feminist scholars have been able to interpret to generate a concrete illustration of the negative impact of such schemes on women and gender relations (see Dey 1981:109–122). The following account builds upon the feminist analyses of Agarwal (1985) and Lewis (1984), which, themselves, synthesize the primary studies.

The aim of the scheme was the cultivation of rice, both as a food and as a cash crop, to raise household income. The settlers came from a farming system where unirrigated crops such as maize and beans were grown on women's plots for consumption and coffee was grown on mens' plots (with women working on the crops to produce a cash income for men). As many studies of the Kikuyu (the dominant ethnic group of the region) show, the production on women's food plots was sufficient for occasional sale of surplus, as well as for subsistence (for an overview, see Stamp 1986). At Mwea, because men did not like to eat rice, women were required to grow the customary food crops. The plots allocated for nonrice production, however, were small and marginal in quality; hence, they could not adequately supply the family (plots for subsistence were not initially designed into the project). Furthermore, women were required to work on their husbands' rice plots (men being the official tenants and "their families" once again being relegated to an ancillary status and role). The workload of women was thus substantially increased over that of customary agricultural production, especially at harvest time. As is typical for Africa in the past and today, women spent longer hours in production than men.

With regard to control over their labour, women traditionally could allocate their own time, within the bounds of customary responsibilities, whose designation was the prerogative of the corporate kin group as a whole (i.e., the lineage) and not the individual husband. In the Mwea scheme, however, the labour of wives and children was entirely under the control of the husbands and men had complete claim to the income from the paddies. Women were paid by their husbands with rice, the amount varying arbitrarily. To buy customary foodstuffs and other household goods, women would then have to sell the rice on the black market, circumventing the rule that all rice be sold to the National Irrigation Board. The proceeds from the rice were rarely adequate to cover household expenses, however. An additional problem was that firewood was no longer a free commodity to be gathered; women had to purchase it, often begging money from their husbands to cover the expense. Moreover, the wood was inferior, requiring more constant attention to the fire than usual. Ironically, if men hired labour to work the paddies, women's work burden was further increased, as they had to cook for the labourers.

> Hence, on the one hand, women found themselves working harder, with much
> less independence and control over their use of time, and, on the other hand,
> there was a marked decrease in their subsistence output, their access to and
> control over cash income, and their say in decisions concerning the family.
> Not surprisingly, cases of women deserting their husbands and returning to the
> old settlements were not infrequent.
>
> (Agarwal 1985:104)

The loss of women's power and autonomy chronicled here is backed up by the law of the land, given that the contract between the National Irrigation Board and each household is legally drawn up with the male "head of household". As the sole legal tenant, the husband thus receives the full payment for rice sold to the Board. Furthermore, because women have no legal status vis-à-vis the family's productive land (this applies to nonscheme areas as well, where male heads of household have been registered as sole land owners), they have no collateral with which to obtain credit to buy inputs to enhance production. African land in settler colonies such as Kenya, South Africa, and Zimbabwe was massively alienated (Newman 1981:125–129). The land remaining to Africans in reserves suffered a major transformation in land tenure law, to the disadvantage of the community, which could no longer plan its use on a rational village basis. Women, in particular, lost out (see pp. 85–87, 103–105).

According to several important indices, the subversion of women's position is linked to a decline in the well-being of the family. Although water is plentiful, it is badly polluted. The studies do not mention the health implications; however, one may speculate as to the likelihood of a serious bilharzia (schistosomiasis) problem in Mwea as well as infant diarrheal diseases associated with contaminated formula. Studies reveal that there was a decline in nutrition between 1966 and 1976; Lewis (1984:181) showed that more than one-third of children between 1 and 5 years old were less than 80% of normal weight for their ages. The women are clear about the problem: on the one hand, they do not have the means to produce for their families and are thus heavily dependent on commodities; on the other hand, they do not have enough cash to fulfill their responsibilities to their families. With this loss of ability to fulfill their customary role, they have lost self-respect. One can thus argue that women and families are subsidizing the monocropping of rice in Mwea economically, socially, and with their health.[2]

Lewis (1984:182) summarizes the Mwea experience as

> prototypical of an extractive mode of development. It appears to encapsulate
> the colonial economy both in the role assigned to women and in the manner
> male profits are dictated by official rather than by market forces. Its design
> precludes the diversification of productive activities among both men and
> women — a precondition for the development of a regional economy
> responsive to the communities' perceived wants. Such schemes are predicated

---

[2]An interesting problem is the availability of rice in the Kenyan marketplace and the impact of cereals dumping by Western nations upon African countries. During a research visit in 1981, I found rice to be extremely scarce, in spite of record yields at Mwea. Rumours circulated that the five truckloads of the National Irrigation Board's rice had been hijacked across Kenya's borders into several neighbouring countries — a black market activity substantially beyond the petty infractions of Mwea wives. I saw local rice on sale in country markets not far from the scheme at KES 7 per cup (about 1 Canadian dollar). At the same time, imported US parboiled ("Uncle Ben's") rice was on sale in an elite Nakuru supermarket for KES 9/kg — less than one quarter the price of rice in the country markets (in September 1988, 16 Kenyan shillings [KES] = 1 United States dollar [USD]).

on a given level of profit in a given form, obtained through a hierarchy of state, scheme management, and male household heads: women's labor is assumed to be an asset of the male head of household.

The summaries of Lewis (1984) and Agarwal (1985) are useful. Neither mentions, however, a significant negative aspect of the Mwea scheme. By its design, the scheme precludes traditional, village-based, decision-making structures including both women and men and women's traditional patterns of association for social and economic cooperation. It was these associations that, in the past, provided women with a counterbalancing measure of power and ensured that village decision-making was balanced to favour all the community.

The Kano River Irrigation Project (Nigeria)

Cecile Jackson conducted an extensive study of Hausa women in northern Nigeria between 1976 and 1978 and has produced an important monograph (Jackson 1985) on the Kano River Irrigation Project (KRP). Jackson (1978) also studied the seemingly unlikely phenomenon of a Muslim women's strike held by Hausa women in 1977. Her assessment of the impact of KRP upon women confirms the insights on the Mwea scheme and demonstrates the ability of women to engage in collective resistance to the subversion of their power. Her work on the 1977 strike goes beyond the understanding gleaned from the Mwea experience and, in that measure, represents a synthesis of political economy insights and WID concerns called for in Chapter 5. Although she does not investigate Hausa gender relations in depth, Jackson's (1985) study is an example of the direction that WID work should be taking. Given their traditional participation in the market economy, Hausa women have been at a greater advantage economically than the Kenyan women in the Mwea scheme. At the same time, however, the Hausa women are relatively disadvantaged socially, given the predominance of Islam and its associated practice of the seclusion of women.

A large-scale irrigation project of 120 000 acres (48 600 ha) was established 50 km south of the city of Kano, Nigeria, in 1971. KRP was designed to increase agricultural productivity. In the way that rice was the innovative monocrop for which Mwea was constructed, wheat for urban bread supplies was the intended crop of KRP (tomatoes were also planned for). The decision was made not to purchase the land and turn the peasants into tenants; this process of appropriation would have been difficult because of the high population density ($179/km^2$), the complexity of land tenure arrangements, and the inevitable resistance of the peasantry. Instead, the government registered individual land titles, installed the infrastructure of canals for irrigation, and exchanged the individual owner's unirrigated land with equivalent irrigated land nearby. Farmers usually had the same neighbours. Credit was provided by the scheme for the first 2 years; thereafter, the farmer was expected to have generated enough capital to sustain the new technology required for irrigated agriculture. Management was supposed to level the land and provide fertilizer, seeds, and water at cost. The crop was to be marketed through the local trading network.

The stated objectives of KRP were "to increase food supply, to provide employment opportunities, and to improve the standard of living" (Jackson 1985:xiii). Examination of the project documents, however, led Jackson to the conclusion that there were also implicit goals. These were similar to the aims of the

Mwea scheme: to convert subsistence farmers into producers for the market. In spite of the massive change envisaged,

> it was also hoped that the social fabric would not be fundamentally changed, that inequalities between irrigators and nonirrigators would not develop, that new skills would be acquired, and that outmigration would be stemmed. The scheme was predicated on the assumption that the local population would move from isolated and dispersed farmstead types of settlement to nucleated villages provided with services.
>
> (Jackson 1985:xiii)

Jackson found that the goals of the project were not reached in several important respects and that, moreover, there were serious consequences for local production and nutrition, the economic power of women, and gender relations. KRP caused a loss of traditional crops: sorghum; tree products such as dates, baobab products, and locust beans (an important weaning food, see p. 34); vegetables; and other food produced under the traditional riverside shaduf flood irrigation system (this system was wiped out by the construction of the Tiga Dam; see Jackson 1985:23). Furthermore, the traditional symbiosis between the agricultural Hausa and the nomadic Fulani — a relationship particularly beneficial to women — was undermined. Project organizers considered the wandering herds of Fulani cattle a problem and, therefore, designed the scheme to prevent the Fulani from passing through. Consequently, a vital food for both groups, *fura* (millet paste balls) could no longer be made and eaten at the midday meal because Fulani women could no longer sell Hausa women the milk to make the nutritious snack. Meanwhile, there were unrealized plans to produce fresh milk for Kano and the region from imported dairy cattle. "This is an example of the planners' blindness to the food needs of the local population and to the entrepreneurial contribution of women" (Jackson 1985:24).

Another example of such blindness related to small livestock. Despite KRP's stated objective to improve the standard of living and the traditional importance of poultry, controlled by women, to family nutrition, the project banned household poultry-keeping. In the face of drastic constraints on this practice and the lack of any support in the form of technological know-how, the women persevered in raising domestic animals, which continued to be an important food source.

Overall, the intention of KRP was that wet-season farming would meet the local food needs and all dry-season farming would be surplus. After 6 years of operation, however, rising food deficits were being recorded in the region along with a decline in the availability of sorghum, millet, beans, and cassava. Nevertheless, on KRP farms, families benefited from the tomatoes and rice grown thanks to the entrepreneurship of the project women.

It is evident that the local political economy was dramatically changed by KRP. The decline in the region's food self-sufficiency was part of a transformation:

> The range of choices available to the farmer has been reduced, as to what to grow and how to grow it. He has become dependent on the KRP management for inputs to irrigated agriculture, certain land has acquired a relatively high value, there is progressively more renting of land and so on. Although the area has been integrated into a market economy for many years there is little doubt that the KRP has accelerated certain trends and initiated others whereby the region is becoming further and further integrated into the world capitalist system....
>
> (Jackson 1985:22)

What this greater dependence on the state and upon the wider economic system meant for women is something that would be hard to call "development."

> For farmers wives[3] generally, the KRP has meant increasing seclusion and their progressive withdrawal from most agricultural tasks — with the exception of wheat harvesting. However, the specific way in which women have experienced this irrigation scheme depends on a variety of factors; age is an important one, for older non-secluded women have found a variety of wage labouring opportunities now available to them.
>
> (Jackson 1978:22–23)

Many studies have shown (e.g., Cohen 1969; Callaway 1984) that, in African Muslim societies, a substantial increase in men's income, as was the case with the wheat crop returns in KRP, leads to a power imbalance in the sex-gender system that is manifested in, and reinforced by, purdah (*shulle* in Hausa). In other words, increased productivity is often linked with increased control of women. Women who formerly worked outside their compounds are secluded once their husbands become wealthy. It is important to note, as Cohen (1969) does, that it is a mark of status, rather than a sudden access of piety, that leads men to desire that their women be secluded. The point, of course, is that religious ideology responds flexibly to political and economic conditions. Jackson reports that even when women's labour was required in KRP wheat fields, informants would refuse to acknowledge that they engaged in this work.

Within the seclusion of their homesteads, however, women showed ingenuity in converting aspects of the project design to their own use while receiving no technological input. The drying and selling of tomatoes and the previously mentioned poultry management are examples. Women were able to generate meagre incomes and some food for the family from such activities in this restricted context; i.e., they had a measure of economic security, if little autonomy in the homestead. For older women, less constrained by rules of seclusion, a solution was found to the worsening gender relations, whereby male "heads of households" increasingly controlled the farm labour and income of women. Many moved to low-paid agricultural employment (at one-seventh the daily wage of men). The women were hired by a multinational company growing vegetables for the European winter market (Jackson 1978). The explanations for this seemingly irrational pattern are complex and are explored in the context of Kenya in Chapter 4 (see also Stamp 1975–1976, 1986). Briefly, Jackson (1978:23) argues that working for the company provided women with much more autonomy than working for "husbands or brothers or male kin of any sort," whom they would find it impossible to defy.

> The authority of men over their wives in the household, which is not altogether a product of Islam, provides a model for the agricultural work relations, such as in the wheat harvest, and this makes rebellion by the women workers a much more difficult matter. In this sense we can see again how the household is part of the reproduction of structures of domination for it is only when operating outside of kin, marriage and village connections that women were able to protest against their exploitation [in the strike against the bean-growing multinational; Jackson 1978:24–25]. And paradoxically it is also the household that enables them to make this challenge for marriage can

---

[3]I disagree with Jackson's (1978) use of the term "farmer's wife." The term implies, once again, that women are ancillary to farm production. The logical absurdity of talking about "farm husbands" makes my point.

give women tactical mobility. For women, the household allows some
material independence but also entails ideological oppression....
Unsurprisingly, given the value Hausa women place on independence, the
wage they are prepared to work for is very low. Wage labour, indeed female
production generally, seems to be motivated not by the desire to accumulate,
nor by the need to reproduce, nor by the need for subsistence, nor by the
demands of the state but by the quest for autonomy.

(Jackson 1978:33,36)

Jackson (1985) draws the conclusion that KRP created no incentive for Hausa
trading women to make investments in production within the household and made
no link between women's entrepreneurial activities and the project's goals for
agricultural production. The complete neglect of women's concerns simply
confirmed for the Muslim women that their best interests lay in removing
themselves as much as possible from the household economy, creating a separate,
women's world into which to place their energies and generate independent
resources, however meagre, with which to endow their daughters (Jackson
1985:57). Clearly, a vital resource for the community, the energy and initiative of
women, was diverted from the community. Consequently, women contributed far
less to local self-sufficiency than might have been the case had the impact of the
scheme on the sex-gender system been taken into account (for another study of the
impact of development schemes on sex-gender systems that makes important
theoretical points, see Conti 1979.)

The importance of women's grass-roots organizations

In practically every study that has considered the decision-making role of
women within African communities, women's organizations have been identified
as central to the authority they wield. Even though cowives in a polygynous
marriage have some collective say within the context of the marital economy, it is
village-based groups, organized by age or by voluntary membership, that provide
women with the power that can counterbalance the dominant position of men (see
the case studies in Chapter 4).

In development literature, development policy, and much of the WID material,
however, women's organizations have suffered from the "target group" approach
previously criticized. With little analysis of how, when, and where women have
formed their own groups, development researchers and planners have no awareness
of the importance of distinguishing between types of groups, particularly between
those generated from within the community's own customs and needs and those
imposed from outside. Thus, it was possible for the 1976 USAID-sponsored survey
of women in rural development (Mickelwait et al. 1976:xiii–xv) to conclude that in
many situations, "new women's associations, backed by educated urban women,
might serve as a non-male-threatening agent for overcoming societal restrictions to
an enlargement of women's roles."

This is the precise approach now taken by many agencies and governments.
Therefore, there is the common phenomenon in African countries of nationally
sponsored women's organizations (such as Maendeleo ya Wanawake [Progress of
Women] in Kenya), which are safe showcases of the government's formal
commitment to women's interests and allow them to coopt national feminist efforts
and ideology. In most cases, the organizations are deeply divided between the elite

women who run them and the alienated local women whose interests are not served; Wipper (1975) analyzed this problem in Maendeleo ya Wanawake. The situation has not changed since the time of her study, as revealed by the 1986 scandal over the embezzlement of the organization's funds by part of the leadership.

Because they have remained invisible, indigenous women's groups have not been identified as institutions to be protected and enhanced through development efforts. Consequently, women frequently lose, through the introduction of new technology to their communities, the opportunities upon which their social activities were based. For example, in removing water collection from the daily routine of women, new water systems (such as pumps) remove an important occasion for women to gather and talk while working. Although nobody would argue that women should go back to collecting water from polluted rivers, the loss of this social time must be recognized as a serious setback for women's ability to network and, hence, for their ability to sustain the social and economic life of the community.

Another aspect of development efforts that has undermined women's groups is the widespread shift to cash cropping, with the attendant shift of production returns from women's control to men's control. An interesting study of work attitudes in a Nigerian city by a Kenyan scholar (wa Karanja 1981) revealed that almost all men and women believed that both husbands and wives should keep separate bank accounts to maintain marital harmony. The women believed that the separate accounts were necessary because of the different spending patterns of men and women (wa Karanja 1981:57–59). These findings reveal a continuity from the past to the present in the division of economic responsibility between men and women. Contemporary women use their income to fulfill their responsibility as primary contributors to the family's well-being in the same way that, in the past, they shouldered the responsibility for production of food and maintenance of family health. Studies on women's groups (see Chapter 4) reveal that the major channel for resources, in the past and present, whether cash or produce, has been through women's groups. The village welfare and production system was in large part maintained, and, in many cases, is still maintained, through systems of fees and pooled resources circulating among women.

The loss of control over the product of their labour has seriously undermined women's ability to fulfill these responsibilities. Furthermore, once out of their hands, the returns from their efforts often no longer go to the sustenance of their families. When men appropriate the cash returns from women's work after commodity production or a new technology is introduced — as in the case of the hydraulic oil-palm presses (p. 59) and as Muntemba demonstrates in the study summarized in Chapter 4 — they treat this income as a legitimate part of the male financial domain. One example of this, personally encountered in Samburu District, Kenya, in 1973, was the case of a husband of four wives who banked the earnings from his wives' industrious production of beadwork for tourists and, with the money, paid the bridewealth for a fifth wife, 50 years his junior. The other wives complained bitterly that the stock of cattle supporting the polygynous family was inadequate to support another wife and her children, and that their husband was satisfying his vanity rather than the needs of the family.

Given that the former relationship between women's productive capacity and their capacity to care for their families has been broken by the diversion of a significant proportion of their economic return to the male economic domain, women's groups have lost the secure economic basis for their activities. It is not surprising, therefore, that women prefer to work outside the family network for a small wage that they control rather than labour on the more productive enterprise of cash crop cultivation on family land. In this regard, I disagree slightly with Jackson's (1985) conclusion that there is only a political and not an economic rationale to women's wage labour outside the family farm.

Despite its lack of historical analysis of women's groups, the WID literature has identified some important priorities regarding the group participation of women in development. The 1984 workshop in Tanzania on resources, power, and women (ILO 1985) was particularly forceful on this topic. In particular, participants stressed the necessity of moving beyond the castigation of development efforts for their negative impact on women, to focus on those rare projects that, by genuine development criteria, succeeded. Only through a careful analysis of such successes, in contrast to poorly designed projects, would planners generate the basis for more consistent success in future.

> The purpose of the workshop was to exchange information and views on successful and innovative projects for rural women, to draw lessons from successful experiences, and to strengthen ongoing projects and stimulate the initiation of new ones..... Women's issues are central and not peripheral to development. The struggle for equality is not a struggle between women and men — it is a struggle to change social structures and attitudes.
>
> (ILO 1985)

Two projects in Sierra Leone deemed successful by their designers and the government were presented to the workshop by the eminent African feminist, Filomina Steady (ILO 1985:13). Their comparison provided a useful lesson on women's organizations and development. The first project, cosponsored by the governments of the Federal Republic of Germany and Sierra Leone, introduced new fish-smoking technology to Tombo, a fishing village. The aim was to improve the returns to fishing as an artisanal activity. The project, through the new technology as well as better storage facilities, made it possible for women, who traditionally processed fish for sale, to raise their productivity and control fish prices. To control the supply of fish and circumvent the necessity of buying fish from men, some women purchased their own boats. Although the project had many successful elements, there were serious questions as to the sustainability of women's self-sufficiency in the fish processing business. The need for foreign exchange to maintain the imported technology, the dependence on foreign experts, and the purely profit-making purpose of the scheme meant a greater dependency than before for women upon elements beyond their control. By feminist and grass-roots definitions of development, therefore, the project was not successful.

By contrast, the second project was a self-help effort. In 1977, the Gloucester Development Association Project was founded to promote village development. It did this by encouraging improved farming methods, providing market stalls for the sale of produce, creating day-care centres and adult-education schemes, and developing a system of bulk food purchase. Its operating budget was a minuscule SLL 500/year (compared with the SLL 900 000 cost of the 6-year fish-smoking project; in September 1988, 36 Sierra Leone leones [SLL] = 1 United States dollar [USD]). "Its achievements are significant, self-sustaining and replicable" (ILO 1985).

Scattered through the literature are similar success stories. The corn mill societies in Cameroon have already been mentioned (p. 53) (see Wipper 1984:75–76). On the basis of 15 mills loaned to villages in the 1950s, corn mills societies were formed, members paying a monthly fee to use the mill. After 1 year, 30 villages had paid off their loans and more mills were bought. Eventually, there were 200 societies with a membership of 18 000. As is often the case when women form associations for a specific purpose, the associations soon expanded their concerns from food processing to other issues typically of concern to African village women (Keyi 1986). Wipper (1984:75–76) summarizes the Cameroonian village experience:

> From the social gatherings that took place around the corn mills came the idea of holding classes in cooking, soap-making, child care, hygiene, and nutrition. The women then set about making bricks and cutting bamboo in order to construct a meeting hall. As the societies' strength increased, the women began to handle long-standing problems. They bought barbed wire on loan and put up fences to protect their gardens from stray cattle. The loan was repaid by putting more land under cultivation. Department of Agriculture assistants introduced a new and better strain of corn, which yielded an abundant harvest. The women began to understand the need for contour farming. Poultry schemes were begun, village plots reforested, and water storage facilities built. The societies' most ambitious scheme was the establishment of a cooperative store to allow women to import articles unavailable locally. Five thousand women raised the initial capital and several stores were soon in operation.

Even in conditions of deep impoverishment, women are able to create collectively the means for improving their community's well-being. Chege (1986) reports the manner in which women in a Nairobi slum formed a communal food production group, the Mukuru-Kaiyaba Women's Group, to farm a 10-acre (4-ha) piece of wasteland owned by the Kenya Railways that was adjacent to their shanty village. Organized along the well-structured lines of traditional Kikuyu women's groups (labour contribution and sharing of returns are carefully regulated, see the Mitero case study in Chapter 4), the group grew maize, beans, and vegetables. The group's purpose extended beyond collective cultivation, however.

> The women sell the food they grow to get income for the group and to plan for other projects. As well, each member gets a portion of the food for her family. A major project they have proposed is the levelling of their land next to the Ngong river, so that it can be irrigated. Another is to fence in a small dam on the river, and stock it with fish. The Health Inspectors from the City Council of Nairobi have approved the proposed fish project. Once they have raised the funds and fenced the dam, the women plan to rent the dam to fishermen, charging entrance fees.
>
> (Chege 1986:77)

Despite growing evidence as to the innovative capacities of Kenya's many grass-roots women's groups, their efforts and abilities have not been harnessed to development as they might be. This is because, once again, the "welfare approach" hampers viewing them as the progressive force that they are. Officials who interact with the groups are usually community development officers or home economics extension workers (Ventura-Dias 1985:209–210). If one can identify genuine development in Kenyan villages, however, the cause may usually be located in the efforts of the village self-help groups.

4   Feminist Political Economy

Feminist political economy is the small but pluralistic body of literature that I have identified as having most successfully elucidated African gender relations (see Chapter 1, pp. 19–24). The historical materialist method of socialist feminism makes up its theoretical core; its substance also includes studies using a liberal approach. The reason for including certain liberal studies in the proposed new conceptual framework is that they contribute a vital local perspective on gender relations and economy. Through the rigour of their empirical analyses and through their sensitivity to local constructions of gender ideology and practice, these studies work to overcome the Western biases and assumptions inherent in of much of the feminist and nonfeminist scholarship on Africa. The three studies summarized in this chapter and the work of Mbilinyi (1984, 1985a,b, 1986) rely on an adapted historical materialist method. Several studies cited in Chapters 5 and 6 for their clarity on gender relations (e.g., Ladipo 1981; Wilson 1982; Badri 1986) start from but transcend the liberal framework.

Although the feminist political economy scholarship has only treated development issues incidentally, as aspects of women's loss of power and autonomy in the village and the family, it provides the grounds upon which an understanding of the phenomena discussed in Chapter 3 can be based. In particular, the centrality of women's organizations to African community life and the gender ideology that empowered women politically can be understood in their historical complexity.

In a recent article on Kikuyu women's self-help groups in Kenya (Stamp 1986), I used the experience of the women of Mitero village to develop theoretical tools for an understanding of sex-gender systems in precolonial Africa, and of the way in which these systems have been transformed in colonial and postcolonial times. The study draws on many feminist political economy texts, including non-African material, in the development of its theoretical argument. Other political economy studies of gender relations in Africa substantiate many aspects of the empirical findings, and point toward the theoretical construct presented here.

The first part of this chapter presents the Mitero study as a case exemplifying the feminist political economy approach. The second part of the chapter summarizes studies by two African scholars, substantiates the case for feminist political economy, and demonstrates the development of this school of thought within Africa. Although details about women's organizations differ and much more work needs to be done on sex-gender systems (e.g., in matrilineal societies), the categories of analysis developed here (see also Stamp and Chege 1984; Robertson and Berger 1986) provide a valid template for the consideration of gender relations in other African societies.

Gender relations and women's self-help groups

The Kikuyu are a vigorous, Bantu-speaking, ethnic group of over 2 million that have dominated the Kenyan political economy for much of the postindependence period. They inhabit a fertile hilly region of central Kenya. Patrilineal, polygynous, and horticultural (i.e., tracing descent through the male line and practicing hoe cultivation of crops), they were typical in many ways of sub-Saharan African agricultural societies. Their communally organized political economy and gender relations based on bridewealth were shared by most Bantu societies (and by many societies belonging to other linguistic groups).

A society such as the Kikuyu has traditionally been considered patriarchal, but an analysis of its gender relations demonstrates that the concept of patriarchy cannot be uncritically applied. Many feminist theorists, seeking to explain what they perceive as the universal domination of women by men throughout history, have used the concept of patriarchy to designate the gender system under which all forms of oppression occur. As Rubin (1975:167) states, however, "the term 'Patriarchy' was introduced to distinguish the forces maintaining sexism from other social forces, such as capitalism. But the use of 'patriarchy' obscures other distinctions. Its use is analogous to using 'capitalism' to refer to all modes of production." Rubin (1975:167) argues that "sexual systems have a certain autonomy and cannot be explained in terms of economic forces." By contrast, "sex-gender system" is a neutral, overarching concept. It may be used to classify all forms of gender relations, from patriarchal and oppressive to egalitarian. Patriarchy, then, is one of a number of sex-gender systems.

Focusing on the sex-gender system as a sphere of human activity and as relationships separate from, but intimately linked to, material production and reproduction allows the restoration of gender relations to their rightful place at the centre of political economy. More specifically, such a focus contributes to a better understanding of the complex interactions between the economic, social, and ideological aspects of male–female relationships in a society such as the Kikuyu, both in the precapitalist era and today. Rubin (1975) draws on the flawed but useful work of Lévi-Strauss (1969) on kinship to define her concept of sex-gender system. Lévi-Strauss (1969) classified the types of "exchange of women" that are integral to human kinship systems (e.g, women exchanged for women, women exchanged for bridewealth, women accompanied by dowry to the groom's family). Rubin (1975:177) suggests that "the 'exchange of women' is an initial step toward building an arsenal of concepts with which sexual systems can be described."

There are problems, however, with the emphasis by Lévi-Strauss (1969) and Rubin (1975) on exchange. Kettel (1986:55) stresses the importance of avoiding a view of women as "primordial pawns in the affairs of men" and, specifically, as a form of "capital" controlled by men (as indicated in Chapter 3, it is precisely this view of women, as assets of men, that has stymied development efforts). Leacock (1981:234) is similarly critical of the view of women as passive objects in the marriage game. She questions the current view that men are "the universal exploiters of women, albeit at times gentlemanly exploiters, who graciously acknowledge women as 'the supreme gift,'" to use Lévi-Strauss's (1969:65) expression. On the basis of much ethnographic evidence, Leacock (1981:24) makes an assertion that is central to feminist political economy:

> The authority structure of egalitarian societies where all individuals were
> equally dependent on a collective larger than the nuclear family was one of
> wide dispersal of decision making among mature and elder women and men,
> who essentially made decisions — either singly, in small groups, or
> collectively — about those activities which it was their socially defined
> responsibility to carry out. Taken together, these constituted the "public" life
> of the group.

These decisions concerned marriage, among many other things. Going beyond
Rubin's idea of woman-exchange, we can view women not as passive objects in
their own exchange but as active agents participating with men to "make
marriages" (Collier and Rosaldo 1981:278), organizing women and men into social
relations for biological reproduction. A categorization of sex-gender systems, then,
will examine the different ways in which marriage is organized and seek to link
them to different patterns of economic and political organization. In turn,
arrangements by which women circulate vary and can be correlated with
differences in their autonomy and authority from one society to another. A number
of studies confirm Rubin's (1975) proposition that there are regularities to types of
marriage exchange by which we can precisely define sex-gender systems.

To establish the main features of the bridewealth sex-gender system, a simple
comparison will suffice. In a society with reciprocal exchange of women between
kin groups, such as the Lele of Zaire (Douglas 1963, cited in Rubin 1975:205), to
get a bride, a man must have a kinswoman whom he can give in marriage.
Furthermore, each marriage incurs a debt. The web of debts and schemes for the
control of women leaves them little latitude for independent action. Where a
woman's family receives bridewealth (which the family can use in turn to obtain a
bride), such a web of debts and staking rights does not exist. "Each transaction is
self-contained" (Rubin 1975:206); however, it places the bride in a network of
"social ties" that constrains her action throughout her marriage. Bridewealth
systems vary considerably, and some involve the conversion of bridewealth into
male political power (for a fascinating account of this network among the Kikuyu,
see Mackenzie 1986:Chapter 5). The fulfillment of the material contract always
depends, however, upon a wife's performance as a procreator and producer; a
number of political and economic considerations rest upon her marriage.
Conversely, the success of her marriage depends on the ability and willingness of
her affinal kin (her relatives by marriage) to fulfill their obligations to her family.

Thus, a marriage, rather than being a concrete, once-only expression of a debt
fulfilled or incurred, is the ongoing manifestation of contractual relationships
among a web of kin. The advancement of these relationships largely depends on the
actions of the woman. As Leacock (1981:241) puts it, "In some societies, women
move back and forth as valued people, creating, recreating and cementing networks
of reciprocal relations through their moves, which are recompensed with
brideprice." The substantial rights of wives in precolonial Africa to control the
means of production and own the product of their labour indicates the power of
their central position in the bridewealth system. Conversely, the bridewealth system
may have been favoured in political economies where economic and historical
opportunity fostered a structure of economic participation for women that allowed
them such control. In this regard, it is significant that the dowry sex-gender system,
with its concomitant poor position for women, is associated with the plough
societies of Asia and the bridewealth sex-gender system is associated with the hoe

cultivation societies of Southeast Asia, sub-Saharan Africa, and other parts of the world (Boserup 1970:48,50).[1]

The bridewealth sex-gender system is also correlated with polygyny (marriage of one man to two or more women). Contrary to the received truth that polygyny always oppresses women, the polygynous household may offer women a basis for solidarity and task sharing. At the household level, cowives cooperate to organize production, consumption, and child care. Although friction between cowives is widely reported, many studies stress the economic and political advantages of polygyny, including the autonomy made possible by shared responsibility (Boserup 1970:43; Mullings 1976:254; Obbo 1980:34–35). There is evidence that cowife jealousy is a construct of patrilineal ideology, whereby brotherly solidarity among men is the social glue that holds kin-based societies together.

In societies with the bridewealth sex-gender system, there are often organizations that express the political power of women (e.g., Kikuyu women's age-grade organizations, and the market trading organizations of Ibo women in Onitsha, Nigeria, in the 18th century; Sacks 1982:3). Thus, although women come under the jurisdiction of their affinal kin (often oppressively so), they have, in the bridewealth sex-gender system, the material, political, and ideological base for relative power and autonomy. The relatively powerful position of women in African societies, compared with many other precapitalist cultures, is due to the prevalence of the rich, complex kinship organization based on bridewealth.

The Kikuyu were organized by descent into clans and lineages and by rank into age grades. There were no chiefs or centralized political authorities, although individual men could become influential by manipulating material wealth to create political prestige. Women were affiliated with their husband's patrilineage through bridewealth, which legitimized the marriage and secured lineage membership for their offspring. Women retained membership in their natal lineage however, and, as lineage sisters, could exercise rights in lineage resources if necessary (see Sacks 1979). Usually, the major economic ties of women would be through their children to their husband's lineage; however, sisters would be expected to participate with brothers in lineage decisions, and widows and unmarried women would have use rights in their lineage land. As Sacks (1979) clarifies, the position of women vis-à-vis their natal lineage was higher than their position in relation to their husband's lineage. In other words, women had a higher status as sisters than as wives (see also Mackenzie 1986).

The mode of production associated with this form of social organization is the communal mode of production. In this mode of production, kinship is the basis of production relations. All people are members of a kin corporation (the lineage or the clan), which owns the chief means of production, the land. In principle, all members, male and female, stand in the same relation to the means of production and share political and economic decision making (Sacks 1979:115). Relations of production are thus cooperative rather than antagonistic. The authority to make decisions, however, is vested in elders, who, in practice, exercise ideological, political, and juridical power. Moreover, the male elders have preeminent authority.

---

[1]When considering Asian sex-gender systems, it is important to avoid the kind of simplistic judgments that have the dogged understanding of African society (for a subtle analysis of gender, class, and caste in India, see Liddle and Joshi 1986).

Among the Kikuyu, as elsewhere, elders were organized for the formal exercise of this authority by the age-grade structure (Muriuki 1974; Leakey 1933). Male elders had privileged status and could largely appropriate the labour of women and younger men as well as make decisions on access to the corporately owned land. Thus, the elders exercised considerable control over the means of production.

The counterbalancing rights of different categories of people tempered this control. Sons had rights to bridewealth and to land and stock with which to set up their own homesteads. Daughters had rights that lapsed on marriage but could be reactivated if necessary. Lineage wives had rights to the use of land and livestock, owned the produce they were responsible for growing, and, to a large degree, controlled the distribution of this produce. Furthermore, lineage wives owned their own houses and controlled the resources of their subhousehold within the polygynous homestead (Routledge and Routledge 1910:47; Kenyatta 1938:11–12, 171–172; Middleton and Kershaw 1965:20). Women as elders had collective authority in a wide range of matters (Hobley 1922:274; Kenyatta 1938:108; Kershaw 1973:55; Stamp 1975–1976:25; Clark 1980:360).

Kikuyu society demonstrates the point that the communal mode of production, although fostering unequal relationships between elders and youths and between men and women, is fundamentally a classless mode of production: no group is free to appropriate and accumulate the surplus produced by another group for their own benefit. The bridewealth sex-gender system was vital to the communal mode of production among the Kikuyu, and gender relations were a shaping force in the nonexploitative relations of production.

Some scholars have argued that such kin-based societies have a class structure based on the appropriation by elders of the labour of women and young men. I consider this argument incorrect, however, in that it is based on a misunderstanding of class. Class is a category that is self-reproducing through the relations of production (e.g., a bourgooisie maintaining itself through the production of capital from the value created by a working class). In that all members of communal societies become elders, the ability to appropriate value produced by others is a function of the life cycle rather than of class division. Moreover, the value appropriated is shared through a complex web of kin and associational obligations; it is not hoarded by elders. In communal societies, prestige depends on generosity.

An accurate understanding of the communal mode of production is necessary for a clear perception of the transformations in contemporary African society. Feminist political economists argue that a lack of such understanding is the reason traditional gender relations have been distorted and are now becoming exploitative. It is the past pattern of relative egalitarianism and autonomy that women are now trying so hard to recapture or retain. Much of the behaviour of women with regard to development schemes (e.g., that of the Hausa women in KRP, discussed in Chapter 3) can be explained in these terms.

It is true however, that gender relations were only relatively egalitarian. The bridewealth sex-gender system involved an element of female subsidy whereby female labour could be transformed into male wealth or prestige. Clark (1980:360–365) and Ciancanelli (1980:26) both confirm this for the Kikuyu before British contact. The subsidy was an important factor in the development of *athamaki* or "big men" among the Kikuyu. Men achieved the position of *muthamaki* (singular) by successfully manipulating the tangible and intangible assets of kinship contracts. Clark (1980:361) summarizes the means whereby gender relations were organized to yield such assets:

> Through the exchange of bridewealth–livestock, marriages were legitimated, and women whose children increased the size of the group were incorporated into the family. These women put more land under cultivation, and enabled the distribution of more foodstuff. The mobilization of wealth in the form of land, livestock and people is a single, though complex, process which collapses the division between subsistence and political economy.

Women could directly enhance a *muthamaki*'s position by agreeing to cook and distribute the food and beer required to attract work parties of young men to clear new land. These men would then become his tenants and political followers. There was nothing to compel women to contribute this effort: consequently, they wielded considerable bargaining power through their monopoly of the beer-brewing craft. (With the colonial importation of beer factories, women lost not only an occupation but also a valuable basis for social influence.)

It is clear that the constraints and obligations of the bridewealth sex-gender system (to bear children for their husband's lineage, to produce food and offer hospitality, and to act as the linchpin in a wide network of affinal kin relations) gave women the opportunity to exercise political power and the authority to make decisions. The age-grade system was the main way in which women exercised this opportunity. It provided the base for their strategies to generate resources and the forum for their collective decision making. Being based on the childbearing cycle, the age-grade structure of women was simpler than the male system (Kertzer and Madison [1981:125–128] discuss the different relations of men and women to the life cycle as it pertains to age-grade structure). The two active age grades were *nyakinyua* (elders whose first child had been circumcised) and *kang'ei* (women with uncircumcised children; i.e., children younger than 15 years).[2]

The anthropological data on women's organizations in former times is meager and contradictory. Mackenzie (1986) thoroughly considers the age-grade and age-set structures of women. In this study, based on recently conducted fieldwork, she has added essential new elements to the understanding of women and age grades, which have been largely ignored in the East African literature. Her interpretive reading of the literature on the Kikuyu is a model for feminist political economy research.

Women elders interviewed in the Mitero village study (Stamp 1975–1976) gave detailed accounts of ongoing organizations known as *ndundu* that had operated since before their grandmothers' time and that combined economic, social, and juridical functions. *Ndundu* is often translated as "council" and it is significant that the same word is used for the council of male elders. A central purpose of the *ndundu* was cooperative cultivation, but they also provided women with organizational and affiliative bases for nonagricultural pursuits. *Kang'ei* women operated under the authority of *nyakinyua* and were required to perform services for the older women to progress through the organization's ranks. Thus, the control of younger lineage wives by their female elders was a legitimate authority counterbalancing the patrilineal control of women. This control also put considerable human labour at the disposition of the women elders as a group. Clark

---

[2] Girls and boys were customarily circumcised among the Kikuyu, although clitoridectomy was banned in Kenya in 1982.

(1980:368) gives an apt summary of Kikuyu gender relations: "Despite an ideology of male dominance pervasive in many kin relations and in areas characterized as the 'prestige economy,' Kikuyu women emerge as the actors with control over resources vital in a system in which relations of production enter into political strategies and are built into the social relations of power." Sacks' (1979) point about sisters and wives coincides with this position. One could argue that lineage sisterhood not only provided women with material resources they could call upon if necessary but also created a metaphor of "sisterhood." This concept extended to all women and constrained the overbearing subordination of wives by husbands. In other words, every wife was somebody's sister.

In the picture that emerges of traditional Kikuyu women's organizations, we can see the lineaments of women's contemporary collective activity, activity that was repeatedly described in Chapters 2 and 3 for societies all over Africa. Variations on the Kikuyu experience have been documented in many studies (e.g., Van Allen 1972; Okeyo 1980; Oboler 1985; for an overview, see Sacks 1982). Women cling to the remnants of these organizations, patterns of authority, and practices of autonomy to resist the negative impact of technology transfer or to convert technological innovations to their advantage.

What happened to women's power and autonomy? The transformation of sex-gender systems is tied up in the transition to capitalism. Whereas in Europe this transition entailed the dissolution of the precapitalist mode of production (i.e., feudalism) and the development of a straightforward capitalist class structure, colonized societies are characterized by the articulation of precapitalist and capitalist modes of production. Precapitalist elements, located in the peasantry, are retained in a dominated and distorted form. These elements include kinship structures and relations of production, age-based organizations, gender relations, and traditional ideologies. The transformed elements subsidize an underdeveloped form of capitalism through the production of cash crops by smallholders and plantation wage labourers. Some of the negative consequences for African communities of such commodity production were chronicled in Chapter 3. One example is the recruitment of elders to promoting cash crop production.

Two important aspects of this underdevelopment are, first, the unequal exchange upon which the sale of primary commodities on the world market is based and, second, the vulnerability of the producing peasants and the exporting nations within which they live to the vagaries of the international market. What makes unequal exchange and an unstable international market possible (i.e., what keeps peasants producing under such adverse circumstances) is the subsidy provided by peasants (chiefly women) who grow food for subsistence and sale on marginal land. Low product prices and low agricultural wages reflect this element of peasant subsidy: the production of the peasant household provides at least part of the subsistence for commodity-producing peasants and wage labourers, so that they are not fully dependent on a cash crop income for survival. Wages or returns to commodity production are rarely sufficient to support a family. In other words, capitalist enterprise in Africa need not provide a "living wage" to workers or producers.

The traditional–modern dichotomy is, therefore, a fallacy: the peasantry, far from being the "traditional" and implicitly "backward" sector of modern African societies, can be seen as an impoverished class created by the relations of production that were imposed on precapitalist societies in the colonial era. It is because of the vulnerability and dependency of contemporary peasants and societies that the present era is labeled "neocolonial."

With regard to gender relations, elements of the bridewealth sex-gender system have also been retained in a dominated and distorted form. At the ideological level, the dynamic tension between formal patrilineal domination and both formal and informal female power has been snapped, and patrilineal domination has united with Victorian and Christian notions of male superiority (Obbo 1980:37–39). Bridewealth in particular, formerly the key to the power and autonomy of women, has become a capitalist transaction and daughters are commodities whose price can be bargained (see Parkin 1972). Furthermore, with the commoditization of land, women not only lost use rights but also saw their rights as lineage sisters attenuated. If husbands became unwilling to share the cash proceeds of the land now registered in their names with their wives, they would be even less willing to accede to the requests of their lineage sisters. There are also ideological consequences for gender relations. With the weakening of lineage ties and the concomitant strengthening of marriage ties, the sister model for interacting with women has given way to the more subordinate wife model (see Sacks 1979).

The consequent loss of women's power in Africa at both the economic and political level, a dominant theme in the Mitero study, is confirmed by many writers (e.g., Van Allen 1972, 1976; Conti 1979; Sacks 1979, 1982; Etienne 1980; Oboler 1985). In Kenya, with the new overarching political authority of the state, the political institutions of precapitalist societies withered. Some place was found for male elders; for example, *athamaki* often became chiefs and subchiefs in the colonial administration. In Mitero, male elders of the Mutego lineage preside over the customary judiciary, which operates parallel to, and in conjunction with, the British common law system (for a discussion of the parallel legal systems, see Ghai and McAuslan 1970). Women elders hold no political positions, however, and women in Kenya are largely absent from formal political power. Direct and indirect pressure by church and state against polygyny and the promotion of the nuclear family have also undermined the former power base of women.

The fact that precolonial institutions and legal structures have largely disappeared does not mean, however, that Africans have turned their backs on the idea of "tradition." Indeed, as I argue subsequently, as Glazier (1985) has shown, and as recent events in Kenya have demonstrated, the idiom of tradition is constantly available to be manipulated by protagonists competing for status, power, and resources in society.

At the economic level, the element of sex-gender subsidy remains and has, in fact, been increased (outlined in Chapter 3). Women are expected to produce to support their husbands as before; in addition, however, they are expected to produce the petty commodity surplus, which their husbands then appropriate. The network of laws and economic practices that characterize the contemporary capitalist state sanction, and, in fact, require, this appropriation. Two of the most important factors are land consolidation and cash crop marketing organizations. Beginning in the 1950s, land was transferred from lineage ownership to individual male heads of households. Legally, therefore, the product of this land is the property of the individual husband, although women continue to lay strong claim to their subsistence products and, in practice, attempt to dispose of them as they see fit. Whether or not they succeed in retaining this control depends on the nature of their individual relationships with their husbands and on their success in participating in the activities of their self-help groups.

Cash crop marketing organizations, such as the Coffee Marketing Board, facilitate the appropriation of the income generated by women's labour. As with other parastatal enterprises, these organizations are oriented toward individual male heads of households. Women therefore carry the burden of production for no wage and under conditions where kinship has been reorganized by the new economic structure into smaller units (i.e., nuclear families). Within these units, their former economic independence and political autonomy is seriously restricted. In the past, even where the *muthamaki* parlayed his wives' labour into personal influence, he used that influence to enhance the well-being of his homestead and lineage, not for personal material gain. Today, the ideology of personal wealth is a primary motive for accumulation, even if wealth is elusive for the peasant. In many areas of Africa, therefore, an exacerbated form of sex-gender domination has become an important element of the general peasant subsidy of commercial production for the world market.

Considering the double subsidy that peasant women provide, their self-help groups take on a special significance. Rather than being simply organizations for coping with development, which is the overt aim cited by most of them, they are vital organizations for resistance to exploitation. Mitero is a sublocation that corresponds roughly with the territory of the Mutego lineage of the Acera clan, which lies just to the north of the late President Kenyatta's home village. The descendants of Mutego, unlike many Kikuyu on the plains just to the east, were not dispossessed of their land by British settlers. Mutego's descendants engage in petty commodity production centering on coffee, which they cultivate on a family basis on a scale ranging from a few hundred bushes to plots of several acres. The community continues to engage in subsistence hoe agriculture on reduced acreage, growing maize, potatoes, and beans of various species for their own consumption and cultivating some food crops for cash.

Whereas many men habitually leave the sublocation for work, in the typical migration pattern of neocolonial Africa, women represent the more demographically stable component of the community. In Mitero, women began to come together in the contemporary form of self-help groups in 1966, with the encouragement of community development officers and the Provincial Administration.[3] The original objective was organization for the utilization of new agricultural inputs, such as fertilizers. Informants stressed that the old style *ndundu* no longer existed; however, it is clear that the self-help groups are successors to these organizations. The groups perform the traditional functions of cooperative cultivation, *ngwatio*, and cooperative household management for women in childbirth, *matega*. Significantly, these terms now incorporate additional meanings. *Ngwatio* is organized to generate funds for self-help projects, such as a nursery school, water piping, and other amenities directly related to reducing the burden of women's labour, or to community improvement. Funds have also been used to establish small businesses, such as a dressmaking shop. *Matega* continues to provide group help to members for weddings and funerals, as well as for childbirth. *Matega* also designates a savings society that collects funds from the sale of surplus

---

[3]Of the 10 women's groups in Mitero, 8 were studied during field research in 1974, 1981, and 1985 through in-depth interviews with the group leaders and members.

food crops and wage labour on nearby plantations and, in turn, provides a lump sum for each woman. With these funds, a woman may buy a major household requirement, such as a cow, a water tank, or furniture. March and Taqqu (1986:60–65) analyze "rotating credit associations" (as well as rotating labour associations), citing them as a widespread phenomenon among women around the world, but particularly among African women.

Interpreting the activities of Mitero women in terms of the analysis set out earlier suggests two purposes. First, by channeling cash from crops into self-help organizations, women were preventing the appropriation of their product by their husbands. Second, the women were attempting to accumulate capital as a means of protecting and enhancing their fragile incomes and compensating for lost subsistence production. With regard to the first purpose, women sought to counteract the onerous obligation of generating surplus for their husbands that arose with land consolidation and commodity production. Engagement in wage production on neighbouring coffee plantations, in a manner similar to that reported for Hausa women in KRP, can be seen as an integral part of this economic strategy. Although work on their own coffee bushes yielded good returns, it represented cash for their husbands. Wage work provided only meager earnings; these earning, however, could be channeled directly into group funds.

The struggle within capitalism over the acquisition and distribution of peasant-produced commodities has been studied by political economists. The resistance of producers may take many forms, such as "refusal to adopt new cultivation practices…, refusal to grow certain crops or cutting back on their production" (Bernstein 1977:69; also see Cutrufelli 1983:119–120). The women and technology literature records many instances of such subversion by women of new technological processes. Women's choices in disposing of their labour time and channeling their earnings into self-help groups may be seen as a form of the peasant resistance Bernstein (1977) describes. Specifically, it is resistance to the appropriation of their product by the international commodity market through the agency of their husbands. As such, it is a resistance to dual exploitation: by both the sex-gender system and the underdeveloped capitalist processes.

Informants in Mitero indicated a considerable struggle over women's labour and earnings. They referred to the male control of coffee earnings: "Men drink the coffee money." Although coffee was seen as a valuable crop, it involved the loss of control of their labour. Vegetable crops for cash sale in the market were preferred. The objections of men to the appropriation by women of the products of their own labour were evident in informants' accounts of husbands who beat their wives for participating in the self-help groups. "Men fear women when they are in a group." Overt hostility between men and women points to the dramatic sharpening of sex-gender contradictions in the contemporary era.

A further dimension is added to these contradictions by the fact that women's resistance is taking place under the banner of development ideology. Since independence, the Kenyan government has encouraged self-help activity, known as *harambee* ("pull together"), which has served to supplement state development efforts in the social services. The ideology of *harambee* is thus a powerful tool for women's assertion of control over their labour and earnings. A number of informants pointed out that men often disapprove of women's business activity and seek to undermine it on countervailing ideological grounds. Such activity has become a major focus of tension in contemporary sex-gender relations; the

83

widespread assimilation of the Western ideology of male dominance — by men, in any event — has added fuel to the fire. In a 1981 interview, a prominent women's leader recognized the power of this ideology and the need for strategy to counter it.

> How does a man exercise power as head of the home? So he has to try all means to suppress women's group activity, to make it not succeed.... We try not to be too aggressive, or to break the link with the family and even community.... We can't expect to break that myth right away — it must be gradual. If you want to change it abruptly, you encounter a stronger resistance.

It is precisely such practical thinking that leads African women to reject the individualist demands of Western feminists. Use of a discourse of family solidarity and welfare is a sophisticated and tactically sound ideological strategy on the part of African feminism.

Thus, while men protest in the name of "traditional" family values, women cautiously argue for the maintenance of their rights and for the improvement of their economic lot in terms of those same family values. The independent economic activity of women is, they say, in the service of children and the home, and progress in this sphere in the modern nation requires new tactics for the fulfillment of their time-honoured tasks. The ideological discourse in sex-gender relations can draw on different elements of precapitalist sex-gender ideology because of the contradictions in this tradition: the ideal of men's dominance over women and of women's primacy in their own realms of authority were held simultaneously. The idea of male dominance is reinforced by Christian and capitalist values, but precapitalist African values regarding the power of women in the political economy of the village remain a forceful weapon in the discourse.

There are problems with the manipulation of women's cooperative traditions both by the community and individual women. Recent research (Stamp 1987) has shown that the productive capacity of women's groups may be captured by advantaged women or by male-dominated institutions within the community (e.g., church, political party) and diverted to ends incompatible with the goals of the groups (see the summary of this research in the section on women's associations in Chapter 5). Nevertheless, women's groups remain the chief means by which rural women empower themselves politically and economically within the community; indeed, efforts at co-optation over the past few years are evidence of this.

In conclusion, women's self-help groups have fused precapitalist sex-gender elements (economic, political, and ideological) with contemporary practices to provide women with a means to resist exploitation and counter the negative effects of development programs. Therefore, the sex-gender system appears as a dynamic aspect of the peasant struggle for self-sufficiency. If women, through their organized activity, can retain even a part of the income they produce and convert new technology to the benefit of their community, the peasantry as a whole is stronger in the face of economic uncertainty and inequity. Given that self-sufficiency is now the major goal African governments are seeking to meet, recognition of, and support for, the complex ways in which women contribute to self-sufficiency would seem to be a matter of the greatest urgency. It is in the pragmatic strategies of peasant women that grassroots solutions to Africa's development dilemmas reside.

Cases in feminist political economy

Land reform and Luo women's rights

In a case study of a Luo women (a western Kenyan ethnic group belonging to the Nilotic language family), Okeyo (1980, in Etienne and Leacock 1980) demonstrates the value of a synthesis of anthropological and historical methods and provides a model for feminist research in Africa.[4] Okeyo (1980) sets the transformation of Luo gender relations in the context of colonial imperatives as they evolved in Kenya from the declaration of the East Africa Protectorate in 1895. The chief of these imperatives was that the colony "pay for itself through agriculture." This was accomplished by the appropriation of African land and the diversion of labour from the autonomous indigenous community to the colonial effort. "The choice to develop the colony by means of agriculture, managed by white settlers exploiting African labor, entailed the disenfranchisement of Africans and the entrenchment of white control over human and natural resources of the area" (Okeyo 1980:187).

Central to the colonial state's agricultural policy was the system of reservations, whereby racial and ethnic groups were segregated on designated lands; the best land was granted to white settlers. On African reserves, the former owners became "tenants-at-will of the British Crown." The aim of these reserves was to supply a stable labour force for the export sector run by the European settlers. In the course of the development of colonial land policy, "African culture, tradition, and economic and political institutions were co-opted to aid the administration of political control and economic exploitation" (Okeyo 1980:188), although customary land use patterns were initially allowed to continue.

The focus of Okeyo's analysis is "the impact of the individualization of land tenure on the traditional precolonial landholding unit (the lineage) and on the position of women. Since Luo women play a key role in the rural economy, especially in food production and reproduction, they are a major category of producers whose land rights are bound to be affected by changes in land tenure" (Okeyo 1980:188). As previously mentioned, the policy to shift land ownership from the lineage to individual male heads of household began in Kenya in the early 1950s; the reform was part of a late colonial effort to stem African resistance to colonialism by creating a conservative African middle peasantry. Following independence in 1963, the reform was continued as a development strategy. The reform process was slower in Luoland than among the Kikuyu; nevertheless, almost all land was adjudicated, consolidated and registered by 1975, with only 6% of women having land registered in their own names (Okeyo 1980:206).

Although the Luo, as a Nilotic people of pastoral ancestry, differ from the Bantu-speaking Kikuyu in their historical experience and culture, they shared the lineage-based communal mode of production and bridewealth sex-gender system described for the Kikuyu. Although Okeyo does not engage in a theoretical investigation of the concept of sex-gender system, the similarities in the experience

---

[4]Achola Pala Okeyo (who formerly published under the name of Achola O. Pala is a Kenyan social anthropologist. A Research Fellow at the Institute for Development Studies, University of Nairobi, and an international consultant, she has published many papers on the status and roles of African women in development.

of Luo and Kikuyu women regarding precolonial political economy as well as colonial and postcolonial land reform confirm my generalizations about sex-gender systems and the position of women, both precolonial and postcolonial. Moreover, Okeyo's study provides an exhaustive analysis of the means by which women lose their use (usufructuary) rights in land during the reform process.

As with the Kikuyu, land rights amongst the Luo in precolonial times resided with the corporate group, the lineage, rather than the individual: men inherited land from fathers; women had use rights as daughters or as wives. Land could not be alienated from the group, and equal access for the purpose of subsistence production was a cardinal principle. The usufructuary rights of individual men and women were complex and well defined. "For instance, each household has a precise knowledge of where fields, pastures, and homesteads are located and to which their use rights apply" (Okeyo 1980:188).

Okeyo draws three major conclusions in her analysis of the changes wrought by land tenure reform. First, the customary land-tenure system of the Luo is a product of a changing political economy. From 1000 to 1400, ancestors of the Luo lived in southern Sudan and practiced transhumant pastoralism. Under this system, men owned and managed livestock; the economic role of women was marginal. Following migration from the Nile valley "cradleland" to the west Kenyan region in the 15th and 16th centuries, the Luo settled down. By the 18th century, they had adopted a mixed economy predominated by agriculture (much like the precolonial Kikuyu). This shift in emphasis drew women into the centre of the economy, as is the case in horticultural societies throughout Africa. "During this period the labor of women and children became critical to agriculture, and the rights of women in land became anchored in their role within the lineage as wives and mothers" (Okeyo 1980:208). As well, control of land became important as the now-sedentary population increased. Consequently, lineage became a more precise instrument for land control, pasture management, and water management. "The woman's economic position was enhanced by the fact that the house (ot), which is the minimal unit of production and of which she is head, became a major channel for the transmission of agricultural land between male agnates [blood relatives]" (Okeyo 1980:189).

The second conclusion relates to the distortions introduced by colonialism.

> The integration of the Luo economy and society into a colonial system had the result of distorting the population-to-land relationships, as well as the structure of the access to land, in a very special way. On one level, the reservation system led to increased demographic pressures on land because it left no option for expansion outside the reserves. Customary tenure adjusted to this artificial population crisis by redefining and restricting the corporate holding of land in such a way that the larger lineage control of land was in some areas reduced to family control. On another level, the reduction of corporate holding also jeopardized women's usufructory rights which had previously benefited from the flexibility and multiplicity of rights in corporate landholding. The trend toward the individualization of land-tenure reform which was thus set off was further exacerbated by the institution of land-tenure reform which, in effect, negates customary principles of landholding and land use. The reform translates corporate, allocative rights in land (the final authority to dispose of land) into individual male titles to land and creates uncertainty as to the legal status of women's usufructory rights in land.

(Okeyo 1980:208–209)

In particular, Okeyo notes that tensions between men and women with regard to the control of land were exacerbated by both land-tenure reform and the colonial reservation policy. Regarding the latter, the colonial government demanded space (usually land alienated from the community) to build schools, churches, commercial and administrative centres, and roads. Regarding the former, individual male statutory owners often ceased to observe the customary rights of wives and children in the use and disposition of what had become "their property."

Okeyo's third conclusion has special significance for contemporary thinking about agricultural development, technology transfer, and the position of women. It has been assumed (if the subject has been thought about at all), that customary use rights can coexist with individualized land tenure. Okeyo challenges this assumption. On the basis of her contemporary empirical research and historical analysis, she argues that

> Customary and statutory rights are different and, in theory, mutually exclusive. It may be predicted that over the next five to ten years [i.e., during the 1980s] the basis and practice of corporate landholding will be eroded and that women as a group will be virtually deprived of their security which had hitherto been protected by the principles of corporate descent and land tenure. In this process the lineage becomes subordinated to the nation-state because the latter assumes authority over resource allocation. By the same logic the house could lose its proprietary control and, therefore, the proprietary link between the mother and son within the house and that of the father and son within the lineage could be severely challenged.
>
> (Okeyo 1980:209)

Okeyo's case study provides an analysis of the historical and social factors behind the loss of control and autonomy described in the women and technology and WID literature. As such, it is a model for the methodology required for future research. For example, the question of compromised inheritance patterns and concomitant insecurity within the family (for men as well as for women) is invisible in the literature as a factor influencing family decisions regarding the adoption or rejection of a new technology. A more visible aspect of Okeyo's research is the question of legal title. The large-scale exclusion of women from statutory title to land in which they have usufructuary rights means they have no collateral to obtain loans. This is a factor widely cited as a barrier to the involvement of women in development efforts (e.g., the Mwea rice scheme, pp. 64–67). Why they have the right and, indeed, the obligation to farm land to which they do not hold title is explained by Okeyo (1980). Development planning must take account of this historically created anomaly if local agricultural improvement schemes are to succeed.

Women as food producers and suppliers in Zambia

A milestone seminar, organized by AAWORD and the Dag Hammarskjöld Foundation, was held in Dakar, Senegal, in 1982 (DHF/SIDA 1982). The seminar's purpose was "to move beyond simple truisms about the situation of women to a more profound analysis of the mechanisms perpetuating the subordination of women in society. The aim of the discussion was, therefore, not to focus exclusively on women but to look both into male–female relationships in society and into how the system of economic organization affects these relationships" (Savané 1982:7).

A valuable contribution toward this purpose was the study of Muntemba (1982b) on the women of Zambia as food producers and suppliers.[5] Applying a rigorous historical methodology and a broad knowledge of research and action on women's concerns in Africa, Muntemba (1982b) succeeded in both delineating the outlines of an African feminist political economy and providing a model for an empirical case study within the framework. Her analysis complements that of Okeyo (1980). It reaches many of the same conclusions regarding gender relations, land rights, and production, but focuses on a different aspect of the feminist political economy effort. The analysis of Muntemba is similarly useful in providing a framework within which the problems identified by WID literature may be understood and more effectively tackled. As a historian, she is concerned with a thorough exposition of the policies and practices of the colonial and postcolonial state as they have broadly affected gender relations in all Zambian ethnic groups. This is in contrast to Okeyo's study, that explored in depth the consequences of changing gender relations within one particular group.

Whereas Okeyo implicitly challenges the traditional anthropological understanding of the position of women in lineage-based societies, Muntemba tackles one of the more recent social science trends in Africa: peasant studies. The plethora of peasant studies during the 1970s was a valuable corrective to earlier neglect of internal socioeconomic structures in Africa. Muntemba faults peasant studies, however, for their neglect of women in production.

> Most works conceive of the peasant as a male and use the male gender. They also largely deal with issues affecting male peasants: cash crops, marketing, agricultural education, mechanization. Even such important questions as land dislocations, migration and social stratification, which affect women most poignantly, are analysed in relation to male peasants.
>
> (Muntemba 1982:29)

Three themes frame Muntemba's inquiry: land, labour, and the sexual division of labour. She develops these themes first in a general African context and then in the context of Zambia's concrete historical experience. In Zambia, women are the primary producers and suppliers of food. Starting with the premise that the ability of women to carry out these responsibilities has deteriorated, Muntemba examines their position in terms of the social relations of production, distribution, and surplus appropriation.

> Control over, and access to, the physical means of production — land or fertile soils, communications, transport — and the productive forces — human labour, implements and inputs — coupled with more efficient methods, ensure labour's productivity. But that is not enough. To ensure non-appropriation and fair distribution there has to be control over one's own labour and the product of that labour. At every reconstructible period in history there has been a struggle over these factors at household, village, national and international levels. How women fared in this struggle influenced their ability to produce and supply food.
>
> Evidence suggests that although this struggle may have existed in pre-colonial times, it was not until the penetration of capitalism and the money economy

---

[5]Shimwaayi Muntemba is a Zambian historian. She has written extensively on the Zambian peasantry, with a focus on peasant women. Currently the Director of the Environmental Liaison Centre in Nairobi, Kenya, she has engaged in development research for several international organizations, including ILO.

that the position of women was most markedly and devastatingly challenged. Then, the struggle heightened at every level.

(Muntemba 1982b:30)

Muntemba surveys this struggle throughout Africa, citing the following developments:

- alienation of land to mining and agricultural companies and to settlers;

- land shortages and landlessness for peasants resulting from intense peasant cash crop production (with constraints upon food-producing land in particular);

- the struggle over labour as males were drawn or forced away to work for colonial enterprises or as competition mounted within households for labour to grow cash crops instead of food; and

- a shift in the sexual division of labour, whereby women not only experienced a dramatic increase in their workload as they took on the tasks of men and tended the cash crops but also suffered a loss in control of their own labour.

Using the Zambian case to substantiate her generalizations (and, in doing so, confirming the conclusions of the Mitero and Luo studies), Muntemba divides the country's history into four stages: the precolonial era; the colonial period from 1900 to the end of World War II; 1946 to independence; and the neocolonial era from 1964 to 1981. In discussing precolonial Zambia, she draws on anthropological and historical evidence to delineate the sex-gender system and mode of production of the predominantly matrilineal societies of the region. Even though male control of women existed in matrilineal societies (fathers and brothers, rather than husbands, exercised this control), inheritance of land through the female line ensured direct access to land for women and, in practice, women exercised considerable control over their own agricultural production. Muntemba describes the complex division of labour between men and women, emphasizing the importance of the gathering of wild foods by women; this was done in poor seasons or when powerful chiefs raided or demanded tribute (gathered foods provided "relishes," which, despite the connotation of this word in English, provided vital nutrients to complement the substantially carbohydrate diet).

The structure of a mining and settler colony was laid down in the colonial period to 1945. Women's position and, hence, their role as food producers differed according to the local experience regarding colonial incursion. In the more densely settled and fertile south-central portions of Zambia, men remained on the land but Africans experienced an intense struggle over land. It was here that the colonialists concentrated their communication and urban centres and appropriated land for their own use. A formal land policy was enacted in 1924, when the Colonial Office took over from the British South Africa Company and set up a colonial administration. As in Kenya, the territory was divided into native reserves and crown lands (the latter being for towns, mines, and white settlement, existing or anticipated). Africans were forced to move to the reserves, which were often on poorer land and became severely overcrowded. This was a major factor in undermining the ability of communities to produce food, a problem exacerbated by the pressure to supply food to the mine workers.

The position of women as food producers was compromised by land dispossession in the south-central agricultural region; in the rest of the country, however, it was the migration of males to serve in the mines that had the sharpest impact on women's production. Most of the agricultural tasks formerly performed by men fell to women. Some tasks could no longer be performed (e.g., lopping and felling of trees and the land rotation required by the poor soils of the region). Consequently, women were forced to overcrop. This, combined with their inability to fertilize, as before, led to serious deterioration of the land. Muntemba's meticulous investigation of the factors involved in deteriorating food production demonstrates the importance of understanding all the elements in a system of production, including the seemingly mundane:

> The men's contribution to scaring birds and harvesting was important because, although these tasks could be, and were undertaken by women, both were undertaken in the morning and evening. At the latter time, women's labour was also required for food preparation. During the dry months, relishes were not plentiful and women had to cover huge distances to fetch them. The heavier burden which started to fall on them sometimes resulted in their getting too tired by the end of the day to prepare the major and, in some cases, only meal of the day. As agricultural production became too onerous, women started to rely more heavily on gathering. Paradoxically, on account of the increasing burden, some found it difficult to supplement their agricultural shortfalls through gathering. In an already precarious agricultural system, villagers experienced actual hunger during the three dry months, the "hunger months".... Another development, which became accentuated later with urbanization, was that as their agricultural burden grew, in some instances they started to shift to less onerous but also less nutritious foods such as cassava.[6]

(Muntemba 1982b:40–41)

Muntemba (1982b) also discusses in detail changes in land, labour, and the sexual division of labour. The period between World War II and independence was characterized by an intensification of commodity production and the entrenchment of a huge urban labour pool, requiring the support of rural production. Men's control of the purchase and use of any new technology introduced to increase farm productivity ensured that women's subsistence food production lost out in the competition within households over the allocation of labour. Moreover, the food that they did manage to grow for the family was not sacrosanct: "Some women informed me that direct or indirect pressure was brought on them to sell women's crops such as groundnuts and vegetables. This was particularly the case if implements [bought by men] were used in the fields" (Muntemba 1982b:43). Muntemba also demonstrates that the question of inheritance is again a factor. Because men owned the implements, their agnatic relatives, rather than their wives, inherited them, even though the wives' labour had generated the income to purchase them. Consequently, the stability of the rural food supply, particularly in the families of older women, was always threatened.

On gaining independence, the new government committed itself to "rural development." As the price of copper started to decline on the world market in the 1970s, however, to make up the shortfall in foreign exchange, even more pressure was placed on agriculture to contribute to the cash economy. Peasants were exhorted to grow cotton, sunflower, tobacco, groundnuts for oil, and maize to feed

---

[6]Mackenzie (1986) gives a similar explanation for the shift from millet to the less nutritious maize amongst the Kikuyu. Maize has replaced other grains throughout much of Africa; this change has been neglected as a serious cause of undernutrition in the continent.

the urban population. In some cases, settler land was returned to peasant production; however, this did little to relieve the mounting pressure on land. In agricultural development schemes, men rather than women were targeted. Asked to analyze their position, women replied, "the government has forgotten us" (Muntemba 1982b:46). Precisely because it controlled distribution and was the agent for increased productivity, the government was the target of women's blame: "in their view the state systematically operated against them" (Muntemba 1982b:46). Women's strategy, in response, was to reduce production to avoid having a surplus for appropriation (this could backfire if food was extracted anyway in hard times). Said two cowives: "Our household production has been deteriorating over the last five years. How can it not when we, the women, have decided to work as little as possible?" (Muntemba 1982b:47).

Muntemba concludes with the following question: What happens when women's capacity to produce and supply food is compromised in nations still dependent on peasant production?

> Control by women of land, of the productive forces, of their labour and the product of that labour must be viewed as the most urgent priority. Thus land reforms and schemes resulting in privatization as the means of bolstering small-scale production must be challenged: they do not take women into consideration. It is imperative to consider women not because they are women but because, as we hope we have shown, they are central to food strategies. Instead, socialized forms of land systems in which *all* producers have usufructory rights must be fostered. But this is not enough. Peasant women have to participate in the political machinery to assure equitable distribution of the productive forces and non-appropriation of food from them. Women must be conscientized to challenge the sexual division of labour which subjects their labour to men.... But the forces at national and international levels are so strong that, alone, women cannot succeed and through this success move toward alleviating some of the food problems bedeviling many African countries.
>
> (Muntemba 1982b:48)

Muntemba, like Okeyo, has analyzed a circumstance widely described in the literature: in this case, the decline in women's food-producing capacity. Consequently, Muntemba has delineated the problem and suggested solutions that go far beyond the technical and individual-oriented panaceas promoted by much of the development establishment. Although some might consider that "socialized forms of land systems" are not politically feasible or economically desirable in most African countries, the issues of land-use rights, political participation, and women's loss of control over their own labour emerge as vital issues to be tackled at national and community levels. Development efforts in Africa, including practical research on technology transfer, require as their groundwork the kind of rigorous historical and socioeconomic analysis demonstrated here.

Part III

New Approaches

5   New Issues in Technology, Gender, and Development

Introduction

In the foregoing survey of conceptual frameworks and findings regarding technology, gender, and development, I have raised a number of issues that bear further investigation. Chapters 5 and 6 organize these issues into categories and indicate some interrelationships that the literature and development policy have not addressed.

The overarching issue is the serious problem in conceptualizing development accurately and recognizing appropriate paths to its attainment in the Third World. Much of the WID literature criticizes "developmentalism," attributing its flaws to inadequate attention to women and gender relations. This critique is, of course, valid: any vision of human progress that is based on an ancillary, dependent status for half of humanity is bound to be epistemologically paralyzed. The WID studies, too, however, accept fundamental Western assumptions about gender relations. The possibility that non-Western societies conceive of family, household, work, and even gender subjectivity differently is rarely contemplated. Furthermore, the WID literature seldom challenges developmentalism on the grounds of its economic premises. Consequently, the literature sabotages its own attempts to clarify relations of women and gender. As long as a faulty conceptualization of economic and political processes in the Third World prevails, whereby relations of dependency are ignored and falsely conceived "tradition" is viewed as the obstacle to "modernization," there is no theoretical space into which to insert a more accurate understanding of gender issues.

It is particularly important to expose the ideological biases and political interests inherent in much development thinking. It would be unrealistic to expect donor countries to abandon their political interests; it is reasonable, however, to require that these countries be clear about the consequences of their policies for Third World societies and that damaging, development aid programs are not justified through a process of mystification. The stark reality is that "development," as commonly construed in the West, has meant underdevelopment for women and, consequently, for children and communities as well. Acknowledging the benefits of many aspects of technology transfer in the fields of health, nutrition, and agriculture, I would argue that the worsening of the quality of life for African women (economically, socially, and often physically) is an indictment of Western attitudes and actions toward Africa that cannot be overlooked. The culpability of African governments also poses serious dilemmas for the protocol of donor noninvolvement in national political affairs. Given that much aid unwittingly supports negative political practices, aid givers must recognize the uncomfortable fact that noninvolvement is a political stance and, as such, needs examining.

The six categories

My call for clarity about technology, gender, and development in Africa is given a concrete form in the following six categories. These categories organize the new issues and interrelationships I have identified. The task of addressing these new issues and interrelationships is the work of future research; some practical guidelines for this task are given in Chapter 7. This chapter discusses the first five categories (A–E), with illustrations where appropriate, to demonstrate the importance of the questions raised. Chapter 6 explores the six conceptual problems outlined in category F.

Category A

A synthesis of feminist political economy and the WID approach, overcoming the limitations of each, will generate a powerful research tool for investigating the precise ways in which technology disadvantages local communities and the ways in which communities are sometimes able, in spite of the liabilities of dependency, to turn new technology to their advantage. Identifying the success stories and the reasons for that success will lay the groundwork for replicating positive experiences. Identifying the reasons for negative results will facilitate a more critical assessment of current technology-transfer schemes. Past mistakes may then be avoided in the future.

Category B

To facilitate the endeavour in category A, a more rigorous investigation of community structures and processes and, in particular, the relationships between village organizations and sex-gender systems, is needed. An important part of this investigation will be research into relationships among women. Women have tended to be treated as a homogeneous group in the literature; there are indications, however, that serious contradictions exist between categories of women. Realistic development planning must account for the impact of these contradictions upon research priorities, policy-making, and implementation.

Category C

Certain foci of societal transformation have been neglected, both in feminist political economy and WID literature. Effective development policy depends upon a clearer understanding of the following factors:

- Women's rights, both political and economic;

- The role of the media (traditional and modern) in disseminating appropriate new technology;

- Social dimensions to the participation of women in family health care and nutrition;

- The logic of traditional technology, both social and physical, and indigenous technological innovation; and

- The "conscientization" of men: how sexist bias and practice at the level of nation and village may be overcome.

Category D

The boundary problem in research and policy has prevented the diffusion of insights and information between research/action loci and even between branches of a given locus (e.g., within an aid agency). The most brilliant understanding of issues concerning technology, gender, and development will have no impact upon Third World societies unless the boundary problem is overcome.

Category E

Who does the research? Is the answer to this question as straightforward as insisting that only African women, and any African women, are capable of generating valid analyses of technology, gender, and development in Africa? Africa is unique as a region of the world: the major portion of knowledge about its peoples and societies has been, and continues to be, generated by outsiders. For Africa, therefore, more than for any other region of the developing world, the issue of who does the research is politically sensitive and methodologically complicated. African researchers themselves are beginning to address this question.

Category F

An aspect of more rigorous inquiry into gender and power in the village and family is the identification of certain conceptual problems in the literature. These problems contribute to the dilemmas identified in categories C, D, and E. Although the following subjects have been debated occasionally in the cross-cultural or feminist scholarly traditions, the challenges to them have not been drawn together into a coherent, sustained critique; rather, the criticisms have been piecemeal, or, in the African context, absent:

- The public/private dichotomy;

- The nature of the "family" and the "domestic realm";

- The economic as the determining factor in society;

- The nature of the "traditional" in society; and

- The nature of "nature."

Misconceptions of these topics are embedded in the literature, particularly in WID writing, and these misconceptions have had a negative impact on development policy.

Inherent in all five conceptual problems is an epistemological dilemma that remains almost invisible in the literature: the subjugation of local "knowledges" to a dominant Western "knowledge" about Africa and, in particular, about African women. Flawed development policies can only be corrected if the flawed nature of our knowledge is addressed.

Toward a new synthesis

A requirement of a good WID study is fieldwork that goes beyond describing the declining power and increasing workload of women (as much of the WID literature does) and does more than document statistics on health and nutrition correlated with women's status (as much of the social medical literature does). It is essential to investigate sex-gender systems and women's groups, and an attempt to record, through oral history and other means, changes from the past to the present. Meanwhile, political economists should be prepared to apply their theoretical insights to concrete contemporary development issues. Two examples of a synthesis of WID and feminist political economy concerns are cited to demonstrate the value of this approach.

The first is a concrete case study. Badri's (1986) study of women, land ownership, and development in the Sudan is important not only as an example of synthesis but also because it focuses on a category of African women that has been neglected in the literature: pastoral women. Much is made in the WID and political economy literature of the connection between horticultural women's production and their concomitant rights and autonomy. Pastoral women have been characterized as having a comparatively low position, in that they are believed to have had little control over the major means of agricultural production: livestock. Traditionally, men "owned" livestock, although the Western concept of ownership does not apply, given the complex communal web of rights and obligations in livestock and the practice of placing animals in age mates and relatives' herds.

Once again, however, Western bias has focused (rather romantically, as endless television shows about the Masai attest) on the connection between men and cattle; the substantial stake women held in livestock has been overlooked. Recent studies show, however, that the difference between the status of pastoral and horticultural women was less marked than has been thought (e.g., Kettel 1986). Evidence is emerging that pastoral women, like men, have age-grade associations, despite the lack of reference to women's age-grades in the anthropological literature. Llewelyn-Davies (1979) has recorded the bases of solidarity among Masai women. Balghis Badri, a sociologist at the University of Khartoum, has conducted research and drawn on the fieldwork of several University of Khartoum dissertations to generate an analysis that demonstrates the importance of women's rights in livestock. Her study (Badri 1986) shows how contemporary neglect of the collective economic contribution of women through dairying has had serious consequences for Sudan's food self-sufficiency.

The first part of Badri's work deals with two cases involving agricultural communities and documents the connection between the loss of rights in land and control over labour and the exclusion of women from the development process. The second part of the study deals with pastoral women. Badri (1986:90) asserts that "this case shows how planners' assumptions that women's domain is primarily private has an adverse effect on development." There are 55 million head of livestock in Sudan and the country is self-sufficient in meat; in fact, meat accounts for nearly 13% of export earnings. Men are chiefly responsible for the herding of livestock, moving with them in search of pasture and water. Women are responsible for milking, milk processing, and marketing of dairy products. Given the potential of the dairy industry in Sudan, both for domestic consumption and export, it is surprising to discover that SDP 11 million is spent annually on importing milk powder and other dairy products (in October 1988, 4.4 Sudanese pounds [SDP] = 1 United States dollar [USD]). Badri sees the problem lying in the government's neglect of the dairy industry — a business monopolized by women, based on their traditional use rights in livestock (these rights parallel those of horticultural women, who have use rights in land owned by the patrilineage).

> I think that if policy makers had concentrated their efforts on helping women to construct woman-run dairy farms and on introducing only appropriate technology for milk processing, a better situation could have been achieved. However, the government policy makers attempted to solve the problem of milk shortage by importing milk and giving licenses to big companies to invest.... Women's traditional work is being taken from them as these companies introduce advanced technologies which women do not know how to use. Any expansion along these lines means a loss to women. The present situation of starvation compels us to take more notice of nomads in general and nomadic women in particular. Instead of introducing handicraft projects to nomadic women...our priority should be given to milk in order to save ourselves millions of pounds annually and to better the situation of women whom we should consider not as belonging to the private [realm], but as part and parcel of development plans.
>
> (Badri 1986:90)

Badri's study sets the agenda for synthesizing, development-oriented research on dairying technology in Sudan.

The second example demonstrating the value of the synthesis proposed is the excellent review article of Benería and Sen (1986) assessing Boserup's (1970) contribution to women and development. (I agree with Benería and Sen's [1986:14] assessment that "probably no single work on the subject of women and development has been quoted as often.") I do not wish to engage in yet another round of "Boserup-assessing" by reporting their critique; however, it is worth summarizing their overview of the issues of population control and birth control, issues intimately tied with health technology transfer. Their conclusions are particularly relevant to Africa, where governments are facing increasing pressure to tackle the stupefying birth rate.

Benería and Sen's (1986) pragmatic assessment of population control and birth-control policies and practices is grounded in a wealth of feminist political economy literature. They argue that even though issues of (biological) reproductive freedom were openly pursued in the West during the 1970s, in the Third World, the issue was much less clear (Benería and Sen 1986:154–156). Complicated by the question of overpopulation and by resistance to imposed Western values and schemes for population control, the question of reproductive freedom has not been directly addressed in literature on the Third World. Benería and Sen (1986) assert that feminist analysis must modify conventional approaches to population control and birth control. In the course of their discussion, they raise the question of women's rights: the right to bear or not bear children and the right to space childbearing. Decisions about childbearing not only affect the woman, however;

they also affect her household and the class interests of her community (even the propertied classes, who depend on the reproduction of labour, have a stake in decisions about birth control for peasants). In particular, the social strategies of the woman's peasant class place powerful constraints on her choices.

> For example, in very poor peasant households that possess little land and that are squeezed by usury and rent payments, the labor of children both on and off the peasant farm may be crucial to the ongoing ability of the household to subsist and maintain land. Pronatalist tendencies in rural areas may have a clear economic basis.
>
> (Beneriá and Sen 1986:155)

After surveying the economic analyses, both neoclassical and Marxist, that point out the conflict between economic rationality and social goals, Beneriá and Sen (1986) discuss the impact on women of both community norms and imposed policies. Their summary assessment is succinct and worth quoting at length:

> While leftists have correctly opposed forced sterilization and have pointed to the social causes of unemployment — the real population problem — there has been a tendency to ignore a critical aspect of childbearing: it is performed by women.... In conditions of severe poverty and malnutrition where women are also overworked, this can and does take a heavy toll on the mother's health and well-being. The poor peasant household may survive off the continuous pregnancy and ill-health of the mother, which are exacerbated by high infant mortality. The mother's class interests and her responsibilities as a woman come into severe conflict.
>
> The result of this conflict is that a poor woman's attitude toward birth control, contraception, and even sterilization are likely to be different from those of her husband or mother-in-law. Research on these problems in the Third World should address questions such as: (1) Who makes decisions about childbearing and birth control within rural households, families, and communities, and on what basis are the decisions made? (2) What indigenous forms of family limitation are available to poor women, and how are they used? (3) Are there differences of opinion and interest between the childbearers and other family members? (4) How does childbearing affect women's participation in other activities?
>
> Answers to these questions require careful empirical research of a sort that is barely beginning in the Third World. The insights gained from empirical research must affect one's assessment of birth-control programs, especially the more enlightened programs that focus on the health and education of the mother. Reduction in the infant-mortality rate, improvements in health and sanitation, and better midwife and paramedic facilities can give poor, rural women more options than having to resolve class contradictions through their own bodies. Such programs, however, clearly cannot be a panacea for the basic problems of extreme poverty and inequality in landholding; the contradictions of class and capital accumulation in the countryside can be resolved only through systemic social change.
>
> (Beneriá and Sen 1986:155–156)

Underpinning this analysis is a sophisticated understanding of the contradictions inherent in contemporary sex-gender systems as well as class contradictions. Beneriá and Sen (1986) have not lost sight of the heart of feminist concern: the well-being, rights, and autonomy of individual women. Their list of research questions provides a ready agenda for research by health technology planners in Africa.

Women's associations and sex-gender systems

Chapter 4 defines a model for the concerns that researchers may fruitfully address to create an understanding of the interrelation between sex-gender systems and communities. Other studies, such as Sacks (1979;1982) and Mackenzie (1986) have engaged in a similar exercise. WIN (1985a:94–107) identifies women's associations and networks as focal points for social and economic transformation in Nigeria and argues that they should thus receive the concerted attention of researchers and aid donors. Feminist scholars have not, however, charted the influence of community organizations, including women's organizations, upon the introduction and sustained use of new technology. Conversely, technology-transfer studies mention women's organizations only in passing. Cooperatives, which receive some attention, are usually discussed in terms of the impact of technology upon the organization rather than vice versa. An exception is Ladipo's (1981) study of two Yoruba women's cooperatives. Lapido (1981) determined that cooperatives attempting to adhere to government guidelines do not succeed as well as groups that create their own rules. "Cohesion, personal development, and financial growth were found to be greater in the self-regulating group" (Lapido 1981:123). Even though a few other studies mention the importance of the contribution of women to decision-making, Lapido's study is exemplary in the context it sets for understanding successful adoption and adaptation in one set of circumstances, and failure in another.

In 1976, women sought to overcome their disadvantage in cash crop production by asking the Nigerian government to include them in the Isoya Rural Development Project, founded in 1969. The project gave access to agricultural training, technology, adult literacy, home economics programs, and, later, new cash crops, particularly yellow maize. In a familiar fashion, however, women had been relegated to the "welfare" aspects of the Project. In requesting inclusion in the economic aspects of the Project, they argued that "as a bird uses two wings to fly, so must a family use the progress of its husband and wife to get ahead" (Lapido 1981:124). The organizations being promoted by the Project were multipurpose cooperatives designed to facilitate agricultural extension efforts, the introduction of new technology, and the distribution of credit. Following permission to form such organizations, the first women's cooperative to constitute itself, *Irewolu*, attempted to meet the guidelines set by government policy and regulations. By the time the second group, which named itself *Ifelodun*, decided to organize, *Irewolu* had failed to live up to the guidelines. Consequently, *Ifelodun* was allowed to formulate its own, more appropriate set of rules. "Thus, an experiment was begun wherein there were two groups trying to reach the same goal of government recognition by different means" (Lapido 1981:125).

Ladipo's discussion of the different experiences of these two groups is intricate and intriguing. It is impossible to convey here the richness of her analysis. The following summary, however, places Lapido's findings in the context of the synthesizing framework I have developed in this book. In an initial assessment of the findings I would assert that the prognosis, according to developmentalist criteria, would have been for greater success for the first group, *Irewolu*. It was a larger group, it followed government guidelines, and its membership was younger. It selected a leader who was "literate and well traveled and had a keen sense of the events which were modernising the country" (Lapido 1981:127). The group's name

100

translates as "good things come to town". From the feminist political economy perspective, however, *Ifelodun* had the greater chance of success. The *Ifelodun* members, being of an older generation, had more experience with other organizations, such as "religious groups, trade associations, savings societies, and associations of household (lineage) wives" (Lapido 1981:126). Surprisingly, the literacy rate was slightly higher among the older women. Being freer of responsibility for small children and having had the opportunity to build enterprises, the older group had a higher proportion of produce buyers and were generally more prosperous; in contrast, the majority of *Irewolu* members were petty traders.

The pattern of wage work identified by myself for the Kikuyu (Stamp 1986) and by Jackson (1985) for the Hausa in the KRP also applied to the *Ifelodun* women. Given the evidence from these studies, it is likely that *Ifelodun* members pooled their income from agricultural labour in the group enterprise. Half of the *Ifelodun* membership worked as agricultural labourers; none of the *Irewolu* membership did. Furthermore, 20% of *Ifelodun* prepared meals for sale; in *Irewolu*, only 3% of the membership engaged in this enterprise. Finally, more members of *Ifelodun* had secure title to land, providing them with a source of income.

Ifelodun's president was seemingly more passive than the *Irewolu* president:

> She had never learned to read or write, rarely left the village, and never voiced an awareness of any event outside her own community. She practiced her religion, Islam, within her home. She was rarely seen to exercise any influence on the conduct of meetings, but it was apparent that she had considerable authority, probably stemming from her role as the village's traditional midwife. It seems she was elected to ensure harmony and stability to a group whose name can be translated as "Friendship is Sweet."[1]
>
> (Lapido 1981:127)

Ladipo (1981) identifies other factors important to her conclusions, including the fact that *Ifelodun* was allowed to restrict its membership to its own village (*Irewolu* membership was drawn from six villages), and to withdraw its savings in the "hungry season." *Ifelodun* members were lineage wives and, I would add, were organized as age mates. *Irewolu* members, however, were prevented from organizing along such traditional community lines. They wished to divide amicably into three groups, six villages being too dispersed a community for any successful group effort. Furthermore, *Irewolu* members resented the domination of Isoya town in the group's affairs. The members' husbands, however, prevented the group members from carrying out this decentralization. The men of Isoya, who wished to retain the prestige of the town's leadership, were particularly stubborn.

This description is almost a casebook of how to, and how not to, organize for development. Because the *Ifelodun* women were the decision-makers, they turned to the skills and practices that had worked for them and for their grandmothers in other associative contexts. Elements of the traditional sex-gender system and the associative structure and practice of women both adapted to the modern context. This facilitated the successful adoption of new technology, the acceptance of new farm methods and materials, and the use of credit to expand their economic

---

[1]This is a slogan women's self-help groups across Africa would approve of — focusing on the prerequisite for group effort. The younger women's "good things come to town" is revealing, by contrast, of a more "modernist" approach. How are good things to come, if not by sweet friendship?

activities. Even though the *Irewolu* women were socially and economically less equipped to handle the communal effort, they had a sense of what would work organizationally. However, they were prevented from making the necessary structural changes. Policy that aims to draw women into cooperatives for the purpose of rural development needs to be based upon this kind of community-specific, sophisticated analysis of community and gender. It must also recognize the necessity of giving decision-making powers to the village women.

Lapido (1981) identified problems of mistrust among *Irewolu* members. These problems suggest contradictions in relationships among women; Lapido touches on these contradictions but does not explore them. She also does not discuss contradictions within *Ifelodun*. Such contradictions inevitably exist, however, and may undermine self-help efforts. Mbilinyi (1984:294) expressed concern about the lack of attention to differences between women. Wealthier peasant women are in a position to hire labourers; these labourers are usually other women. However, few studies focus on this labour group, their working conditions, and their family life. The same problem applies to the treatment in WID literature of entrepreneurs. The liberal approach is concerned with obstacles to the success of these women rather than with the ways in which they exploit other women. Mbilinyi (1984) set out a research agenda for the consideration of such class contradictions among women.

In a recent study, I explored these contradictions in terms of ideological discourse among the village women of Mitero (Stamp 1987). The study demonstrates how women's egalitarian ideal of shared resources is sometimes violated in practice. *Matega*, in both its traditional and modern meanings, is a powerful word in the Kikuyu lexicon: it stands for the ideology and practice of sharing among women. As explained in Chapter 4, in the past, *matega* stood for women's aid to women at childbirth. From collecting firewood to tending her children and fields, village wives would rally around each childbearing woman. In keeping with the spirit of modern development, *matega* has taken on a new meaning. It now designates the savings activity of village women's self-help groups. The communal savings account, in addition to funding community projects (e.g., primary schools), is intended to contribute a lump sum to each woman in turn. With this, she can afford an otherwise financially inaccessible household improvement.

Recent research in Mitero indicates that enterprising women enhance their material well-being and prestige by exploiting the tradition of *matega*. They receive a disproportionate share of the group savings and possibly divert resources intended for community-development projects for their own use. It is these enterprising women, however, who have played the greatest role in creating the modern idiom of cooperation.

Urban elite women have also adopted the practice of *matega*. They hold parties at which guests are expected to contribute substantial sums of money to their hostess. A recent report from Chad indicates a similar process at work amongst the elite women of Ndjamena, where the *pari vente* ("a gamble to sell") has become an important substitute for an inefficient banking system and where popular or influential women gain unfair advantage. It appears that the traditional credit club system found in many parts of Africa, of which *matega* is an example, is everywhere facing manipulative pressures of the kind identified in the Mitero study.

Matega is not only coopted by individuals: certain male-dominated rural institutions are also manipulating the concept for their benefit. The Catholic church holds regular *matega* to raise funds. The Catholic women's self-help group has been absorbed into the church structure and women no longer practice typical group functions; instead, they devote their energies to fund-raising according to the instructions of the male leadership. The local administration used the women's groups to fund its own events and projects, as well as weddings. As the local subchief said, "for every one of these functions the group is told how much money it will contribute." The resource-generating power of *matega* has not been lost on the village men, some of whom have pushed their way into group membership. Finally, the district-wide umbrella organizations of the women's self-help groups have engaged in a massive transfer of group capital from the countryside to nearby cities by investing in urban rental buildings. Our research charts the mismanagement and even embezzlement of the groups' funds, as well as the lack of return on women's *matega* activities.

In its focus on the ways in which the "common language of custom" is used to subvert the goals of self-help groups, the Mitero study draws important insights from Parkin's (1972) monograph on economic change among the Giriama of coastal Kenya and Glazier's (1985) work on the uses of tradition regarding land acquisition among the Mbeere of central Kenya. The study also draws on the growing body of literature on gender relations in East Africa, and on certain concepts from theory on discourse and ideology. We hope the study contributes to the theoretical understanding of ideological discourse in contemporary African society and that it will join useful works such as Ladipo's to increase the understanding of the problems and the opportunities provided by women's self-help activity.

Neglected focal points for social transformation

Women's rights

Women's rights are one of the aspects of development that have been neglected in the push to understand women's economic role. Case studies presented here have charted ways in which women have lost customary rights, particularly in land. There is some important work on the consequences for women of changes in land tenure (as the synopsis of Okeyo's study in Chapter 4 attests); the WID literature, however, does not address precolonial legal systems as thoroughly as it should.

There needs to be a much more specific focus on the question of women and the law (for the direction such enquiry might take, see CWS/cf 1986). There are often glaring inequities in the national laws of African countries: a legislative attempt to criminalize wife-beating was laughed out of the Kenyan Parliament several years ago. Apart from these obvious inequities, there has been a drift in recent years "into de facto attenuation of women's rights" (Guyer 1986:415). While discussion of women's rights in Africa is often linked with concerns about importing Western "women's liberation," claims that the rights issue is just another form of ideological imperialism are specious. As Howard (1984:46) says, "While the provision of women's rights cannot be separated from the attempt to develop sub-Saharan African countries, neither can women's rights be put aside until such a Utopian time as the government of a newly developed society sees fit to grant them."

Rights are more pertinent to the issue of technology and development than may appear to be the case. The ability of women, individually and in associations, to adopt and sustain new technology for development depends on their civil rights. Many studies show that women rationally choose not to invest energy and income in the application of new technology to productive resources that are no longer theirs by right. Female assessors on customary tribunals, for example, could ensure that customary rights[2] are not whittled away further (Guyer 1986:415). One aspect of women's rights, addressed by some feminist political economists, is the issue of use (usufructuary) rights. Especially in patrilineal societies, where most property was collectively owned by men and inherited through the patrilineage, use rights were the preeminent form of rights in productive resources. The imposition of Western notions of the primacy of property ownership has rendered these indigenous rights invisible or illegitimate. There is an urgent need for research into appropriate legal reform to protect and enhance the rights of women under the adopted British common law or French Napoleonic law. At present, the parallel operation of indigenous and Western legal systems works to the disadvantage of women. Bridewealth remains legal, for example, as a touted cornerstone of "traditional" marriage. Yet there are no modern laws to control the violations of indigenous law that are often practiced with regard to such customs.

A valuable conference on women's rights in Zambia in 1985 made a number of these links (ZARD 1985). For example, Chintu-Tembo (1985) examined women's rights and health and concluded that, although women have the same rights as men with regard to health care, a lack of education regarding these rights has seriously undermined the delivery of health care to women. Chintu-Tembo (1985) also examined dilemmas with regard to rights and health that are unique to women. For example, the law does not insist on hospital delivery of babies; a woman's right to choose between hospital and home birth is subverted, however, by the lack of facilities for home delivery and policy of the University of Zambia's Teaching Hospital "to achieve 100% hospital delivery or medically supervised delivery" (Chintu-Tembo 1985:65). Provision of some training for traditional midwives appears to be at odds with hospital policy.

A particularly sensitive but important area for future research on women's rights is the impact of new, Draconian versions of Shari'a law on Muslim societies in Africa, in the context of the modern fundamentalist movement (see El Naiem 1984). Apart from basic questions of human rights, there are serious implications for the ability of women such as the Hausa of KRP to contribute meaningfully to the development of their societies. Again, sensitivity to the historical aspects of the oppression of women under Islam is required. As Muslim women at Forum '85 in Nairobi insisted, the view of Islamic ideology as unchanging and primordially sexist is ethnocentric and unscientific. These women expressed resentment toward Western feminists for the condemnation of their religion in the name of Western-defined human rights. Feminist reform within Islam depends upon

---

[2]I use the term "customary rights" with reservations, as the term connotes a dichotomy similar to the formal/informal dichotomy discussed in Chapter 6. The implication is that there is "law" (Western law introduced with colonialism) and then there is "custom," which does not have "the force of law." Present customary law is subordinate to common law; yet, it is another example of ethnocentrism to assume that Africans in the past had "customs" but no "laws." A woman's use right to the milk of her husband's herd or to a plot of land from her husband's lineage was as legally binding and as litigable as a title deed to an office building today.

interpretation of the Islamic tradition and upon an appeal to aspects of its texts that are supportive of women.

Role of the media

Little attention has been paid in either the WID or the feminist political economy literature to the relationship between the media and women. There are two issues that need to be addressed: first, the dissemination of negative stereotypes of women; second, the use of the media for the transmission of information about new technology and techniques. In the past, African women's organizations, notably AAWORD and WIN, have drawn attention to the problem. AAWORD has focused its attention on the first issue. It hosted a meeting (funded by CIDA) of professional media women and researchers in Dakar, Senegal, in 1984. A similar meeting for women journalists of Eastern and Southern Africa was held in Nairobi, Kenya, the same year. Of particular concern to the Dakar meeting were the "trivial images of women in the media." The conclusions, substantiated by an ATRCW research project on the mass media in Africa (ATRCW 1985b), indicated that Western images of women as housewives and dependents, reinforced by appeals to a reconstructed and false African "tradition," were common. Clearly, the media trend undermines an accurate perception of the real position of African women in society and hampers efforts to have women taken seriously by policymakers.

WIN has identified a disturbing trend in the media with regard to the portrayal of Nigerian women (WIN 1985a:108–125). In addition to the perpetuation of erroneous stereotypes of women, there has been a misogynist tendency to report negatively about women's activism and to neglect their achievements.

> The Nigerian media tends to give disproportionate prominence to reports of negative activities.... The news that a female engineer has been elected to head an international body, or that a female scholar has been awarded an honorary degree abroad, is tucked away in the inner pages. Women in the establishment are given news space (although hardly headlines), when they appear at important functions as gracious hostesses, giving charity, or performing one welfare role or the other.... However, on any occasion that female activities indicated that they (normally regarded as exceptions) could be a rule, the media embarks on a trivialisation campaign. Witness the contrast between the awed reports of the first set of women in civilian government 1979–83, and the boisterous jokes bandied about [regarding] the female upsurge in the Legislature and Executive post-1983.

> Condemnation and ridicule are meted out to female activism that does not emerge from the ruling classes. For instance, market women who adhere to their traditional locations of trade, are portrayed as "stubborn," while as tail-ends of the middle-man chain, they are reported to be "economic saboteurs." When they try to let the government know how they are affected by various policies, they get less coverage than statements by women of the upper classes who urge them to obey government's directives.... Whenever an issue concerning women crops up, the overwhelming majority of editorials, cartoons and news analysis bring pressure on women to conform. For instance, crime is not only seen as a societal ill, but as a direct result of women neglecting their homes, husbands and children, in their "inordinate" pursuit of wealth. Male criminals are actually pitied for having succumbed to pressure of greedy womenfolk, who demand what their men cannot afford to supply....

In the main, attention is paid to the worst side of women, witness the series introduced by the *Sunday Sketch* at the tail-end of the UN Decade of Women: "The Wickedest Women in History." Media opinion also reinforces the societal unequal status of women, pays grudging lipservice to benefits granted women, exhorting them to be grateful for the "concessions" and not to regard them as rights.... Perhaps the most startling indication of the deep-seated antipathy to women was the furor over women in drug trafficking. Relentlessly the editorials, cartoons, and news analyses harassed women to the extent that by January, 1985, the word "cocaine" was synonymous with woman, and female criminality was analogous to women's liberation.

(WIN 1985a:108–125)

The concern with media imagery, which has remained a preoccupation of African women alone, is an important area for investigation by research/action loci.

The role of the media as a development tool is a less thorny issue. Studies have revealed that the media have been underused as such a tool, chiefly because of poor planning and inadequate research on the media-related behaviour of women. For example, Subulola and Johnson (1977:107), in a survey of beliefs on infant feeding and child care among 143 Benin City mothers in Nigeria, found that only 5 mothers cited radio and television as a source of information. This in spite of regular programs on nutrition and child care. Odumosu (1982) reached a similar conclusion. Both these studies identified the use of English rather than the vernacular as a barrier. As well, Odumosu (1982:108) discovered that "women's programs" were broadcast in the middle of the day, when most women, who were petty traders, were occupied away from the home.

Odumosu (1982) put in a plea for "the traditional media," i.e., word-of-mouth method of disseminating information, and the use of bell-ringers dispersed to strategic points. In a survey of 200 pregnant women, Odumosu found that over 90% had received tetanus shots. Although 79% possessed radios, only 4.5% heard about the immunization program via this medium. The rest learned of the program via word of mouth. Odumosu's conclusions are suggestive of the kind of research on media that might yield a significantly higher return for technology-information programs. It is also worth noting that concern for the media as a tool appears to be restricted to health and nutrition researchers, a fact that social scientists and development planners should remedy. Correcting program times, using the right language, and researching methods to utilize the "traditional media" would seem to be among the more easily solved development dilemmas.

Social dimensions of health care

Several examples of the importance of social context were given in the section of Chapter 2 dealing with health technology. The discussion of women's rights also draws attention to the wider context of health-care delivery. The issue of health must be connected with other development concerns: for example, health cannot be separated from agricultural issues. If women are disequipped economically and socially, then their ability to retain control of family health maintenance will be undermined. "Appropriate technology" for childbirth is a particularly pressing social issue. Several studies in the social health literature have pointed out that Nigerian midwifery, if improved with a better understanding of cleanliness and of pathology requiring a physician's intervention, is the most suited to low levels of state-provided health care. Given the supportive social conditions prevailing in the village, midwifery also makes the most efficient use of society's resources, including women's familial and community organizations. In particular, obstetrical practices that are under criticism in the West but have been introduced to Africa (such as the use of the lithotomy position, where a woman gives birth on her back) are criticized. Problematical in a context where high-technology inputs are available (such as fetal monitors), such practices are even more problematical where such equipment is not available.

Pamela Brink, a nurse–anthropologist who conducted a detailed study of Nigeria midwives involving observation as well as statistical methods, reported that women will attend hospital or community health centre antenatal clinics but are reluctant to deliver there, preferring their local midwives. They give the following reasons:

> The hospital will not allow them to squat for delivery and that the midwife is not in constant attendance upon them during the entire process as their village TBA [Traditional Birth Attendant] is. When asked why they attend antenatal classes if they do not intend to be delivered by the nurse-midwife, they state that they attend antenatal clinics to receive the medicine and the vitamins necessary to make their baby healthy.
>
> (Brink 1982:1887)

Brink's report of sound midwifery techniques and the supportive family environment substantiated the women's choice of home delivery.

Another social aspect of health care is the importance of involving women's organizations in health development. In Nigeria, Feuerstein (1976) compared a cholera-prevention program in one community, where traditional Western methods of attempting to influence people individually were used, with a program in another community that aimed at obtaining community approval for the health policy. In the first community, only 45% of villagers reported for immunization; there was 73% participation in the second village. Feuerstein (1976) discovered, however, that the medical profession showed little appreciation of the contribution communities could make to health care. She found a sentiment among doctors and nurses that public health was secondary to hospital medical care, and that training professionals was more important than training health leaders. "[These] attitudes are as difficult to change as traditional health beliefs because of their cultural and psychological aspects" (Feuerstein 1976:52).

A survey of 400 Kenyan village women by Were (1977) to determine their attitudes toward equal rights and their opportunities within the community yielded a clear consensus. The women felt that their organized groups were the appropriate basis for managing health care. They felt that they could achieve more through collective action than through individual effort in moving toward what they called "healthy living" (Were 1977:529).

These findings, when combined with the tools for analyzing social and economic process developed in Chapter 4, show a possible direction for future work on the social context of health technology transfer.

Indigenous technology and invention

Given the success of Africans in populating a continent and creating a culturally rich and diversified civilization over several millennia, it would seem self-evident that indigenous technology was well adapted to African conditions. However, little has been done to determine what aspects of the indigenous technology should receive active encouragement for retention. Indeed, little is known of inventions and technology that lost out to cheap industrial imports over the last 100 years. The Haya of East Africa were making steel in blast furnaces almost 2000 years before it was invented in Germany; the decline of smithing of all kinds as a result of colonial trade in implements from Sheffield is a better known phenomenon. Mackenzie (1986) has recorded in detail the sound agricultural practices of Kikuyu women (use of fertilizer, contoured fields, windbreaks, etc.).

Many case studies presented in this book imply the appropriateness of indigenous technology in physical terms, social terms, or both. Charlton's (1984) case of the rejected oil-palm presses (see p. 59) demonstrates both. The account of new stove technology (see p. 59–60) illustrates the great social significance of traditional cooking technology. The starting point for research into this important issue is the assumption that African technology is adaptive, not inherently "backward." The conditions to which the technology was adapted — social, economic, and environmental — may have changed and, thus, new technology may be required. However, it cannot be assumed that, in every circumstance, a new way of doing things is better than the old way.

For example, I doubt if any researcher has considered the possible connection between the short-handled hoes of women, which are often decried for the way they make women bend over for hours every day, and the women's strong backs and necks, necessary for carrying heavy head loads. In a continent where draught animals have been historically barred by tsetse fly or where terrain or economy has made the use of such animals difficult or impossible, the human head has been the chief means of transportation. Yet back problems are not common among African women engaging in traditional work patterns (unless the women are overworked). It is unrealistic to assume, given the conditions of poverty in Africa, that head loading will be abandoned in the near future. Changing other aspects of women's physical work, however, such as providing them with hoes that do not require them to bend over, might prevent the development of strong backs that are not injured by heavy head loading.

Given the discovery that our own unexamined assumptions about our artifacts and our bodies have caused problems in technology transfer, to break free of our biases, imaginative connections such as this need to be made (see discussion of Kirby [1987] in Chapter 6). One might wonder, for example, what effect Western attitudes to women's muscular strength might have had on "appropriate technology" design. The idea that anything weighing over 20 lb (9 kg) would require a man's help in carrying would flabbergast a Kikuyu woman, for whom loads of 100 lb (45 kg) are possible over long distances. The point of thinking about interrelationships between technology related tasks and about such questions as muscular strength is that we cannot assume to know the connections between one kind of technological practice and another unless we conduct the research.

As for invention, a phenomenon observable in any African village or town is a perfect example: a child running down the street with a marvelous wheeled contraption, full of moving parts and complicated hardware. To argue that Africans are uninventive or that invention does not continue daily is to be, at best, ignorant of ordinary African life and, at worst, racist. What must be examined are the social and ideological reasons why African inventiveness has not been translated into a culture of mechanical competence as, by contrast, exists among Asians.

The "conscientization" of men

Sexist bias at all levels of policy-making was one of the major findings in the review presented in Chapter 3. Western feminists have agonized for years, in academia and in aid agencies, about how to make their male colleagues read their articles, attend their workshops, and integrate the substantial analyses and findings of feminist research into their own work. We have yet to find a solution, although there have been advances on some fronts. The problem of "conscientizing" African men exists in a worldwide context of massive indifference toward the efforts of feminists, both male and female, to insert women and gender into the knowledge about human society. In Africa, the issue is politically sensitive. It is ironic that in a continent where women once enjoyed greater power and autonomy than women in most other regions of the world, efforts to change men's minds are now seen as profoundly threatening. From the level of political theory to the level of putting technology-transfer schemes into practice, research on sexist ideology and how it may be overcome is required.

The boundary problem

The boundary problem has been extensively documented in Chapters 1 and 2 and demonstrated in several of the case studies presented. Rather than repeat the assertions already made, concrete research guidelines to overcome the problem are spelled out in Chapter 7. One suggestion that it is important to make, in spite of its self-evident value, is that agencies should identify the bridge-building suggestions in the studies they commission and actively work toward using them within the structure of their organization.

Who does the research?

The sensitivity of African women to the question of outside researchers was addressed in Chapter 2; the problem of the subordination of local "knowledges" is discussed in Chapter 6. The goal should be for Africa to take charge of the production of knowledge about itself. It is important to recognize, however, as some African feminist researchers do, that a simplistic attitude favouring any African research over all outside research will inevitably lead to certain biases and to the perpetuation of conceptual errors that indigenization is intended to overcome. Mbilinyi (1985b), in particular, is clear-sighted about the problems of an "African women only stance."

As previously mentioned, unequal access to research resources and channels of dissemination will ensure research efforts are dominated by elite women and that the voice of ordinary African women will once more be silenced. Feminist political economy has revealed how elite women have been ideologically, economically, and politically coopted to the Western-dominated interests of their class. Only research organizations that have analyzed class structure and sought to account for it in their research design may succeed in overcoming the limitations of existing conceptual frameworks and generate research and development programs based on an accurate knowledge of sex-gender systems and the local community. Such organizations (e.g., WIN, WAG, WRDP) seem to be operating on the best principles of women's (genuinely) traditional cooperation: research *ngwatio*.

A review of the literature on women, technology, and development in Africa has revealed that the significant divide in conceptual approaches is not between Africans and non-Africans. No magical insights are bestowed on intellects simply because they are African, and white skin does not doom a researcher to error. The distinction between valuable and inappropriate research lies in the conceptual framework used, and African scholars have contributed to each conceptual framework so far discussed. To suggest that an African's ethnic background is the key determinant of the validity of his or her ideas trivializes the complexity of the intellectual issues involved; the suggestion may, in fact, be considered ethnocentric and condescending (equivalent to the backhanded compliment that "blacks have rhythm"). Projects that uncritically seek African researchers, failing to scrutinize their credentials or the quality their work, convey the message that the issue is not important enough for the application of our own rigorous standards of analysis and criticism.

Given our relative advantages and the unequal power relations between the West and Africa, however, the task of critiquing African scholarship and action is extremely sensitive. On the one hand, the criteria by which judgment is passed must be scrupulous in avoiding the ethnocentric bias described for so much of the literature and policy on Africa (i.e., we must avoid the often-leveled charge of "intellectual colonialism"). On the other hand, we must ensure that the standards we apply are as rigorous as those we demand for research on our own society.

Beyond this, the reality that a substantial proportion of the resources for research and action reside in the West, both in agencies and among scholars, ensures that work on Africa will inevitably continue here. Our moral responsibility in this regard is twofold. First, we must ensure that our efforts genuinely serve African interests and are derived from a sounder knowledge than we have displayed. Second, we must identify and support those research efforts in Africa that are tackling the biases and assumptions of development activities and are engaging in useful, development-oriented feminist political economy. Both responsibilities require respectful participation in current African attempts to uncover and assert local "knowledges." Chapter 6, dealing with the conceptual problems inherent in feminist as well as nonfeminist scholarship on Africa, addresses this important task.

6   Conceptual Problems in the Study of
Women in Development

Introduction

The WID literature on Africa has explored the negative consequences of contemporary trends in national and international political economy and of development activity in particular, and it has also generated prescriptions for the amelioration of these consequences. As previously suggested, the literature is tied, not always firmly, to a much smaller body of more theoretical writing, largely by anthropologists and historians, who have sought to explain the culture and political economy of gender in Africa (for reviews, see Robertson 1987; Strobel 1982). However, the increasing visibility of WID discourse and the growing challenge to conventional social science assumptions have not generated a coherent approach that overcomes past theoretical errors and asks the right empirical questions. There are two reasons for this:

- the relationship between WID and feminist literature and

- the relation of WID literature to the wider body of literature on the Third World.

WID/feminist literature relationship

With few exceptions, conceptual problems inherent in feminist literature have been incorporated into the African material. Far from breaking with conservative problematics, as they hoped to do, many feminist scholars argue from the same assumptions that underlie the arguments they are challenging. For example, many feminists accept the idea of women's universal subordination.

> Some feminist analyses...come to social darwinist conclusions in spite of themselves.... Feminists and marxists seem haunted by an unrealistic fear: What if the social darwinists are right when they assert that women have never been the social equals of men? I think this fear has retarded inquiry into the question of women's position. Instead of tackling the problem head on, many have often found it easier to make end runs or apologies, conceding that women are subordinate but reasoning that culture, not biology, has put us in that position or that the conditions for equality have not yet been created.
> (Sacks 1982:5)

Sacks (1982:60) demonstrates her point through a critique of the still-influential article of Ortner (1974). Sacks argues that in studies such as Ortner's,

> The essence of culture...as it pertains to women, is to select those themes and attributes that reinforce female subordination and to project them as the totality of femaleness and maleness. And so the concept of culture becomes the science of stereotyping; culture becomes the enemy of women; and we are led by this logic back to [the 19th century writer] Bachofen where women really are rooted in nature, and hierarchy, or culture, is a male creation reflecting reality. There is not much to recommend this logic.

Rosaldo (1983:76–77), in a critique of her own earlier work as well as other studies, makes a similar point, targeting the nature/culture duality as the central "biased dichotomy" in need of redress.

> Few social scientists writing today would deny the fact that feminists have changed our intellectual horizons. At a minimum, we have "discovered" women. More important, we have argued that certain categories and descriptions that at one time made good sense must be reformulated if we are to grasp the shape and meaning of *both* men's and women's lives...[but] feminist scholars over the past ten years provided challenges to certain biases in traditional accounts without supplying the conceptual frameworks necessary to undermine them. While recognizing enemies and blind men among teachers and peers, we failed to recognize *ourselves* as heirs to their traditions of political and social argument. Simultaneously, we embraced and were at pains to redefine some of the gendered dualisms of past work. We found a source for questions in the most egregious errors of the past. But at the same time we stayed prisoners to a set of categories and preconceptions deeply rooted in traditional sociology.

WID/Third World literature relationship

The problem of unexamined preconceptions in the feminist literature is related to the second problematic connection for WID literature: the wider realm of Third World scholarship from which WID also draws inspiration. In this academic tradition, scholars have again been unsuccessful in breaking free of Western discursive practices, in spite of radical attempts to do so. An example of this is the failure of Marxism to escape Western economic concepts in its intensive effort to theorize non-Western class relations and precapitalist modes of production. For instance, the debates in ROAPE discussed in Chapter 1 reflect a preoccupation with Western categories of understanding (e.g., see Kaplinsky et al. 1980). Furthermore, in their productivist emphasis, Marxists accept the privilege accorded to the economic realm by the "modernization" or "developmentalist" school of thought: both developmentalists and orthodox Marxists view noneconomic motivation as irrational. In the first case, it is seen as backward tradition; in the second, as a superstructural chimera or, at best, a mystified, ideological representation of relations of production.

Baudrillard (1975) asks whether capitalist economy can illuminate earlier, non-Western societies. His answer to this question is an emphatic no. "Starting with the economic and production as the determinant instance, other types of organization are illuminated only in terms of this model and not in their specificity or even...*in their irreducibility to production*. The magical, the religious, the symbolic are relegated to the margins of the economy" (Baudrillard 1975:86–87). The dilemma, according to Baudrillard (1975:88–89), is that "Western culture was the first to critically reflect upon itself (beginning in the 18th century). But the effect of this crisis was that it reflected on itself also as a culture *in the universal*, and thus all other cultures were entered in its museum as vestiges of its own image."

The work that I have identified as feminist political economy comes closest to addressing the epistemological dilemmas raised here. Nevertheless, there has not yet been a coherent, sustained critique of the conceptual problems embedded in WID and other literature on the Third World. I have organized my discussion of the problems into six interrelated categories. If future development efforts are to help rather than harm African women and African communities, each of these categories requires investigation and correction.

The public/private dichotomy

A component of most conceptual frameworks for the consideration of women in the development process is the identification of "public" and "private" social spheres, the domain of men and of women, respectively. This division is the basis for the "welfare" approach and the emphasis on "income generation" to the neglect of women's productive role (discussed in Chapter 4). The division is also a powerful component of sexist ideology and policy. Few liberal studies, including most WID literature, however, challenge the dichotomy. Rosaldo (1974:35), in her earlier work, exemplifies the theorization based on the public/private concept:

> Characteristic aspects of male and female roles in social, cultural, and economic systems can all be related to a universal, structural opposition between domestic and public domains of activity. In many ways this claim is far too simple.... Yet the complexities of particular cases do not undermine our global generalization, which points not to absolute, but to relative orientations of women and men. Furthermore, by using the structural model as a framework, we can identify the implications for female power, value and status in various cross-cultural articulations of domestic and public roles.

While Rosaldo went on to become her own best critic regarding this analysis, as her reflections cited on p. 112 demonstrate, the influential textbook in which the analysis appears (Rosaldo and Lamphere 1974) continues to inform most liberal thinking on the subject. Many argue that the solution to women's disadvantage vis-à-vis development programs is either a more active role in the "public" sphere or a better recognition of the potential contribution of the "private" sphere. That the public/private dichotomy is an inaccurate conceptualization of present and, even more so, past African life needs asserting in the strongest possible terms.

Some Western feminist theorists have focused on the public/private dichotomy (for an overview, see Jaggar 1983). Spender (1980:191–197), for example, links the public sphere to the written, male-dominated word. She argues that the private world and language of women are subordinated to the dominant world of men. There are some interesting insights for Western women in Spender's (1980) analysis; however, the study displays both the problems of radical feminism's atheoretical approach and the ethnocentrism that characterizes much feminist writing. (Spender universalizes from Western experience, without acknowledging that she is doing so.)

Armstrong (1978) argues that the growth of a public/private distinction is due to the growth of the state and the declining ability of women to control and distribute resources: features characteristic of Western society and African nations today. Western theory, however, does not explore the possibilities of a world where the

113

distinction between public and private is absent; indeed, where such realms are not perceived. Such therapy, therefore, cannot speak to the African past, when women controlled and distributed resources and when state structures, where they existed, did not "privatize" women. Even under present, adverse conditions, women retain a measure of control over the distribution of resources that has been absent from Western society for centuries.

The feminist literature on the Third World, with a few notable exceptions (e.g., March and Taqqu 1986), has not systematically debated the dichotomy. Many studies on African gender relations, however, including some WID studies, do implicitly challenge the public/private dichotomy. The best of them document the porous boundary between what is kept from general view (the "private") and what is out in the open for all members of the community to see. The world of women is indeed separate from that of men, marked by a sexual division of labour and gender-specific ideological discourse. It is far from private, however, in the sense Westerners understand the concept (where a private world of the home is supported by law, residential patterns, and political practice). The community of women is as full a participant in the decision-making structure of village life as the community of men.

Even Muslim societies, which practice the seclusion of women and appear to lend themselves most readily to Western notions of public and private, challenge our understanding of these concepts. Callaway (1984:430) uses Ardener's (1975:vii–xxiii) concept of the "muted group" to explore the ways in which women in some societies, seemingly silent with regard to their own interests, are able to have an active community life (see also Dwyer 1978).[1] Indeed, "the 'muted group' construct implies that the seeds for total independence exist within the women's experience of total suppression" (Callaway 1984:430). Under conditions that may appear unbearable to a Westerner, the value system of a separate world for women, within which women are fully autonomous and active social agents, "stimulates and sanctions an assertiveness which could ultimately be the foundation for political efficacy" (Callaway 1984:430–431). It is precisely upon such ideological and structural foundations that it was possible for the Muslim Hausa women in the Kano River Irrigation Project of Nigeria to mount a successful strike for higher wages in 1977. The success of this action was a good example of political efficacy (see review of Jackson [1985] in Chapter 3).

For the great majority of African women who are not secluded on religious grounds, the distinction between a public and private world is even less valid. Wipper (1982), Van Allen (1976), Mackenzie (1986), and Mbilinyi (1986) are among the many scholars who have documented women's resistance movements during the colonial era. They have demonstrated the ability of women to mobilize for political action. The importance of such action in colonial history has, outside such studies as these, remained invisible, however (Mbilinyi 1986).

---

[1] In criticizing Ardener's concept of "the muted group," one can ask the question, silent to whose ears? Women are neither silent to each other nor to men in the local community (Dwyer 1978; Etienne 1982). Much of the feminist writing that sees women as ideologically dominated fails to recognize the tautology of their argument: the voice of women is absent from the world of male discourse; therefore, women are silent; therefore, men are ideologically dominant. Many of the studies in Ortner and Whitehead (1981), for example, are guilty of this tautology. In focusing on the absence of women from male discourse and failing to investigate women's ideology and how they think it relates to male ideology, feminist scholars perpetuate notions of the universal subordination of women. The problem is not the silence of women but the privileged status of the community of men gained through contemporary socioeconomic processes.

Although women are largely absent from contemporary national and "formal" political institutions, their political efficacy continues to be manifested at the community level. It is at this level that we must investigate the nature of the African "public." As all the detailed work on women's organizations reveals and as substantiated in a theoretical work on women's associations (March and Taqqu 1986), women's communal organizations are one of the most vibrant, effective institutions at the local level. Given that the "formal" juridical and political institutions imposed by colonialism upon Africa are weak, "informal" structures have a local legitimacy that sanctions their decision-making authority in the community. March and Taqqu (1986) analyze the reasons for the emergence of "rational-legal authority" (Max Weber's term), which led to the formation of the large-scale political structure known as the state. This structure was imposed on the precapitalist, small-scale African societies by colonial conquest.

> Perhaps because jural–political authority superseded other kinds of authority in our own history, it has largely superseded them in our thinking as well. The historically specific, political–jural form of authority that evolved in the west appears to have come, by itself, to signify the total concept of "legitimate" authority. From this perspective, formal associations appear legitimate because they are empowered by rational jural–political charters. The fact that informal associations do not have such charters, however, neither makes them illegitimate nor excludes them from political processes. Public acceptance and sanction, not charters, constitute the primary basis for authority.
>
> (March and Taqqu 1986:2)

March and Taqqu (1986) attribute confusion over legitimacy to "failure to distinguish between several meanings of the word 'public.'" The summary by Van Allen (1976:64) that they use to clarify these meanings is worth repeating:

> One notion of "public" relates it to issues that are of concern to the whole community; ends served by "political functions" are beneficial to the community as a whole. Although different individuals or groups may seek different resolutions of problems or disputes, the "political" can nevertheless be seen as encompassing all those human concerns and problems that are common to all members of the community, or at least to large numbers of them. "Political" problems are shared problems that are appropriately dealt with through group action — their resolutions are collective, not individual. This separates them from "purely personal" problems.
>
> The second notion of "public" is that which is distinguished from "secret," that is, open to everyone's view, accessible to all members of the community. The settling of questions that concern the welfare of the community in a "public" way necessitates the sharing of "political knowledge" — the knowledge needed for participation in political discussion and decision. A system in which public policy is made publicly and the relevant knowledge is shared widely contrasts sharply with those systems in which a privileged few possess the relevant knowledge — whether priestly mysteries or bureaucratic expertise — and therefore control policy decisions.

Therefore, there are two meanings to the concept of "public": "the nature of the collectivity involved, and the nature of the space or style in which that collectivity operates" (March and Taqqu 1986:3). In the West, such distinctions have been forgotten and only one meaning is accepted: a supposedly uniform total public in whose name policy is made. "This assumed uniformity gives rise to an idiom of public interest or common welfare which is essential to formal political action" (March and Taqqu 1986:3). Something is considered politically legitimate only if it

115

serves this hypothetical "public interest." Because this idiom of public interest is part of a political discourse that has become dominant in the Third World, systems of authority that fall outside the definition are not acknowledged as legitimate.

This is why women's organizations are seen as "informal" and not considered part of the legitimate political structure. Another problem for the legitimacy of such associations is that they operate in a sphere rendered less visible by contemporary, male-dominated structures and discourses: the world of "women's affairs." However, this does not make their activity "private." The lower profile does not correspond to a low level of public acceptance and political power. In fact, the case of the *Ifelodun* Yoruba women's group described in Chapter 5 suggests the opposite conclusion (see also Van Allen's [1972] classic study of Ibo women's custom of "sitting on a man" and O'Barr's [1982, 1984] important theoretical contributions to the topic of women's political power). To understand the nature of "public life" in Africa and the role of women within it, the Western conceptualization of opposing private and public spaces must be abandoned.

The WID literature has argued that the public realm has been favoured over the private realm in the development process. I would argue instead that it is the community of men that has been favoured over the community of women. Outsiders, from missionaries to colonial officials to contemporary governmental elites, have recognized men's networks as the sole, legitimate "public" with which they should deal — the uniform, undifferentiated "public" that embodies "public interest." Consequently, the complex links between the male and female communities, which serve to make of a village a functioning "public" whole, have been broken or distorted. Concomitantly, women's community has been relegated to the status of "private" or informal, to conformity with Western ideology. As March and Taqqu (1986:5) say, the view that "informal life is personal and hence apolitical — especially among the poor and the powerless — obscured the legitimacy of associations that are not constituted through rational-bureaucratic and legal charters." The denial of the African concept of public, implicit in almost every development effort, has done a profound disservice to the political life of African communities.

"Family" and the "domestic realm"

The problems in conceptualizing "family" in Africa have been considered in Chapter 3. The foregoing discussion on the public/private dichotomy also bears intimately upon this issue. The notion of "household" is necessary (see Bryceson 1985:11). Far too much of the literature assumes that the "household" is an undifferentiated unit, however, with no internal divisions or contradictions. Liberal and developmentalist approaches assume that the household may be taken as a unit of statistical analysis that acts rationally as a corporate entity in the marketplace. Thus, development policies have often targeted the household without considering the differential impact upon its different members (see Guyer and Peters 1987).

African sex-gender systems pose special problems for considering the household. For example, the complexities introduced by polygyny are overlooked. Even though a majority of African marriages are now monogamous, the idioms, practices, and organization of space are still often structured according to the polygynous marriage. Because of the lack of subtlety in perceiving family and household, writers reduce women's problems within the family to "male

116

domination" — a vague and ahistorical notion. Bryceson (1985:8) argues that, in most of the women and technology literature, "male domination in its cultural and institutional sense, is treated as an historical given fact. Having identified the extent and incidence of the edge that men have over women in the acquisition and control of technology, the analyses rarely offer an in-depth dissection of its nature." The consequence is that analyses of family and household are "primarily descriptive."

A more rigorous, historically grounded understanding of gender relations therefore requires a clearer conceptualization of the African household and, in particular, the politics of space. A starting point is the recognition that African households have indefinite social boundaries. "Not only do households vary in structure, but also in function, often with household members resorting to participation in other groupings for some of their production and consumption functions" (Bryceson 1985:11). The recognition that women's labour is not domestic in the Western sense is particularly important. Not only is women's agricultural work not domestic, but their transformation (consumption) activities must also be seen in a different light. These tasks are an "enabling function for agricultural production. Women spend a great deal of time in drudgery which directly or indirectly contributes to production. A case in point is the provision of water, which has most frequently been defined in terms of social welfare. In fact it is properly a matter for agricultural policy" (Fortmann 1981:208).

The spatial boundaries of families are also indefinite. Members of a household often reside in different dwellings within a village or, indeed, in different settlements. It is common in Africa for households to be divided between urban and rural members, with constant circulation between physical residences. Much of Africa's economic resources move back and forth between city and countryside (and sometimes between countries) through these family networks.

Another erroneous aspect of the concept of "family" commonly applied is the implicit assumption that inheritance and genealogy centre around the husband and father. For the large areas of sub-Saharan Africa characterized by the matrilineal descent system, this assumption has had serious consequences. Rogers (1980:129–138) provides an insightful analysis of the active suppression of matriliny by the World Bank and other agencies. Using the World Bank's Lilongwe Land Development Program in Malawi as an example, Rogers (1980) shows how the complexities of land tenure, cooperative production and distribution, and inheritance are reduced in the understanding of project officials to a set of "socialistic" obstacles to progress. In the evaluation documents, matriliny is described "somewhat emotively as 'matriarchy'" (Rogers 1980:132). This, of course, misses the point about matriliny, which according to most anthropologists is a system of inheritance and obligation revolving around the uncle–niece and nephew relationship, rather than around the father–children relationship, as in patriliny. Although men are still dominant in matrilineal systems, studies reveal a greater authority for women and more control over communal assets than in patrilineal societies.[2]

---

[2]The relative authority of women in matrilineal societies has become a subject of debate, however. Poewe (1981), amongst others, challenges the assumption that male members of matrilineages are automatically more authoritative than female members. I suggest there is a tautology in much of the reasoning on matriliny: "everywhere, men dominate women, thus women's authority in matrilineages cannot be real: it is only apparent authority."

To illustrate the conceptual errors perpetrated in the World Bank project, Rogers (1980:131) comments on a document that deals with present attitudes to inheritance:

> [The evaluators] cite survey responses from the people they define as "growers" (mostly men): "The survival of Matriliny in Africa is a talking point among Sociologists and there is certainly considerable evidence of an increased desire amongst growers that inheritance should pass to their children...." The problems with this rationale are [that] the answers are likely to have been influenced by what the enumerators (themselves very Western-orientated, with salaries paid by the project) wanted to hear. In addition the question of what was understood by "their own children" is an open one: if, for example, a man felt his nephews or nieces to be his own children, and entitled to inherit his goods, he would probably have responded in the affirmative.

How and why an ideology of the family emerged that was at variance with the African reality is another subject of inquiry. Mbilinyi (1985a,b) locates the emergence of such an ideology in the political economy of colonialism and neocolonialism (see also Bryceson 1980).

> Ideology about the male dominant-female dependent nuclear family has been used in an effort to legitimise the periodic expulsion of women from the wage labour market and/or towns during times of crisis. The ideology pertaining to the countryside, where villagers supposedly can survive so long as they work hard enough...helps to rationalise their forcible return "home" to what is described as their tribal homeplace. Both sets of imagery have arisen in the context of consistently lower wages for women than men in all occupations and at different education levels.... Both imageries conflict with the growing rate of urbanisation and the increasing number of female-headed households in villages and town.
>
> (Mbilinyi 1985b:81)

Analyses of this kind rescue the concept of "family" from the received truth of a "natural" state and locate it firmly in the African historical context (see The "traditional," pp. 121–124).

The task of reconceptualizing the family is particularly urgent in the light of a dramatic world demographic trend toward households headed by women. Youssef and Hetler (1983) provide a useful comparative survey of this trend, but also stress the difficulties in collecting data given biases in statistical research methods. "Even when questions on the sex of the household head are incorporated into data collection procedures, there are still major obstacles to determining the incidence of woman-headed households because of the definitions, or lack of definitions, of 'family' and 'household head' in censuses and surveys" (Youssef and Hetler 1983:225). The circumstances of female household heads have been well described, however (for summaries of recent studies, see Momsen and Townsend 1987). Chipande (1987) discusses the innovative strategies of female household heads in Malawi; Wilkinson (1987) presents the particular problems faced by rural Basotho women in the context of Southern Africa's labour reserve system.

Women head households in Africa both from necessity and by choice. Many are widowed, divorced, or left to run households when men migrate to find work. Increasing numbers of women are choosing to become single mothers to circumvent the daunting inequities of married life and to ensure security for their old age (the appropriation of their income by husbands, the loss of property rights and, hence, access to credit, commoditized bridewealth, and the patrilineal control of children are some of the problems facing married women). Only when the ideology of the male-headed nuclear family is abandoned and it is recognized that female-headed families are not anomalous and marginal to African society, will development planning adequately account for the needs of this significant household form.

The economic as the socially determining level of society

Both neoclassical and Marxist economics assume the primacy of economic motivation in human life (although the structural Marxist school of Althusser, Poulantzas, and Laclau discussed in Chapter 1 challenges this assumption). Much of the WID and feminist political economy literature sees economic relations as the source of ideological and political structures and practices. Gender relations, are also analyzed in largely economic terms, in spite of attempts to theorize the sex-gender system as an autonomous structure in human society. This preoccupation with economic roles is now reflected in many aid documents (e.g., ILO/INSTRAW 1985). As I have shown, a focus on the economic contribution of women and the economic dimensions of gender relations is an important corrective to perceptions of women as marginal, noneconomic beings, inhabiting a "private" realm and requiring "social welfare" to correct their problems. Fortmann's (1981) critique of "domestic" work, cited previously, is a demonstration of the utility of this approach.

Nevertheless, it is time to take stock of the recent preoccupation with the economic. Although it is beyond the scope of this study to critique "economic determinism" or to enter the current theoretical debate about it, I suggest we should examine our assumptions in this regard. The invisibility of the politics of space is a case in point. Another example is Jackson's (1985) conclusion about women making choices on political and ideological grounds rather than on economic grounds (see the discussion of KRP in Chapter 3, pp. 67–70). Particularly serious is the practical invisibility of the "social welfare" (or "social reproduction") issues of nutrition and health care in the WID and feminist political economy literature. Given the intimate connection between economic factors and the ability of women to fulfill their social welfare responsibilities, the overemphasis on economic factors is all the more dismaying. As Cecelski (1987:45–46) points out, for example,

> When families are really hard pressed, food production and cash earning take precedence over women's household tasks such as cooking and fuel and water collection, even though these are also essential for family welfare.... When more time has to be spent on particular tasks, whether in farming or in fuel collection, women's other work suffers.... In villages where women had to spend more time on fuel collection, they spent less time on cooking. This, however, can result in a lower nutritional level.

With regard to technology transfer, Carr and Sandhu (1987) have shown that much "appropriate technology" planning has been based on the assumption that the primary impact of new technology would be economic, in the form of more time available for either food production or income earning. The errors in this thinking (discussed in Chapter 3, pp. 56–61) again demonstrate the dangers of reducing the complexities of women's activities to simple economic dimensions. As an example of unintended outcomes, Carr and Sandhu (1987:51) present evidence that "technologies related to household tasks are unlikely to save women time since they may simply result in other family members offering less help, or lead to increased expectations regarding the quality or quantity of household services."

Baudrillard (1975) argues that our theories of economic causality are in fact a metaphor derived from the experience of 19th century industrial life, where production was indeed the dominant element shaping society. He critiques the application of Marxist models of political economy and the Marxist method of historical materialism to earlier and non-Western societies.

> The analysis of the contradictions of Western society has not led to the comprehension of earlier societies (or of the Third World). It has succeeded only in exporting these contradictions to them. At times not even the contradictions have been exported but very simply the *solution*, that is, the productivist model.... Through its most "scientific" inclinations toward earlier societies, [historical materialism] "naturalizes" them under the sign of the mode of production.
>
> (Baudrillard 1975:89–91)

Political economists may find Baudrillard's judgment overly harsh. Nevertheless, perhaps we should ask whether the "productivist model" is appropriate for theories of African social relations, either in the past or the present. Certainly, attempts to explain all aspects of sex-gender relations in terms of relations of production have proved difficult. With regard to WID research, an overemphasis on production issues at the expense of other aspects of development problems has created a theoretical and empirical imbalance in the literature. Mbilinyi (1984) identifies economism as one of the chief priorities for research in East Africa, and criticizes her own earlier tendencies toward such reductionism. Admitting that undue emphasis has been placed on "women's place in production and reproduction" and that definitions of these concepts have been overly mechanical, Mbilinyi cites an example of such economism in her bibliography on women in Tanzania (Mascarenhas and Mbilinyi 1980:12) to which a colleague drew her attention:

> Our conceptualisation of the women's question refers to women in production and reproduction, that is, the nature of women's work, and how women are situated in production and in the reproduction of the labour force and society itself.... This is why there are so many items on women peasants and women workers, on ideology and education, on health and nutrition, and *none on fashions of dress and hair style. The problem of integration of women into development is not a problem of hairstyles.*

Mbilinyi confesses

> As we later noted in the same work, harassment of women for wearing short dresses, blue jeans and cosmetics was part of a general campaign to put women in their place as subjugated people. Hair styles had everything to do with women's oppression and the oppression of men as well!
>
> (Mbilinyi 1984:298)

Swantz (1985) pinpoints the preoccupation with dependency theory as part of the problem of economism. She argues that although it is important to recognize and analyze the dependency of local economies on international market forces, the adequacy of dependency theory for explaining women's condition must also be questioned.

> In view of the fact that a mode of analysis may contribute to further subjection of people in general or of women, the theoretical approach adopted is crucial. A dependence theory approaches the problems negatively, concentrating on aspects of deprivation of a class of people, but failing to point a way forward.... When developing a methodology for an analysis of local solutions in social processes, it cannot be assumed that the improvement of the living conditions of peasants and workers in general will suffice for the correction of imbalanced structures in relation to women.
>
> (Swantz 1985:2–3)

As the following discussion of the "traditional" reveals and as suggested in the discussion of *matega* in Chapter 6, a fruitful line of research lies in the application of theory about discourse and ideology to our understanding of African political economy. In discourse analysis, power relations are understood to be shaped by dominant visions of reality. Mbilinyi's (1984) point about the use of cultural discourse to subjugate women and Swantz's (1985) point about the negative consequences of the dependency approach confirm the value of studying discourse. Yet, such theory has only recently begun to be applied to WID issues. The following discussions of "tradition" and "nature" develop an argument about discourse. The final section of this chapter explores the relationships between power and knowledge.

The "traditional"

I have argued against perceiving developing societies to be on a unilinear course between a "traditional" and a "modern" existence. I have also shown how precolonial elements of sex-gender systems have been retained in a dominated, distorted form, providing the ideological raw material to constrain the autonomy and power of women: in the name of "tradition."

Along the same lines of ideological inquiry suggested in the preceding section, it is important to investigate the ideology of "tradition" as it pertains to gender relations. Katz (1985) demonstrates, in the context of African national politics, the power of ideological discourses that recruit "tradition" to their explanations of how society should be. Dominant discourses that support the ruling group are those that have most successfully used tradition to legitimize the group's political power. To distinguish contemporary ideological constructions from genuine historical social structures (especially sex-gender systems), similar work must be done at the local level (e.g., Glazier 1985). Disparate evidence suggests that the challenge of women's demand for rights and improved economic and social conditions is met with the accusation that they have abandoned their "traditional" responsibilities and are seeking to undermine the family. Such gender discourse has a powerful effect in the creation of guilt among women, in stifling their dissent, and in blocking progressive legal reform.

The political pitfalls inherent in an ahistorical view of "tradition" are exemplified by the controversy surrounding the question of clitoridectomy. Western radical feminists condemned the practice as a "barbaric tradition." African apologists defended it, however, and attacked Western feminist interference in the name of "honourable and functional tradition." In neither case is the appeal to a primordial, unchanging "tradition" helpful in understanding and solving this politically sensitive and medically urgent problem. Kirby (1987) provides an incisive analysis of the feminist discourse on clitoridectomy. Focusing on the thinking of Western women who do not believe clitoridectomy to be a problematic topic, she critiques their assumption that they speak authoritatively for non-Western women. Kirby also challenges their belief that clitoridectomy provides evidence of universal patriarchy. The books by these feminists are

> disturbingly consistent in their representation of a mutilated, abject body.... The peculiar and prurient fascination of the viewer/reader is swiftly sanitised behind the impassivity of a medical gaze. In fact medical discourse provides the common thread which weaves through this entire cluster of texts, providing its classifications and, implicitly, the "real" meanings which will secure the argument.... A mind/body dualism is an essential assumption for these arguments.... The vitality of this body's subjectivity, the beliefs and values which have been "incorporated" into its existential significance are pared away as extraneous.... Although clitoridectomy and infibulation are practised in thirty countries in Africa alone, the diversity of its cultural, political and historical experience is summarily negated: medical discourse alone provides the guarantee for this Western positivity of "What you are."
>
> (Kirby 1987:37–38)

Kirby (1987) concludes with some reflections on the dark side of Western philanthropy and suggests that preoccupation with "traditions" such as clitoridectomy have more to do with the West's obsessions than with enlightened altruism.

It is not only Westerners who misconstrue tradition. Wilson (1982) gives an excellent analysis of contemporary African gender discourse.

> *Authenticité* has been a device for consolidating power and legitimizing antidemocratic principles as traditional African values. Today, it is clear that *authenticité* has been used to obtain mass support and to distract attention away from the pressing economic and social problems that confront Zaire.... The rhetoric and reality of *authenticité* is paternalistic, authoritarian, and self-serving.... Under *authenticité*, the entire responsibility for maintaining the morality of the system rests with women. Men do not have moral responsibilities.
>
> (Wilson 1982:190–191)

Wilson's (1982) study, which documents the ways in which an ideology of "tradition" is used to control and oppress women, is an example of the kind of research that might fruitfully be pursued.

Mbilinyi (1985a) adds an important dimension to the critique of ahistorical approaches to "tradition." In Tanganyika, colonialism created notions of "traditional life" to serve its own exploitative ends. According to Mbilinyi's (1985a) conclusions, the colonial Tanganyikan regime constructed a dichotomy between rural, "traditional" African life and urban, "modern" life that transformed indigenous society in the service of "the colonial solution." In reality, the colony consisted of peasant-based economies on the one hand and a capitalist sector on the other. The latter was made up of urban and plantation enterprises that were owned first by German and later British multinational companies, and by individual European and Asian settlers. Both rural and urban enterprises depended on the migrant labour system; in particular, the plantations depended on the largely female casual labour pool. The aim of the regime, therefore, was

> to stabilise the working class and restrict African settlement in town solely to permanently employed workers and the middle classes. In order to successfully carry this out, the African extended family system was attacked, and the nuclear family was encouraged. The secondary economy was heavily taxed, regulated, and wherever possible, undermined. "Staff associations" or "workers councils" were promoted among workers to counter the labour movement. Women became central actors and targets in the struggle to impose the colonial solution.
>
> (Mbilinyi 1985a:88)

Mbilinyi (1985a) critically examines colonial discourse to uncover the economic and political reality served by the concept of a division between "city" and "countryside."

> A contrast between city and country permeates colonial commentary on the society its agents found, and the one they struggled to create and rule. In simple terms, the city was associated with non-Africans, men, adults, wage employment and civilization; the country, with Africans, women, children, "subsistence" and "bush." According to colonial ideology, the country was "home" for Africans, in "tribal areas," and the African in town was considered an "alien" in "foreign" territory who had "immigrated" and was in danger of being "detribalised".... Colonial archives assume this contrast. Moreover, they presume that the past was rural and agricultural. The centuries of urbanisation and economic specialisation which was identified with the development of feudal kingdoms, Swahili culture and the rise of the Zanzibar Commercial Empire, vanish from memory. So, too, do the struggles between slaves and slave-owners, queens and commoners, disappear.[3]
>
> (Mbilinyi 1985a:88)

In addition to inventing a false traditional/modern dichotomy, the colonial discourse Mbilinyi analyzes supports the public/private dichotomy previously discussed: the village being the "private" sphere in Western terms and the town being the only truly "public" domain. On the grounds of both dichotomies, the demands and needs of the "country" could be dismissed by colonial policy as backward and unimportant.

Mbilinyi (1985a) proposes concrete strategies to combat biases in both archival records and the interpretations of historians. Suggesting that "the same facts are subject to different interpretation, depending upon the group or class or sex with which the spokesperson identifies" (p. 96), she argues for the creation of opposing knowledge. However,

> The creation of oppositional history is in itself a political act. By speaking, writing, acting, drawing, or singing their own histories, people teach one another new ways of perceiving themselves and the world. Defiance of "official" histories is an act of empowerment.... The main audience ought to be the speakers themselves and the popular classes they represent.... This suggests the production of easily readable texts and other media in the local national languages spoken by the people.
>
> (Mbilinyi 1985a:96)

---

[3]The process Mbilinyi (1986) delineates is a precise description of the discourse of apartheid and the conceptual underpinnings of the Bantustan system in South Africa, whereby the majority of South Africans are treated as foreigners in their own land.

We have recently seen arguments, by both Western commentators and certain African leaders, that the colonial past is over and done with and should not be used to explain contemporary problems (for a particularly pernicious example of such writing, see Sender and Smith 1986). This argument, again, conspires to reinforce the vision of a backward Africa, where present dilemmas have no history other than timeless African "tradition." I thus agree with Mbilinyi's (1985a) view that the recapture of history, including that of the colonial era, is a vital task for the present. This could be used to correct Western biases regarding Africa and to empower local communities and particularly women.

Mbilinyi's (1985a) proposal (and the work of Tanzania's WRDP in general) offers a valuable tool for inserting women into not only the policy-making process but also the process of constructing accurate knowledge about their communities and problems, in other words, the objects of development policy. The practical importance of such historical research is dramatically illustrated by Kimati's (1986) study of nutritional knowledge amongst Tanzanian women. Kimati (1986:131) protests that

> The word "ignorance" used in the nutrition context by some people implies not knowing about good nutritious foods and how best to use them in the "western sense." Traditional knowledge about food may not have been valued as useful. This word has been used in nutrition for years with an already formed bias that the mothers who have malnourished children...are the ones who are ignorant and we, the educated, know everything about nutrition.

This study found, however, that the traditional combination in Tanzania of prolonged breast-feeding, complex weaning practices, women's food production and higher social status, nutritional supplements for lactating mothers, and family planning ensured sound nutrition for children. Kimati (1986) suggests that rather than ask why one third of Tanzanian children under 5 years suffer protein malnutrition, nutritionists should ask why two thirds are not malnourished. The answers, to be found in traditional nutritional practices, will provide many of the solutions for eradicating malnutrition. Kimati's (1986) argument for the recruitment of local knowledge to nutrition policy could be replicated for every area of development planning.

The nature of "nature"

Along with mainstream development thinking, most WID writing takes the environment as a given: a known entity that need only form the backdrop for development research and action. Assumptions about how the environment works take one of two forms. The first sees it as a neutral, unengaged, and indifferent essence, timeless and "out there," apart from human lives. The studies on the social oppression of women discussed in previous chapters display, through their silence on the environment, such an assumption. Even in studies that deal with environmental resources such as land and water, discussions of women's loss of use rights or control present people relating to each other in a passive, noninteractive, physical context.

The second vision of the environment implicit in development thinking is one of nature affected by humans. Their effect, however, is seen merely as a problem of misuse or overuse, usually because the users know no better; and it is overuse that has caused the environment's catastrophic decline — people have tempted and brought on their heads the laws of entropy. Sectoral analyses of environmental resources often assume that nature is working this way, as does much of the writing on African famine. Studies that often make this assumption are those concerned with deforestation and the problem of fuelwood (cf. Agarwal 1986). Even though this catastrophic vision of nature is more dynamic than the first and includes the idea of human agency, it too is making assumptions about a nature that is "out there" and somehow not part of the social problem. Whether nature is seen as a homeostatic device, as in the first view, or as a decaying, abused body, as in the second, the nature of "nature" has remained unexamined. In both, nature is "natural."

What both of these assumptions about the environment miss is the social dimension of our understanding and practices regarding nature. It is this historically created relation to the environment that now shapes nature itself. Agarwal (1984) challenges us to rescue the concept of "nature" from the realm of timeless essence and give it a history and a dynamic relationship to human thought and action. He explores the national and international socioeconomic processes that have favoured one kind of nature, "a nature that is geared to meet urban and industrial needs, a nature that is essentially cash generating," over another kind of nature, "a nature that has traditionally come to support household and community needs" (Agarwal 1984:9). It is the latter nature, the rapidly vanishing one, that is most supportive of women's responsibilities and needs, and about which women have a deep working knowledge. What Agarwal (1984) proposes is that nature is historically selected by dominant forces in society and actively shaped to their needs. Both the ideas about what nature is and the actual physical transformations it undergoes are the products of society. In other words, nature is far from "natural." This is not, of course, to argue that no "real" world exists apart from human thought about nature and that science has been investigating a chimera. Rather, it is to suggest that the dominant scientific discourse about the environment, as it has historically developed over the past several hundred years, is intimately connected with the social and political world within which it was developed.

Agarwal's ideas are an excellent starting point for a critique of assumptions about the nature of "nature" in Africa. We need to study the concept precisely because the assumptions of experts have contributed to the failure of past development efforts. It is the unwitting (or disguised) selection of Agarwal's first nature by contemporary socioeconomic forces that poses the greatest environmental problems for women and local communities in Africa. By this process, the relationship of women to the environment has been undermined, devalued, and disregarded. It is Agarwal's second nature that we should identify, analyze, and promote if we wish to see solutions to the resource problems of African women and, hence, of African communities. When based on the second nature rather than the commercially oriented first nature, however, local environmental practices are necessarily discredited by the traditional/modern dichotomy and considered obstacles to development. Moreover, competing uses of nature find concrete expression within the African family. Whereas men welcome the commercialization of production fostered by development activities, women often resist it. For men, Agarwal's (1984) first nature appears to offer immediate opportunities; for women, however, the second nature is the only one within which they can continue to carry out their traditional responsibilities. A commercialized nature is one where women have reduced use rights, where their scientific

125

knowledge is devalued, and where resources are directed away from the local community that women sustain.

At the heart of the problem, therefore, is a shift from one kind of nature to another, a transformation that has gone unnoticed. The historical construction of a nature more hostile to women has not been clearly addressed in the WID literature; indeed, the WID enterprise is inextricably intertwined with this problem of thinking about the environment. On the one hand, the issues identified by the WID literature beg questions about the underlying assumptions of development efforts. On the other hand, however, the conceptual problems embedded in the WID literature contribute to the perpetuation of mistaken assumptions about the nature of "nature."

When scholars take on the term "nature" or "environment," they enter a well-demarcated arena of debate. One of the topics that has aroused great controversy in Africa, as elsewhere, is conservation. Environmentalists have colluded in constructing a static, timeless nature, a museum to be protected from human activity. Agarwal (1984:1) suggests that many conservation programs

> seem to be based on the belief that concern for the environment essentially means protecting and conserving it, partly from development programmes but mainly from the people itself. There is little effort to modify the development process itself in a manner that will bring it in greater harmony with the needs of the people and with the need to maintain ecological balance, while increasing the productivity of our land, water and forest resources.

The argument here for Agarwal's second nature does not accede to the idea of nature as museum. Rather, it begins from the premise that humans and nature construct each other in an ongoing dialectical process. The shaping of that process should be an area of concern. Agarwal (1984) states that most environmental groups in India that are succeeding in mobilizing people at the local level to prevent ecological destruction (often in the face of government policies) are not concerned with environmental protection per se. Rather, their concern is "to put the environment at the service and the control of the people, the people being defined as the local communities who live within that environment.... It is this growing understanding of the relationship between the people and their environment, born out of a concern for a more equitable and sustainable use of the environment, that is probably the most fascinating development" (Agarwal 1984:2).

Because arguments against the dominant view of nature are often dismissed as antidevelopment and antipeople, it is important to discuss the conservation view and how it is distinguished from the second nature. Third World governments have a point when they protest that "having got their riches and their affluent lifestyles, Westerners were now simply asking for more affluence: clean air, clean water, and large tracts of nature for enjoyment and recreation, many of which were going to be preserved in the tropical forests and savannas of Asia, Africa, and South America" (Agarwal 1984:3). These arguments, however, are used as a justification for the promotion of a nature geared to urban and industrial needs, i.e., to the interests of Third World elites.

The power of the push for such a nature not only lies in the political and economic power of dominant classes but also stems from the construction of Western scientific knowledge. As Keller (1985:131) argues,

> The very concept of "laws of nature" is, in contemporary usage, both a product and an expression of the absence of reflectivity. It introduces into the

study of nature a metaphor indelibly marked by its political origins. The philosophical distinction between descriptive and prescriptive laws is invoked to underline the neutrality of scientific description. But nonetheless, laws of nature, like laws of the state, are historically imposed from above and obeyed from below.

Cloaked in the respectability of the laws of nature, the proponents of the first nature dismiss the knowledge and concerns of those who hold to the second nature. Given that indigenous scientific knowledge (the "science of the concrete" as Lévi-Strauss termed non-Western sciences) falls within the latter category, this dismissal has profoundly disturbing consequences for the ability of Africans to promote their own understanding of nature.

> A variety of natural and human resources are untapped because, outside the communities themselves, there has been little or no knowledge of their existence. This is especially true in relation to women, whose control over local resources has not so far been sufficiently recognised. [Such resources are] a "power of periphery."
>
> (Swantz 1985:3)

Cecelski (1987:46) gives an example of such resources: "In subsistence economies uncultivated areas provide food, medicines, building materials, tools and utensils. Foods gathered from these areas, mainly by women, are often an important nutritional supplement. Even arid and semi-arid savannas and deserts can provide a variety of wild produce, which are especially important as a fallback during drought." Yet, the destruction of these products of the second, community-oriented nature by development projects and environmental degradation have largely gone unnoticed because local knowledge has not been valued. Agarwal (1986) condemns forestry planning on this account and makes an eloquent case for genuine community participation in policy-making and implementation.

It is important to stress that local knowledge about nature is not merely "folk knowledge," in which there has been no rigorous testing of propositions against reality. The "science of the concrete" may be inextricably woven into everyday practices, where its rigour is invisible to Western scientific methods. The recovery of this science requires subtlety and social expertise. Dahl (1981:201) makes the point with regard to pastoralism.

> A certain type of research for which I think there is still a need is that of pastoral ethnoscience. Sheer descriptive studies of ecological classification systems, ethnobotany, etc. do not receive much academic acclaim but are urgently needed. they are needed both to establish a reasonable platform for communication with pastoralists and to give proper appreciation of the pastoralists' substantial mass of useful knowledge. One may argue that such studies are not the business of anthropologists, but one cannot deny that it is their active duty to interest botanists, animal husbandry personnel, etc. in these fields.

An example of such "ethnoscience" is the work of David Western on Masai cattle management (e.g., Western and Dunne 1979). His work challenges assumptions that had commonly been made by anthropologists working on East African pastoralist societies regarding pastoralists' lack of "scientific" understanding of livestock management and milk production. Decisions regarding homesteads, migration, and other matters were seen to be based on purely social criteria (for a classic case study, see Gulliver 1955). Such a view is possible if one subscribes to the idea of a noninteractive, passive nature, visible only to the eye of an impartial, Western science. In contrast, Western started with the question of the pastoralists' scientific basis for herd-management decisions (Western and Dunne 1979). Interested in the complex, harmonious interaction of humans and animals in the savannas of Kenya, Western educated himself in anthropological issues and methods. In the course of his work with the Masai of Amboseli, he was inducted into an age set, as enthusiastic researchers often are. As a lineage brother, he became an owner of cattle himself.

Thus, as both an honorary Masai and a scientist respectful of the alternate scientific knowledge of a different culture, Western sought to discover whether there was a common ground for his science and that of the Masai. Consequently, he asked better questions about pastoral decision-making and came up with answers different from those of the anthropologists. His enquiries took two directions. First, he surveyed existing and past boma (settlement) sites and, with Dunne, quantified regularities in the sites chosen (see Western and Dunne 1979). Their statistical analysis revealed that boma sites were consistently located at a certain point in the slope of a hill, on certain types of soil and stones, and oriented in particular ways. Second, he asked his age mates why they located bomas in this way as well as other questions about cattle management. Because he asked scientific questions, based on his own expertise both as ecologist and cattle owner, his informants responded with a wealth of information regarding their decision-making process.

In the highlands, Masai favoured black or coloured cows for their better heat absorption properties, which enhanced milk production (melanism as an energy-conserving mechanism has been observed by ecologists studying other species). Contrarily, in hot, lowland areas, white cows reflected heat and, in using less body energy to combat heat, yielded better than dark, coloured cows. With regard to the location of bomas, the site characteristics quantified by Western and Dunne were explained by the Masai in terms of the maintenance of cattle in optimum condition. Points further down the slope would be too dank and encourage disease; sites higher up would be too cold and exposed. In addition, sites were chosen for the nature of the ground: dark soils and stones absorbed the sun's heat and reflected it at night, keeping the cows warm. This prevents the diversion of milk-producing energy to heat conservation. Western came up with a great deal of scientific knowledge about dairying: elders responsible for choosing the grazing location for the day would do meteorological observations to ensure that the green flush following spot thunderstorms was used. They knew to the last cup what each cow could and should produce and constantly strove to meet production targets through sound technical choices in herd management.

One might add a point that even the enlightened ecologist has not yet focused on: this daily subtle use of nature must involve close collaboration between the dairyists: women, who actually controlled and measured the milk, and the male herders or herding directors. The next task in uncovering local scientific knowledge about cattle management, therefore, is a similarly sensitive exploration of the dairying and livestock health-care knowledge of women.[4]

---

[4]Even though work on pastoral peoples has recently taken a more enlightened attitude toward pastoral practice, on the whole, it remains gender biased and ethnocentric (Kettel 1986:48). For a more sophisticated approach to cattle management that, nevertheless, does not pay adequate attention to the role of women, see Galaty et al. (1981).

In conclusion, the bankruptcy of development research and policy is due to not only its gender blindness but also its denigration of the scientific capacities of Africans and, by extension, the denial of a historically shaped nature. What this account of pastoral science reveals is the importance of starting from the assumption that humans in a successful socioeconomic lifestyle are intelligent regarding all aspects of their social and physical world.

Liberating subjugated knowledges

Inherent in all of the preceding conceptual problems is a profound epistemological predicament, exemplified by Mbilinyi's (1985a) call for a struggle to recapture history for Tanzanians. Much of the critique of conceptual frameworks in Chapters 1 and 2 and evidence throughout this study confirm that competing views of reality are a central aspect of development dilemmas. Time and again, this review has chronicled the imposition of the dominant, Western "knowledge" to the detriment of local "knowledges" that are more appropriate constructions of local reality. Part of the problem has been poor science that relies on biased dichotomies: inadequate theories and methodologies for understanding the "family"; the nature of public life; the history of African societies at both the broad and local levels; and local conceptions of nature. This poor science is itself a product of history, emerging as an aspect of, and a support for, the power relations that subjugated Africa. By the nature of these power relations, knowledge of Africa was constructed by non-Africans according to Western categories of thought. The alienation of Africans from their own knowledge of themselves is the other part of the epistemological dilemma. Given the deep differences between the West and Africa in both knowledge and practice of gender relations and in the construction of female identity, the crisis in knowledge has urgent implications for WID efforts.

It would be irresponsible and utopian to suggest the possibility of return to a golden age of African self-knowledge (indeed, the suggestion that the African past is more "authentic" than the African present is implicitly ethnocentric, denying the right of Africans to identify themselves as cosmopolitan members of the world community, sharing its modern cultural values and practices). Nevertheless, researchers can no longer avoid the task of investigating the relationship between dominant power structures, past and present, and the nature of knowledge about Africa. Central to this task is an engagement with the theory of discourse. A start has been made by scholars interested in applying the insights of recent discourse analysis (as well as the ideas of earlier Third World humanist critics such as Franz Fanon) to our knowledge of Western domination. For example, a 1984 conference on the sociology of literature at the University of Essex generated the Group for the Critical Study of Colonial Discourse now based at the University of California, Santa Cruz, CA, USA (Group for the Critical Study of Colonial Discourse 1985; for a relevant study from the Group, see Spivak 1985). Said's (1979) exploration of the concept of "the Orient" in Western thought, already considered a classic study, has provided the inspiration for much of this thinking, including some work on discourse on Africa (e.g., Miller 1985). Mueller (1987) has engaged in a ground-breaking critique of WID discourse.

Michel Foucault, the thinker who is widely credited with having developed during the 1970s a new method for the study of humans in society (and whose later work inspired Said and subsequent discourse analysts), provides a place to begin a theoretical inquiry into the discourses of domination in the Third World (for an introduction to his ideas, see Foucault 1980b). Foucault has been criticized from both left and right, as well as by feminists, for his obscure writing and irrelevance to contemporary social and economic concerns — they view him as a trendy theorist of the avant garde. Nevertheless, an increasing number of scholars in the West, including feminists, are recognizing the value of Foucault's approach for a fresh understanding of the nature of institutions and the mechanisms of power, as Mueller's (1987) work attests. The controversial nature of his vital contribution to recent social thought should not deter researchers in gender and development from assessing his theory and adapting his insights in the African context.

Foucault's (1973, 1979, 1980a) work shows how ideas about madness, illness, crime, and sexuality have been transformed in the modern era to serve the tactical needs of new social systems. Out of his analyses of organized forms of social life, such as prisons, hospitals, schools, and insane asylums, original thinking has emerged about the nature of power and discourse and the way in which our era has constructed humans as objects of knowledge. This is neither accomplished by the deliberate actions of power-wielding practitioners, nor does it follow formal laws or rules. Instead, cultural practices are structured by a "grid of intelligibility" (Dreyfus and Rabinow 1983:121), which emerges through the subtle interplay of power and knowledge. The "grid of intelligibility," according to Foucault (1980b:194) is "a thoroughly heterogeneous ensemble consisting of discourse, institutions, architectural forms, regulatory decisions, laws, administrative measures, scientific statements, philosophical, moral and philanthropic propositions — in short, the said as much as the unsaid."

Although Foucault's work focuses almost exclusively on Western institutions (and there is vigorous debate over the quality of his historical methodology), his relevance to the Third World is nevertheless significant. First, his thinking provides a method for an epistemological investigation into how the African — and especially the African woman — has been constructed as an object of knowledge. Second, his insights on the relation between power and knowledge provide a valuable conceptual tool for understanding the emergence of this knowledge about Africans in colonial and postcolonial contexts. Foucault (1979:26) conceives of power "not as a property, but as a strategy...one should decipher in it a network of relations, constantly in tension, in activity, rather than a privilege that one might possess." Power is not simply exercised in a monolithic way by those who "have it" over those who "do not have it" (the notion of power in much underdevelopment theory). Conversely, knowledge is not something that can only exist apart from power relations.

> Perhaps we should abandon the belief that power makes mad and that, by the same token, the renunciation of power is one of the conditions of knowledge. We should admit rather that power produces knowledge (and not simply by encouraging it because it serves power or by applying it because it is useful); that power and knowledge directly imply one another; that there is no power relation without the correlative constitution of a field of knowledge, nor any knowledge that does not presuppose and constitute at the same time power relations.... In short, it is not the activity of the subject of knowledge that produces a corpus of knowledge, useful or resistant to power, but power-knowledge, the processes and struggles that traverse it and of which it is made up, that determines the forms and possible domains of knowledge.
> (Foucault 1979:27–28)

So far, this study has implicitly argued that contemporary international economic relations and related aid efforts are power relations that have shaped and, in turn, been shaped by particular "forms and domains of knowledge" about Africa and African women. The discourse is not necessarily coherent and unified: indeed, I have argued that knowledge about Africa and its development problems is fragmented among the different research/action loci and between different conceptual frameworks. As Foucault (1979:26) says about discourse: "It is often made up of bits and pieces; it implements a disparate set of tools or methods. In spite of the coherence of its results...it cannot be localized in a particular type of institution or state apparatus."

Foucault (1983) contends that a new kind of power has emerged in the last several hundred years. This power has been advanced by a series of disciplinary practices across an array of institutions, including the state (he deliberately puns in his use of the term "discipline," implying both its meaning as regulation of behaviour, and its meaning as regulated areas of inquiry).

> What is to be understood by the disciplining of societies in Europe since the eighteenth century is not, of course, that the individuals who are part of them become more and more obedient, nor that they set about assembling in barracks, schools, or prisons; rather that an increasingly better invigilated process of adjustment has been sought after — more and more rational and economic — between productive activities, resources of communication, and the play of power relations.
>
> (Foucault 1983:219)

Those power relations are, he suggests, a new secular version of "pastoral power" (in the sense of spiritual guidance, not herding society). The new "pastoral power" resides in the state and other modern institutions and, like the ecclesiastical power that it has replaced, is salvation oriented.

> It was no longer a question of leading people to their salvation in the next world, but rather ensuring it in this world. And in this context, the word *salvation* takes on different meanings: health, well-being (that is sufficient wealth, standard of living), security, protection against accidents. A series of "worldly" aims took the place of the traditional pastorate.... Sometimes the power was exercised by private ventures, welfare societies, benefactors and generally by philanthropists. But ancient institutions, for example the family, were also mobilized...to take on pastoral functions.... Finally, the multiplication of the aims and agents of pastoral power focused the development of knowledge of man around two roles: one, globalizing and quantitative, concerning the population; the other, analytical, concerning the individual.
>
> (Foucault 1983:215)

This quotation reads uncannily like a description of development aid activities. I believe that Foucault's concept of a secular "pastoral power" can be used to illuminate the process by which development discourse and its accompanying disciplinary practices have come to dominate Third World societies. The utility of Foucault's ideas about the relationship between power and knowledge is explored further in Chapter 7.

In thinking about the utility of discourse theory for feminist political economy and practical research on women, technology, and development, the theories of resistance that are being proposed to counter the new globalizing power process should be given special attention. Laclau and Mouffe (1985) argue that old conceptions of social struggle that rely on theories of contradictions between monolithic classes are no longer appropriate. Instead, they call for a "radical democratic politics" that links the interests of marginalized and oppressed groups, allowing them to mount a more powerful challenge to today's hegemonic forces than each group could muster alone. Central to Laclau and Mouffe's (1985) analysis of the pluralistic resistance movements of our day is recognition of the importance of the feminist struggle. As well, they are concerned with the West's domination of the Third World.

Laclau and Mouffe's (1985) thinking about resistance is closely related to Foucault's ideas about "the insurrection of subjugated knowledges," an insurrection that is already under way, according to him.

> What has emerged in the course of the last ten or fifteen years is a sense of the increasing vulnerability to criticism of things, institutions, practices, discourses. A certain fragility has been discovered in the very bedrock of existence — even, and perhaps above all, in those aspects of it that are most familiar, most solid and most intimately related to our bodies and to our everyday behaviour. But together with this sense of instability and this amazing efficacy of discontinuous, particular and local criticism, one in fact also discovers something that perhaps was not initially foreseen, something one might describe as precisely the inhibiting effect of global, *totalitarian theories*.... The attempt to think in terms of a totality has in fact proved a hindrance to research.... I believe that what this essentially local character of criticism indicates in reality is an autonomous, non-centralised kind of theoretical production, one that is to say whose validity is not dependent on the approval of the established régimes of thought....
>
> By subjugated knowledges one should understand...a whole set of knowledges that have been disqualified as inadequate to their task or insufficiently elaborated: naïve knowledges, located low down on the hierarchy, beneath the required level of cognition or scientificity.... It is through the reappearance of...these local popular knowledges, these disqualified knowledges, that criticism performs its work.... With what in fact were these buried, subjugated knowledges really concerned? They were concerned with a *historical knowledge of struggles*. In popular knowledge there lay the memory of hostile encounters which even up to this day have been confined to the margins of knowledge.

> (Foucault 1980b:80–83)

This thinking on "subjugated knowledges" is directly relevant to the point previously made in here on the suppression of local knowledges and the struggle to retrieve them. It is also relevant to the critiques throughout this book of theories and policies that universalize from both Western subjectivity and Western historical experience. Foucault (1980b:83–84) calls for researchers to "establish a historical knowledge of struggles and to make use of this knowledge tactically today." The purpose of such "genealogical research" is to "entertain the claims to attention of local, discontinuous, disqualified, illegitimate knowledges against the claims of a unitary body of theory which would filter, hierarchise and order them in the name of some true knowledge and some arbitrary idea of what constitutes a science and its objects.... It is really against the effects of the power of a discourse that is considered to be scientific that the genealogy must wage its struggle" (Foucault 1980b:83–84).

Geertz (1983) is an important protagonist in this struggle to establish a voice for disparate knowledges. He suggests that the growing interest in interpretation and exegesis is in part

> a result of the growing recognition that the established approach to treating such phenomena, laws-and-causes social physics, was not producing the triumphs of prediction, control, and testability that had for so long been promised in its name. And in part, it is a result of intellectual deprovincialization. The broader currents of modern thought have finally begun to impinge upon what has been, and in some quarters still is, a snug and insular enterprise.
>
> (Geertz 1983:3)

To the extent that development thinking has been such a "snug and insular enterprise," nonchalantly dismissing the dismal failures of its own predictions, tests and methods, it is long overdue for such "intellectual deprovincialization" (for a valuable and highly readable introduction to interpretive social science, see Rabinow and Sullivan 1979).

Feminist scholars such as Mbilinyi are attempting to carry out the tasks proposed by Foucault and Geertz. Indeed, the entire feminist endeavour can be construed as an attempt to give women and gender relations a historical context. This is what Rosaldo (1983) is endeavouring to do in her reflections on the moral and epistemological dilemmas of feminist social science (cited at the beginning of this chapter). The task of Western scholars and aid agents is to take local knowledges seriously: to rescue them from the "margins of knowledge" and to incorporate them into a scientific understanding of African society. Western scholars must also recognize the dominant position of their own knowledge in the hierarchy and the role that knowledge plays in international power relations. Concrete suggestions for research that address the epistemological issues raised here are made in Chapter 7 (pp. 146–157).

Framing Future Research

Chapters 5 and 6 have suggested promising directions for new research, both in terms of specific methodologies and approaches to the problem of technology transfer and in terms of larger theoretical questions that will provide the grounds for a sounder understanding of gender, technology, and power in Africa. This chapter proposes some concrete guidelines for conducting such research, organized around five tasks. The first proposal suggests a checklist of research topics for the task of classifying sex-gender systems. Second, a template for exploring interrelationships between development policy and social systems is explored. The third proposal offers a model for concrete action on technology dissemination that accounts for the need for community participation in such dissemination, and the scarcity of resources for it. Fourth, a program inventory to catalogue successful development efforts is suggested. The fifth and final proposal presents an exercise in the application of theory to a practical aid issue, the aid expert – aid recipient relationship, as an example of how to tackle the task of addressing the knowledge crisis in Africa. These guidelines should not be construed as posing a unified, singular approach to research problems and opportunities; rather, they spin off in several methodological directions with the aim of stimulating an imaginative search for possible methods and objects of more fruitful research.

Classifying sex-gender systems

One of the major findings of this book is the lack of understanding regarding sex-gender systems in both the developmentalist and WID literature. The historical and cultural specificity of gender practices have been almost entirely ignored in developmentalist literature and given only descriptive treatment in WID literature. Meanwhile, feminist political economists have, on the whole, not paid detailed attention to the issues of technology transfer. Knowledge needs to be generated in a systematic way for African societies, using a standardized framework of analysis so that comparisons can be drawn between communities and generalizations can be made (or rejected if they are inappropriate). It would be particularly useful for policy planners to know, for example, that the experience of the Kamba in Kenya with regard to the adoption of a particular program is likely to be similar to that of the Ibo of Nigeria, given similar sex-gender systems. At the same time, the different political economies of these two groups can be taken into account.

What I am suggesting is a typification of sex-gender systems, as they existed in the past and as they have been transformed in the present. From such a framework, one would be able to make the generalization that, in patrilineal bridewealth societies, land tenure arrangements were X and Y, and have become A, B, and C; in matrilineal bridewealth societies, by contrast, land tenure operated according to P,

Q, and R, and contemporary political economy has transformed it in a way different from that of patrilineal bridewealth societies.

Such a typification will, on the one hand, provide the space to analyze each target community in historical and cultural terms, and, on the other hand, provide the framework for generalizing, comparing, and applying successful results from one area to another. The typification must draw upon the following resources and methods:

- Good, nonethnocentric and nonelitist existing studies, especially those of African researchers;

- Interpretive reading of older texts, particularly the early anthropological literature, trader's diaries, etc.[1]; and

- New research focusing on sex-gender systems and, in particular, women's communal activity.

Sex-gender systems may be typified by following a checklist of research questions, to be covered by archival work, interviews, observation, and use of secondary sources. The study should have detailed information about, and analysis of, contemporary political economy, precolonial political economy, and the process of transformation.

Contemporary political economy

With regard to contemporary political economy, the following topics should be investigated.

- National political system (i.e., military dictatorship, nominally democratic, socialist, multiparty, etc.).

- Local formal power structure (i.e., system of local government, power of political parties at the local level, role of government-sponsored cooperatives, etc.).

- Local aspects of economy such as the resource base (i.e., pastoral, agricultural, or mixed), the degree to which commodification of production and integration into the national and international market has occurred, and the nature of crops and their price history.

- Ethnicity: "tribalism" must be treated historically. Ethnic divisions have become much sharper than in the past. What have been the advantages or disadvantages facing the ethnic group under consideration? How does it stand in relation to national political power and distribution of resources?

---

[1] Although many of these texts are sexist, they contain crucial information regarding precolonial sex-gender systems and modes of production. Contemporary oral history is too far removed from precolonial times to be of much use. An excellent example is Leakey's (1933) compendious study of the Kikuyu before 1903. Several feminist scholars, such as Clark (1980) and Mackenzie (1986), have found this text a mine of information.

Precolonial political economy

With regard to precolonial economy, seven topics need examination.

- Kinship and residence system (i.e., patrilineal–patrilocal, matrilocal, etc.); this determination will draw on classical ethnological material.

- Sex-gender system (i.e., structure, ideology, and practice of gender relations). Closely linked to the topic of kinship, this investigation will draw on recent theory and research. Particular attention should be paid to the relationships and rights of cowives, with respect to both each other and to their husband and his lineage. The differing status and rights of women as wives and as sisters should also be explored.

- Land tenure, stock ownership, and inheritance laws.

- Usufructuary (use) rights of both men and women.

- Household and village division of labour, especially the sexual division of labour.

- Local power-knowledge (Foucault 1979; see pp. 129–130) regarding the functioning of society, specifically, with respect to agriculture, health practices, and nutrition. To what degree did this power-knowledge reside in individuals and to what degree did it reside in community organizations (from elders' councils to women's groups to cowives)?

- Organized associations of women. Was this formalized in age grades, trading groups, or secret societies? If not, what kind of ad hoc association characterized women's cooperation among themselves? What functions, responsibilities, and authority did women's associations carry? What was the relation between men's and women's authority? What was the relationship between the position of women as wives and their position as community members?

The process of transformation

Once a picture of precolonial society has been created, the basis has been laid for considering the elements in its transition. For example, the way in which women's traditional organizations have been transformed should be investigated. In particular, the ways in which special-purpose groups (e.g., church group, rent-strike group, weeding group, etc.) become the basis for wider political action or other community tasks should be thoroughly examined. It is important to consider the process of transformation in terms of the community as a whole (linked to the wider political economy), rather than in terms of changes for individuals.

The following seven areas should be examined: kinship and residence, sex-gender system, land tenure and inheritance, use rights, division of labour, local power and knowledge, and women's organizations. The following points give examples of specific questions that may be asked.

- Kinship and residence: What impact have housing projects with a Western design had upon polygyny? Where cowives share a dwelling, how has this

136

affected the wives' rights and responsibilities and the family's ability to perform its economic and caretaking tasks?

- Sex-gender system: The above questions may also be considered as questions about changes in the sex-gender system. What has happened to the practice of bridewealth and what are the implications of these changes in the status and autonomy of wives and daughters? Has there been a shift to monogamy and, if so, how has this affected women's rights and their role and authority as mothers? What has been the impact of Christianity on gender relations?

- Land tenure, inheritance: How has the individualization of ownership of land and stock affected resource use, resource control, and inheritance patterns? Has the shift to individual ownership negatively or positively affected families' self-sufficiency? In the context of the move toward a patrilocal, nuclear family, how have matrilineal land tenure and inheritance rights been affected, and what does this mean for the education and health care of children?

- Use rights: Closely related to the above, how has individualized land tenure affected women's use rights in land and livestock? Have these changes affected the ability of women to carry out their economic responsibilities? It is also important to consider the use rights of sons, who may be excluded from access to family resources by individualized ownership.

- Division of labour: How have the above four issues affected the village division of labour, especially the sexual division of labour? What has been the impact of male out-migration upon the division of labour, especially upon women's work? Has mechanization altered the division of labour, and if so, has this been to the disadvantage of women?

- Local power-knowledge: What has been the impact of the domination of Western knowledge (formerly under colonialism and today in the context of independence and development aid) upon traditional knowledge? How has this affected the ability of local communities to make informed and relevant decisions, specifically with regard to health practices, agriculture, and nutrition? Has community-based knowledge, residing in men's and women's councils and groups, given way to specialized knowledge monopolized by certain individuals in the community or by "expert" outsiders? Have women lost out to their husbands or the community regarding the production and dissemination of knowledge? Given the breadth of this area of inquiry, the questions should be focused on concrete, specific practices.

- Women's organizations: What is the form and function of contemporary women's organizations, from household to district? How do these relate to former organizations? To what degree are women's groups — whether for trading, cultivation, processing, social events, or religious purposes — locally generated or imposed from above? What has been the relative development success of locally generated groups versus imposed groups?

These are selected questions that may be asked about the process of transformation and are, as such, far from exhaustive. Beyond a general analysis of the broad changes of each of these topics, studies should pose questions that directly deal with their specific, practical concerns. Studies concerned with health technology should focus on questions of power and knowledge. Such questions

Table 1. Template of possible interrelationships for studying technology transfer.

Vaccine programs and
- traditional health practices and beliefs regarding the disease in question
- decision-making power regarding health
- usual methods of information dissemination
- community involvement
- etc.

Water procurement and
- sexual division of labour
- decision-making power regarding different types of technology
- impact on daily social routine
- etc.

AIDS education and
- sex-gender system
- decision-making power regarding sex
- customary control of knowledge regarding sex
- the economics and culture of prostitution
- etc.

Information technology (e.g., radios) and
- control within the household over consumer products and their use
- daily schedule of tasks of community members relative to time of instructional programs
- etc.

have a strong bearing on a family's ability to manage its health care or solicit medical intervention.

Overcoming the boundary problem

While the larger political and philosophical issues are being considered at the organizational level, research/action loci may make progress using practical tools. Interconnections must be made between previously unrelated or poorly related areas of concern (Table 1). To begin, using the preceding guidelines, a study should be conducted in every area for which a development program is planned. It may not always be possible to conduct a full-scale study; however, with the use of secondary sources and this focused methodology, an analysis of some degree of depth should be possible. The case study thus obtained is the necessary basis for the applied research that will generate the specific project.

The technique involves asking a series of questions about the proposed technology-transfer program. These questions should determine whether participation, knowledge, and organizational practices as well as abilities and resources of women have been taken into account. The questions should also uncover the impact of any new technology upon gender relations, both within the family and in the community at large. In turn, consideration should be given to the possible ways that existing organizations might divert the proposed program, or support and enhance it, given the nature of their economic and political interests. The template of interrelationships in Table 1 is far from exhaustive: considerable effort should be devoted to developing the lists of correlating factors to be examined according to the practical aims of the proposed research.

Organizing for the dissemination of technology

This study has substantively demonstrated the value of women's grassroots organizations, and their power (even if construed as "informal") to influence village developments. The problems with the top-down approach, from sexist bias in policy to inadequate accounting of women's participation in development, have also been shown. It is also clear that the resources for disseminating new knowledge are limited. This scarcity may be advantageous, however, in forcing a more cost-effective use of existing resources. The use of local human resources is also a more desirable approach from both a political and an ethical point of view. Self-reproducing schemes are the most desirable of all.

Rachlan (1986) discusses the "Human Action Model," developed at the Environment Research Centre of the Institute of Technology in Bandung, Indonesia. This model has been applied successfully in pilot projects for rural development. The project discussed by Rachlan (1986:i) was aimed at "significant and efficient use of available inputs to produce optimum outputs and at the continuous use, dissemination, reconstruction and development of outputs by the target beneficiaries to accelerate the achievement of social and economic welfare of, and most importantly instill sense of independency from outsiders in, the rural population."

The mechanism used to disseminate technology for the improvement of the environment is known as "horizontal dissemination of technology by vertical changes of roles." This method produces

> more and more non-paid village extension agents who continuously try to improve their knowledge and practical skills to get better social status in their community. The physical impact seems to justify this mechanism. By spending about 60% of the originally planned inputs the amount of hectarage treated by the ever improved technologies is 12 times as many as originally targeted.... Experience shows that by applying the horizontal dissemination of technology the government monetized inputs decreases at each phase of the dissemination process. At the demonstration phase the government input is purely advice, and at the diffusion phase the government field extension worker visits the farmer group only by request.
>
> (Rachlan 1986:10)

The full development of this model in the context of African village groups is the research task suggested here. Given the vigour of community-level groups in Africa, the prognosis for the effective functioning of this kind of model should be excellent. Tables 2 and 3 provide a model that could be evaluated for, and tested in, the African context. Table 2 sets out the process whereby villages become empowered as disseminators of technology. Table 3 shows the four project phases: pilot, model, demonstration, and diffusion. The Indonesian statistics in Table 3 reveal the changing ratio of inputs from a majority by the government in the pilot year (year 1) to a majority by the villagers in the diffusion year (year 4).

139

Table 2. Horizontal dissemination of technology by vertical changes of roles.

Year	Extension worker	Target beneficiaries of:			
		Year 1	Year 2	Year 3	Year 4
1	Facilitator	Learners	—	—	—
2	Motivator	Facilitators	Learners	—	—
3	Advisor	Motivators	Facilitators	Learners	—
4	Resource person	Advisors	Motivators	Facilitators	Learners

Source: Rachlan (1986).

Table 3. Comparison between government's and villager's inputs over the course of the horizontal dissemination project.

Year	Development phase	% of inputs	
		Government	Villagers
1	Pilot	70	30
2	Model	50	50
3	Demonstration	30	70
4	Diffusion	10	90

Source: Rachlan (1986).

Inventory of successful initiatives

The problem for gender, technology, and development in Africa is not a lack of material; rather, the material is fragmented, divided among research/action loci, buried in documents that fail to cross the boundary between one area of expertise and another, and divorced from Africans' knowledge of the problems. Of particular concern to African women is the failure to document successful development initiatives (see ILO 1985; also discussed in Chapter 2, pp. 37–44). A crucial research task to meet this concern is the development of an inventory of successful initiatives. The inventory should include both aid agency projects and locally devised efforts. Part of this task is the development of criteria to 'success' (e.g., a water supply project that puts a water tap in a village but leaves women more harried than before should be excluded from the definition).

The time span that should elapse before an initiative's success is judged must also be determined. A review of the continuing benefits of a project several years after completion can reveal a less successful picture than appeared immediately after the project's completion. Setbacks to an initially successful project, however, should not disqualify it from inclusion in the inventory: useful lessons may be learned from both the positive and negative aspects of the initiative, as the following case summary of the Mraru women's bus service demonstrates.

The nature of the inventory

Four kinds of documents should be reviewed. The first three comprise material produced by development-oriented research/action loci; the fourth is more specifically academic. First, case studies that capture the struggles and achievements of women in all their rich texture and detail are invaluable for assessing the interplay of social and technical factors in a successful endeavour. These narrative accounts, moreover, are particularly useful for women in other villages seeking to pursue similar technological innovations. Second, studies that provide overviews of development efforts in a broad area of technology transfer, such as water and sanitation, are useful for the comparative context and the framework of assessment that they generate. The first type of study provides a detailed analysis but few if any comparisons; the second type of study provides comparisons without much detail. Thus, the two types of studies complement each other. A third type of document is the research project that assesses a particular piece of technology (e.g., mechanical flour milling) and evaluates its development and application in the African context. Academic texts comprise the fourth category of document to be scanned for inventory material: case studies, overviews and bibliographies should be found and collected.

Case studies

An example of the kind of case study that should be reviewed and catalogued is the initiative of the Taita women of Mraru, eastern Kenya, to solve their problem of getting their produce to market (Kneerim 1980). The SEEDS (Sarvodaya Economic Enterprises Development Services) pamphlet series, which published this case study, is exemplary of the kind of documentation being called for here. A jointly sponsored project of the Carnegie Corporation, the Ford Foundation and The Population Council, it was developed

> to meet requests from all over the world for information about innovative and practical program ideas developed by and for low income women. The pamphlets are designed as a means to share information and spark new projects based on the positive experiences of women who are working to help themselves and other women improve their economic status. The projects described in this and future issues of SEEDS have been selected because they provide women with cash income, involve women in decision-making as well as earning, are based on sound economic criteria, and are working successfully to overcome obstacles commonly encountered. The reports are not meant to be prescriptive, since every development effort will face somewhat different problems and resources. Rather, they have been written to describe the history of an idea and its implementation in the hope that the lessons learned can be useful in a variety of settings. They are also being written to bring to the attention of those in decision-making positions the fact that income-generating projects for and by women are viable and have important roles to play in development.
>
> (Kneerim 1980:i)

The Mraru Women's Group is typical of the self-help groups all over Kenya, with features much like the Mitero groups described in Chapter 4. In 1971, the Mraru women decided to raise funds to purchase a bus to carry them to the market in nearby Voi. This action was impelled by the difficulties the women faced in getting a seat on the local bus service; people from more remote villages and men usually occupied all the space. Over several years and with the help of various agencies, including a bank in Mombasa, the women raised sufficient funds and solved the logistical problems of ordering and purchasing a small bus. The bus entered service in 1975 and, for several years, made good profits. By 1977, the bank loan was paid off and substantial savings were being realized. The women's group invested these funds in other projects including a village store and a herd of goats. Meanwhile, they succeeded in managing the technical aspects of servicing and repairing the bus.

For some time, the efforts of these women were praised as a model of what women could achieve through their own efforts and on the basis of self-defined needs. The life of the village was improved, with reliable access to Voi (a benefit also for those needing hospital services) and women-managed, local store supplies. There were also substantial intangible benefits: e.g., a greater voice for women in village affairs and the addition of a whole new dimension of organizational skills to the traditional repertoire of women.

When the bus wore out, however, the Mraru women did not have sufficient capital to purchase a new one at the vastly higher prices of 1979. When Kneerim (1980) wrote the review, they were following two main strategies: first, to save the additional 60 000 Kenyan shillings (KES) (about CAD 6 000) necessary for a down payment and, second, to have the land and buildings they owned in Mraru surveyed so that the shop could be accepted as collateral for a long-term loan. The author draws a number of general lessons from both the positive and negative aspects of the Mraru experience that could usefully be applied in other contexts (see Kneerim 1980). One lesson that is particularly important for Kenyan women is that they avoid the inclination of small businesses to diversify hastily without attention to long-term capital needs (for an analysis of this phenomenon in Kenya, see Marris and Somerset 1971).

> The Mraru Women's Group has shown unusual creativity and persistence in identifying common needs and organizing to meet them. They have also demonstrated that a small, private organization with few resources can effectively call on the skills and resources of other agencies, both public and private, to help them achieve their goals, while remaining independent and self-reliant.
>
> (Kneerim 1980:1)

Overviews of development efforts

An example of the second type of study, the overview of technology-transfer endeavours, is the briefing document prepared by INSTRAW and UNICEF for the 1985 United Nations Decade for Women Conference (INSTRAW/UNICEF 1985). Referring to the world water supply and sanitation crisis as well as the International Drinking Water Supply and Sanitation Decade (IDWSSD) launched in 1980, the document proposes a two-pronged plan of action: first, development of a strategy for "the enhancement of the role of women within the IDWSSD" (INSTRAW/ UNICEF 1985:21) and, second, assistance in ongoing activities associated with IDWSSD programs. With respect to the latter, INSTRAW/UNICEF (1985:21) proposed that it "initiate and undertake action-oriented research to improve the data base, following identification of specific issues, countries and pilot projects" and "promote awareness from community through international levels through collation and dissemination of information and experiences about the stake and potential of women in improved water supply and sanitation."

The document summarizes efforts by international agencies (e.g., FAO, UNDP, Unesco, UNICEF, the United Nations Department of Technical Cooperation for Development, the United Nations Development Fund for Women, and WHO) and regional commissions (e.g., ECA). The two main parts of the publication are an annex on "strategies for enhancing women's participation in water supply and sanitation activities" — the recommendations of the interagency task force on women and water of the IDWSSD steering committee (INSTRAW/UNICEF 1985:23–31) — and an annex entitled *Insights from field practice — how women have been and could be involved in water and sanitation at the community level* (INSTRAW/UNICEF 1985:32–45).

The second annex is the most interesting section, with its proposed inventory of successful programs. It surveys a wide range of water and sanitation projects and organizes conclusions about their value or inappropriateness into useful categories. It considers the past and possible future involvement of women in the different aspects of water and sanitation projects: planning at the community level; needs assessment; data collection; design and choice of technology; implementation (construction, operation, and maintenance), monitoring, and evaluation; and the special issues of training, and health and hygiene education. The document also reviews the broader context of primary health care, women's involvement in the community, and women and development. The section on design and choice of technology is typical of the useful (and sometimes humble) prescriptions that the document has produced. For example,

> In reaching technology decisions, full advantage must be taken of women's knowledge in water and sanitation aspects of the environment, including water source and water quantity during dry and wet seasons. Women as water drawers can provide important information. For example...in Panama, women took the engineers to a fresh water source on the shore of the island which had not been found during the feasibility survey.... Consulting with women on the design of latrines can often result in simple technological changes which make latrines more acceptable to users. For example, in Nicaragua the latrine was not used by women because their feet could be seen from the outside....
>
> (INSTRAW/UNICEF 1985:38)

Assessments of specific types of technology

Although many technical assessments ignore or treat simplistically the social factors implicated in the technology being reviewed, some documents do account for these factors. These assessments are particularly valuable because aid policymakers cannot read sociological analyses to put real equipment in place in African villages. Unfortunately, far too much of the criticism of technology transfer has been general and sociological; the interface between the new material objects and the individuals and communities that are to use them tends to be ignored. Well-researched, organized technology assessments should be sought, both to provide concrete, detailed information on the technology under consideration and to provide models of how future assessments may be carried out.

An example of such a document is *An End to Pounding: A New Mechanical Flour Milling System in Use in Africa* (Eastman 1980). This booklet, which considers several prototype dehullers and grinders designed to produce acceptable flour from both cereal and legume crops, "is not intended to be a comprehensive instruction manual; rather it attempts to review the accumulated knowledge and experience gained during the development, testing and operation of the several mills referred to" (Eastman 1980:5). The dehuller that is singled out for its special merits in the context of societies in Africa's semi-arid tropics is from a prototype designed in Saskatoon, Canada, and modified in Botswana. The booklet begins by discussing the need for a special milling system for the semi-arid regions of Africa, in which millet and sorghum are the human staples. The problems with traditional flour-making methods and the various environmental and economic factors contributing to the need for a special milling system are also described. "The most convincing reason for developing a simple, dry mechanical milling process is that people in the Third World want it. In a survey done in several villages in Senegal, the three most desirable additions to village life were reported as a reliable water supply followed by grinding and dehulling facilities that would produce an acceptable product from local grains" (Eastman 1980:8).

The study discusses the development of the technology, giving an account of the first pilot mill in Maiduguri, Nigeria. Following purely technical sections on the dehuller and milling systems, focusing on their suitability for the cereals of semi-arid areas, the booklet gives guidelines on planning a mill. Two types of mill are considered, a continuous-flow mill, which would serve a large market area and operate as a regular factory, and a service mill, designed to process the produce of local growers for their own consumption. Eleven planning steps are proposed for the latter: these include analysis of grain production and consumption patterns; selection of appropriate sorghum-growing areas; conducting a mill-utilization survey; testing existing grain and flour samples to ensure a popular flour from the mill; choosing a mill site; and budgeting, financing, and implementing mill construction.

The final section of the booklet, the most important for our purposes, evaluates the milling systems discussed in the previous sections. On the basis of a number of technical, economic, and social factors, the service mill is suggested as more appropriate than the continuous-flow mill in many rural contexts (the latter being of value for urban populations).

> Mill planners must recognize that mechanical milling is apt to cause some changes in a society. For example, in many rural communities, much of the social interchange revolves around routine household tasks such as dehulling and grinding cereal. A continuous-flow system may remove this focus for community socializing, whereas a service mill still provides the opportunity for social interchanges. In addition, if a continuous-flow mill is functioning with full community support, the local economy is based on trust — trust that the grain that is sold now will be available later in the form of flour. Service processing does not require the same degree of performance from or confidence in the mill and in the marketplace.
>
> (Eastman 1980:43)

Academic texts

In addition to surveying the two types of development-oriented studies, the inventory of successful programs should also review the more strictly academic literature for case studies, project overviews, and bibliographies. Regarding case studies, the corn mill societies in Cameroon, whose success was chronicled by

Wipper (1984:75–76; also see Chapter 3), and examples in Chapter 3 are evidence of the value of this literature. These cases are often amongst the most interesting because they are set in social-science analyses and, often, in the context of feminist critique. Overviews written from an academic perspective are also valuable; they provide a critique that is independent of allegiance to commissioning agencies or governments. Rogers (1980) gave a hard-hitting analysis of the aid process and its impact on women, with evidence from a number of specific development cases. Mascarenhas and Mbilinyi's (1983) analytical bibliography is an excellent example of a focused resource that draws together both academic and nonacademic literature. The result is a picture of the overall state of knowledge regarding women in a specific country (Tanzania).

Research tasks for creating the inventory

The following seven research tasks emerge from the concerns raised in the preceding section and throughout the book and from consideration of the nature of the material to be included in the inventory.

- The criteria by which a project or initiative will be judged successful must be set. (Does the project treat women as central actors? Is the community adequately involved as a collective decision-maker? Does the interface between the material technology and women's physical and social attributes, preferences, needs, etc., work smoothly? Is the technology sustainable at the village level, particularly in terms of the knowledge and work patterns of women? Does the technology transfer enhance or, at least, sustain the authority and autonomy of women in the community? etc.).

- Determine the time span to be examined. Establish guidelines according to different types of technology transfer on the basis of case reports that cover a number of years and identify the point at which problems appear, such as the Mraru study.

- Where the time span is inadequate to evaluate long-term success or where inadequate information has been given in terms of the established criteria for success, follow-up investigation in the field should be considered.

- Specific field research should eventually be designed to recover information regarding initiatives that have escaped the attention of aid agencies, governments, or academics. This is likely to be particularly valuable for community-initiated efforts.

- Information from the investigated initiatives should be organized according to the four types of documents previously described: case studies, overviews of development efforts, assessments of specific types of technology, and academic texts. For case studies, the possibility of a correlation between the origin of the initiative (agency, community, or government) and its success should be investigated.

- In each African country, an analytical bibliography modeled after Mascarenhas and Mbilinyi (1983) should be produced. Covering topics from the theoretical to the applied, such a bibliography can set out the state of intellectual resources in a given country, the political commitment to women's issues, and the concrete achievements regarding women in development. The document can thereby provide an invaluable source of information both for local activists attempting to bring about legislative and other change and for aid practitioners seeking to situate themselves accurately in the gender politics of the country in which they are working.

- Conduct research on how to disseminate the inventory for wide use among research/action loci and communities. The inventory, or parts of it, could be compiled in different ways according to the desired audience. For example, the inventory might be presented in a more narrative form for community groups. Where the inventory has revealed comparable social and economic problems in the application of two different types of technology, a partial inventory that includes both types could be constructed. In this way, villagers concerned with one type of technology could benefit from the lessons learned regarding the other type. A computerized inventory could also be used to generate custom-made part inventories for specific communities or research/action loci.

Transforming the aid expert – aid recipient relationship

This study has identified a crisis in knowledge about Africa and, in particular, the alienation of Africans from their own knowledge of themselves, African women being the most alienated of all. The task of addressing this dilemma is huge and daunting, but a start can be made that has practical value for aid efforts. The relationship between aid expert (as scholar or practitioner, whether African or foreign) and aid recipient (as individual or community) is a transfer point of both power and knowledge. As such, it provides a distinct object of inquiry around which a number of the problematic issues of development policy can be looked at. Most importantly, the conditions for the presence or absence of locally generated knowledge about development problems may be illuminated by such research. The aid expert – aid recipient relationship is thus suggested as a topic of research; at the same time, the discussion here is an exercise in applying theory to practical aid issues. The following argument and suggestions for research proceed by reference to the general problems in knowledge about Africans as aid recipients, rather than through specific reference to women. Implicit throughout, however, is the general purpose of this book: to elucidate the problems for women, technology, and power in Africa.

Thinking about theory

The context for understanding the aid expert – aid recipient relationship as an object of inquiry is, again, the thinking of Foucault.[2] The important task of synthesizing materialism and discourse analysis has been set aside. The dynamics of the aid donor – aid recipient relationship depends largely on how the recipient takes up the discourse. This process, in turn, is partly determined by the recipient's material circumstances. Because the aim of this exercise is to focus on the way development discourse constructs aid recipients as targets of aid activity, the question of the recipient as an active subject, embedded in local relations of

---

[2]The purpose here is to apply theory to a concrete problem and not to review the literature within that theoretical tradition.

production and engaged in a dynamic relationship with the aid donor, is not discussed. Investigation of this important topic is a necessary aspect of the research tasks delineated on p. 154.

It is difficult to characterize the ideas of Foucault without simplifying them; through his "genealogies" of contemporary cultural practices, however, he has diagnosed a trend toward an increased pervasive organization of society. As the excellent commentators on Foucault, Dreyfus and Rabinow (1983:xxvi), put it,

> [this comprises] the increasing ordering in all realms under the guise of improving the welfare of the individual and the population. To the genealogist this order reveals itself to be a strategy, with no one directing it and everyone increasingly enmeshed in it, whose only end is the increase of power and order itself.

Although there are other ways of interpreting contemporary history and other thinkers, such as Nietzsche, Weber, and Heidegger have interpreted it this way before Foucault, his special contribution is his focus on the link between "the most minute social practices" and the "large-scale organization of power." Foucault argues that human beings have, in the last two centuries, been increasingly constructed as subjects and objects of knowledge. This argument is elaborated via several powerful examples, including the evolution of penal institutions and the development of modern ideas about sexuality (see Foucault 1979, 1980a). These examples "show us how our culture attempts to normalize individuals through increasingly rationalized means, by turning them into meaningful subjects and docile objects" (Dreyfus and Rabinow 1983:xxvii).

Following Foucault's thinking, it is seen that first colonialism and then international aid required that the colonized and, later, aid-dependent people become objects of knowledge in a new way. They could then be categorized and rendered manageable first as colonial subjects and, subsequently, as aid recipients. The World Bank's report on Africa (IBRD 1986) (see Chapter 2, pp. 27–28) exemplifies the overt aim of aid discourse to construct manageable populations of aid recipients. Governments are called upon to create a "social consensus" around the World Bank's family planning, resource, and agriculture policies. What will create a compliant population is, quite explicitly, acceptance of the World Bank's understanding of development problems and it is African governments' responsibility to inculcate this understanding.

Given our immersion in the Western system of knowledge, it is hard to recognize the degree to which what is known about Third World peoples, how it is known, and how much is known is not what they have known about themselves. The very categories we employ, the systematization and generalization of knowledge about them, are products of our will for knowledge, rather than theirs. This knowledge is, moreover, a product of the power relations between the West and the Third World, and is a shaping force in those relations (see Payer 1982).[3]

Foucault is "frustratingly elusive when it comes to capturing our current condition in general formulae" (Dreyfus and Rabinow 1983:xxvi). His refusal to give us a grand theory, however, is consistent with his conclusions: "Once one sees

---

[3]This is not to argue that Western aid is devoid of deep altruism. As Foucault (1980:95) says, within the grand strategies by which history proceeds, the "inventors" of tactics are "often without hypocrisy." It is instructive to remember, however, that colonialism was animated by a powerful discourse of altruism, expressed (and eventually caricatured) as the "white man's burden."

the pervasiveness, dispersion, intricacy, contingency, and layering of our social practices, one also sees that any attempt to sum up what is going on is bound to be a potentially dangerous distortion" (Dreyfus and Rabinow 1983:xxvi). Another problem in applying his ideas lies in the interpretive nature of his work:

> Foucault says that he is writing the history of the present, and we call the method that enables him to do this interpretive analytics. This is to say that while the analysis of our present practices and their historical development is a disciplined, concrete demonstration which could serve as the basis of a research program, the diagnosis that the increasing organization of everything is the central issue of our time is not in any way empirically demonstrable, but rather emerges as an interpretation. This interpretation grows out of pragmatic concerns and has pragmatic intent, and for that very reason can be contested by other interpretations growing out of other concerns.
>
> (Dreyfus and Rabinow 1983:xxvi)

To bring this problem into the context of development thinking, critics such as Mbilinyi (1985a) (see pp. 122–124), whose pragmatic concerns lead to a particular interpretation of colonial discourse, could find a challenge from the position of quite different concerns (e.g., male-dominated postcolonial elites). These concerns could insist on interpreting the same evidence differently. "Interpretive analytics" are always open to such challenges.

In spite of this and other problems in Foucault's work (such as a concept of power that is ultimately so inclusive as to weaken its utility), the insistence on standing back from our own systems of meaning creates refreshing possibilities for tackling the epistemological dilemmas at issue here. Precisely because it is an interpretive method, it is useful for drawing "local knowledges" out from under dominant systems of thought. Minson (1985:ix) tells us succinctly what we should and should not do with Foucault's theory:

> The most appropriate respect for Foucault need not necessarily consist in devotedly awaiting and consuming his every last word on every subject. There is something absurd in Foucault's intellectual heroisation. His enduring value will, I believe, be found to lie in a series of quite unspectacular suggestions (including some instructive errors) on a limited set of theoretical, historical and political questions.... To my mind, the most appropriate tribute [to his memory following his death in 1984] is on the one hand unremitting critical attention to his arguments, whilst on the other hand, producing arguments of one's own in the areas he has done so much to open up.

To demonstrate the utility of Foucault's approach, while suggesting a concrete program of research regarding the aid expert – aid recipient relationship, I draw upon his concept of "'local centers' of power-knowledge" (Foucault 1980a:98). He argues that, in discourse, objects of scientific inquiry are not external to the "economic or ideological requirements of power." For example, in the discourse on sexuality that has developed since the 18th century,

> If sexuality was constituted as an area of investigation, this was only because relations of power had established it as a possible object; and conversely, if power was able to take it as a target, this was because techniques of knowledge and procedures of discourse were capable of investing it.

Local centres of power-knowledge are the nexus of this intertwined process. Examples of local centres are "the relations that obtain between penitents and confessors, or the faithful and their directors of conscience. Here, guided by the theme of the 'flesh' that must be mastered, different forms of discourse —

self-examination, questionings, admissions, interpretations, interviews — were the vehicle of a kind of incessant back-and-forth movement of forms of subjugation and schemas of knowledge" (Foucault 1980a:98). The relationship between medical professionals and their patients is another such local centre that has emerged in the last several hundred years and is now a potent force in contemporary society throughout the world.

I believe that the aid expert – aid recipient relationship is such a local centre of power-knowledge. It is a key point in the technology transfer process and, more broadly, a significant site of the formulation of both power relations and knowledge about the aid recipient. To adapt Foucault's (1980a:98) expression, the recipient of development aid was "constituted as an area of investigation" because "relations of power had established it as a possible object." Conversely, people and communities could become targets of power relations because of the development of "techniques of knowledge" that could construct them as aid recipients. In other words, knowledge about Africans as aid recipients constructed during the aid process is used in turn to inform, organize, and expand aid as both a discourse of development and a set of practices. A concrete example of this process can be found in Rogers (1980:120–138) (see Chapter 6, p. 117). Rogers shows how knowledge about matriliny is constructed out of the relationship between the aid expert (the World Bank) and the aid recipient (matrilineal Malawians). This knowledge of matriliny as "socialistic" and "matriarchal" is then used to shape appropriate (i.e., antimatrilineal) policies. It also provides the matrix (or "grid of intelligibility") into which any further information about kinship is inserted. Therefore, the discourse and practice of development in the Lilongwe project both act to suppress matriliny and seriously to undermine women's rights and control of resources.

Because of the overt, intentional, and massive nature of international aid, it is a particularly powerful example of the permeation of new relations of power-knowledge throughout societies. The transformation of penal institutions and of ideas about the criminal explored by Foucault (1979) was piecemeal and followed no overt, global strategy (although the outcome is a global approach to prisons and prison reform). In contrast, aid is based on an immense and obvious disequilibrium in scientific knowledge between the giver and the receiver; a situation that the aid process should at least partially correct. Although it is possible to argue that penology and criminology are pseudosciences (see Dreyfus and Rabinow 1983:162–167) and that much of the supposedly objective knowledge about Africa is pseudoscientific, there is an irreducible core of technical and scientific knowledge implicated in technology that cannot be wished away by critiques of development discourse. Moreover, no liberation of subjugated knowledges can correct the inequality in power-knowledge relationships that are based on this irreducible core. The task of transforming the aid expert – aid recipient relationship requires that truly superior knowledge be separated from ideology or poor science masked as superior knowledge.

What is the intellectual process whereby insights developed in a different empirical context appear as relevant and useful for the study of development aid in Africa? Applying theory always proceeds, in part, by intuition; interconnections do not necessarily emerge at the level of linear reasoning. Given the overt systems of domination in which Africa, in general, and women, in particular, are enmeshed, thoughts about the relations between power and knowledge are obviously useful.

149

Africanists, both indigenous and foreign, have reflected for many years on the history of knowledge about Africa (e.g., Davidson 1969:17–31). A primary impetus for 20th century feminism has been the recognition that knowledge about women and gender relations is entangled in male-dominated power systems.

I have chosen the ideas of Foucault as an exercise in the imaginative application of theory; however, there are other philosophical and sociological traditions that might fruitfully suggest new research possibilities. The most developed, current model for the dual process of critique and application of theory is the ongoing, 20-year debate on the relevance of Marxist thought for the study of Africa. The debate has resulted in a rich and varied adaptation of Marxist method and theory for the illumination of African political economy. The fruitful results of this exercise, specifically within feminist political economy, have been referred to throughout this book.

Given the problem of subjugated knowledges, it may appear contradictory to suggest another use of Western scholarly traditions to clarify the African condition. The contradiction, however, is only apparent. The key here is that useful theories and methods are being identified (in contrast, for example, to the political science of the early 1960s that described new African political institutions as variants of the American or European systems [see the influential Almond and Coleman 1960]). The solution for subjugated knowledges cannot simply be geographic, as Africans are the first to attest. The utility of a theoretical framework is the space it provides for identifying and rectifying culturally relative, ethnocentric, and sexist explanations of non-Western societies. This utility neither depends on whether the theorist addressed non-Western society (Foucault did not) nor on the theorist being free of empirical error and ethnocentrism if non-Western society has been addressed (e.g., Marx's writings on India are regarded as Eurocentric and incorrect [Katz 1989]). The point is that both theorists offer Africans the tools to critique non-African knowledge about Africa and place it in a historical context. It is no accident that Marxist thought has proved so attractive to African critical thinkers; it seems inevitable that African scholars engaged in discourse theory will turn to Foucault in coming years.

The aid expert – aid recipient relationship is but one possible area for applying ideas about discourse (and one of the most important for clarifying the problems of technology transfer and gender). Other objects of aid-related inquiry that may be subjected to scrutiny include the concepts of population and health. For anyone familiar with the current Western preoccupation with birth rates in the Third World, the following statement about the changing politics of health in the 18th century will seem in many ways apt for our own time:

> The great eighteenth-century demographic upswing in Western Europe, the necessity for co-ordinating and integrating it into the apparatus of production and the urgency of controlling it with finer and more adequate power mechanisms cause "population," with its numerical variables of space and chronology, longevity and health, to emerge not only as a problem but as an object of surveillance, analysis, intervention, modification etc. The project of a technology of population begins to be sketched: demographic estimates, the calculation of the pyramid of ages, different life expectations and levels of mortality, studies of the reciprocal relations of growth of wealth and growth of population.... The biological traits of a population become relevant factors for economic management, and it becomes necessary to organise around them an

150

apparatus which will ensure not only their subjection but the constant increase of their utility.

(Foucault 1980b:171–172)

This is not to argue that high birth rates pose no real danger in Africa. Rather, it is to indicate that one of Western aid's most important projects is to define and manage African peoples as "populations," and as the wilful authors of a paramount economic problem for Africa: "the continent's troublesome population trends" (Sai 1986:130). This aspect of development discourse has proved one of the most politically sensitive and controversial among Africans and African governments.

Applying theoretical insights

The following six hypotheses about the aid expert – aid recipient relationship are suggested by the application of discourse analysis to the development literature and to commentaries on development policies. The hypotheses draw on many of the conclusions reached in the preceding chapters. These hypotheses could be useful in shaping questions about the premises underlying aid research and policy, for studying either individual cases or a genre of aid projects (e.g., health technology transfer, agricultural extension work, etc.). It is neither that all aid projects are informed by this development discourse, nor that the aims articulated by the discourse are necessarily inappropriate or wrong. Rather, the source of many of the problems with aid efforts is the construction of a particular kind of knowledge about the problems and their solutions and, in particular, about the relationship between aid expert and aid recipient.

Hypothesis 1

Individuals are constructed, at the levels of both general aid policy and individual projects, as a collectivity of "resources" to be mobilized for development. Thought of in this way, people in developing countries cannot be envisaged as active decision-makers in development policy: "resource" implies an essentially inanimate object, part of a system where useful and unusable elements are decided in advance. The only possible participation for people as "resources" is their passive acceptance of a predetermined vision of their problem and its solutions.[4] The dilemma is particularly poignant for African women, whose active agency in their own societies has been ignored or trivialized since colonial times. The notion of aid recipients as "resources" has come to the forefront in the present era of economic constraints and crises. In the more prosperous, less cost-conscious 1970s, aid recipients were often referred to as "beneficiaries," another passive definition that construed developing peoples as recipients of Western generosity. The discussion of women as "welfare" subjects in Chapter 3 addresses a concrete aspect of the problem of thinking about Africans as passive recipients of aid.

---

[4]Here, Foucault's (1980a:140) concept of "bio-power," developed in the context of his analysis of transformations in Western society over the past 200 years, is particularly relevant. He argues that there was an explosion of numerous and diverse techniques for achieving the subjugation of bodies and the control of populations. On the notion of humans as "resources" for the developing nation, Foucault's thinking about Western society is again useful. Regarding the increasing "intervention of the state in the life of the individual" (see Dreyfus and Rabinow 1983:138), in our context, such intervention is not by the state alone, but by an international apparatus to recruit humans as resources for development.

Hypothesis 2

A more negative perception of Africans can be found in much of the discussion about economic growth. Once growth is taken as a self-evident good, as it is in most development thinking, any factors that do not contribute to the preconceived pattern of growth are inevitably in a position of logical opposition to growth, i.e., they become "obstacles to growth" or "constraints on growth." People's problems, people's attitudes, and, sometimes, people themselves are among the obstacles to be addressed by development aid policy. "Resource" at least connotes an inherent value in a developing country's populace; "obstacle," however, devalues humanity and distorts the problems of the very people the aid is supposed to support. Occasional concessions to local rationality (e.g., "Poor people in Africa, as elsewhere, find it in their interest to have large families" [IBRD 1986:26]) do little to mitigate the negative and punitive approach to aid recipients' own choices found in so many aid documents. This hypothesis is intimately linked to the problem of conceptualizing "the traditional" as a timeless pole of the traditional–modern dichotomy (see pp. 121–124).

Hypothesis 3

Where recipients are not talked about as collectivities ("population," "resources," or "obstacles"), they are constructed as "targets" of aid policy. In many cases, it is the individual rather than the community that is the target. Indeed, Africa's traditional patterns of collective economic activity — with regard to land tenure and use, for example — have been considered obstacles to development; consequently, aid policy fostered the individual at the expense of the collectivity (see Leonard 1986:198).[5] Yet, as development thinkers have come to admit, "it is now clear that these conceptions greatly underestimate the adaptability of collective land tenure systems.... 'Traditional' systems have not in fact inhibited agricultural development.... There are few costs and many benefits to land tenure systems under the control of local communities" (Leonard 1986:198). The aid policy problem goes deeper than a distaste for dealing with communities: the notion of human lives that find their primary identity and expression as inseparable elements of a community is foreign to most Western thought. This is an urgent epistemological problem for aid research and policy, as has been demonstrated throughout this book.

Hypothesis 4

Individual aid recipients are not only "targets" of development policy, they are problematic targets. Project analyses commonly consider the attitudes and practices of women problematic, even when the intent of the project is to involve women in the development effort. Getechah's (1981) useful assessment of the role of Kenyan women in water development (see p. 30) is, nevertheless, symptomatic of the treatment of aid recipients as problematic. Her discussion of the possible contribution of women to water-supply projects is set in "conditions of poverty, ignorance, and lack of technical know-how among rural women" (Getechah 1981:86). This suggests that women lack "self-reliance," a quality that, paradoxically, is to be introduced from above (this paradox is at the heart of the movement in Kenya to prod rural women into self-help groups). Where groups are

---

[5]Note that the language still poses the question of land tenure in strictly economic rather than social or ethical terms.

genuinely "self-help," i.e., originating locally out of the collective needs and practices of women, they often fall outside the net of administrative control and aid. As such, they are either ignored or treated as targets for "assistance," to be drawn into the management net.

The notion of a lack in the qualities of aid recipients has the notion of "potential" as a necessary correlate (e.g., "Although the women are making a substantial contribution, their potential has not been fully exhausted" [Getechah 1981:87]). Thus, even though recipients are problematic, they provide an empty slate of unfulfilled "potential" upon which the latest fads in development aid can be written: from the 1950s preoccupation with promoting the virtuous, clean housewife (see Koeune 1952); to fostering the creative, income-generating craftswoman; to creating the fuel-efficient, tree-planting environmentalist; to restoring the nurturing, breast-feeding earth mother. Once again, I am not denigrating the goals associated with these images; rather, I am seeking to expose the degree to which development discourse is based upon such imagery, which often has more to do with Western political or cultural preoccupations than with the real needs of the women concerned.

Hypothesis 5

Overall, recipients, as communities or individuals, are constructed by development discourse as subjects to be managed; recipient input is limited to "feedback to the research system" (Leonard 1986:197). The site of interaction is "extension," a term with a venerable history in Western agricultural development that poses particular problems for understanding the development task in the Third World. The aid expert – aid recipient relationship, which is the most crucial transfer point for technology and other aspects of development, becomes an outpost of a system, a frontier whose boundary is the extension worker; the aid recipient is on the other side of this boundary. The World Bank's Training and Visit (T & V) System of agricultural extension, one of the most acclaimed solutions to the problems of agricultural development, nevertheless epitomizes the construction of the aid expert – aid recipient relationship as a "management system" (see IBRD 1983:94–95). "A highly disciplined approach to extension management," the T & V System is "the best available solution to these management demands" (Leonard 1986:196–197).

Even Rachlan's (1986) excellent model for the dissemination of technology previously discussed (pp. 139–140) succumbs to the concepts of "resource," "target," and "beneficiary." Obviously, aid programs, by their nature, are "systems" that extend information and technology from an area where these are known to an area where they are unknown. Researchers and policymakers should be more aware of the power relations and domination over local knowledges entrained in this logic of dissemination.

Hypothesis 6

Women's knowledge is invisible in development discourse. Anthropological studies have shown that these are large, gender-specific areas in the production and use of knowledge in Africa. In the older anthropological literature, this fact emerged by default; e.g., the following astonishing entry appears in Lambert's (1956:96) study of political institutions among the Kikuyu: "Men say they do not know for certain whether...gatherings of women are merely called for specific purposes or whether they are *ad hoc* committees of permanent and organized *chiama* [councils]." Like many social scientists, Lambert was content to leave women's areas of knowledge in the shadows, reported vaguely by male informants (the idea of interviewing women directly did not seem to occur to him).

Development studies have continued the tradition, so that women's knowledge about family, agriculture, health maintenance, nutrition, and associated technology has never been systematically solicited and analyzed. Consequently, aid projects have been built on erroneous, incomplete knowledge, as many examples throughout this book reveal. Male-dominated aid institutions and governments seek male knowledge in the "local centres" of power-knowledge, thereby unwittingly reinforcing male domination, disrupting the local power-knowledge relationships and alienating women from the development process. The incomplete male knowledge structure is taken to stand for the entire local knowledge. Women's knowledge is considered, if at all, as part of a private realm outside the responsibility and jurisdiction of the aid project, a type of knowledge on a par with a stereotypical Western housewife's knowledge about which laundry detergent or diaper to use. The suppression of women's knowledge, and the distortion of the local power-knowledge relationships is one of the most tragic consequences of Western aid as it has been practiced in Africa over the last 30 years.

Transforming the expert–recipient relationship

The preceding theoretical exercise only has value (beyond its possible contribution to scholarship) if it provides a means for a sharper understanding of inappropriate aid policy and practice and a means for transforming such policy and practice. By engaging in what Althusser (1977:253) calls a "symptomatic reading" of texts, the six hypotheses have generated a set of concrete ideas about how the knowledge of development problems is structured. Testing these hypotheses against existing aid projects and using them in the design of future aid efforts may open the way to a transformed aid expert – aid recipient relationship. This final section of Chapter 7 suggests research tasks for such a transformation.

First, a survey of aid efforts that have accounted for local knowledges and local agency, with regard not only to women but also to community decision-making structures and practices, is necessary.[6] A starting point would be a literature review in each research/action locus. Some development agencies have made a particular effort to survey and assess such efforts; the IDRC study, *Coming Full Circle: Farmers' Participation in the Development of Technology* (Matlon et al. 1984) is a notable example. The survey should particularly seek studies such as Matlon et al. (1984) that emphasize participatory research. The survey should systematically arrange proposals for, and experiences with, such participation, evaluate the nature of the aid experts' knowledge about the aid recipient, and explore how the experts utilize and characterize local knowledges. In thinking about women as aid recipients, it is necessary, but not enough, to review the position papers and proceedings of all WID conferences; these all too often merely give prescriptions backed by brief project-summary statements (e.g., INSTRAW/UNICEF 1985).

---

[6]It is important not to idealize local knowledge or to assume that successful traditional practices have necessarily survived rapid and overwhelming change. We must also keep in mind the processes whereby influential people in the locality use traditions for their own benefit. The politics of the construction of local knowledge is an important topic to be considered in this research.

Second, the key principles for a transformed aid expert – aid recipient relationship need to be extracted and codified from the documents identified in the survey, both specific cases and overviews such as Matlon et al. (1984). The boundary problem has prevented the circulation of insights from the few good studies beyond the specialists in the field surveyed. The study of Matlon et al. (1984) on farmers' participation exemplifies the possibilities for crossing the boundary. Among other useful tasks, this study presents and assesses the "research–development–production" (RDP) approach to agricultural development, in which "farmers' participation is required, first, in diagnosing the problems, second, in designing technical improvements, and, third, in using and evaluating the innovations" (Matlon et al. 1984:12).

The RDP approach consists of three categories of methods. The first is evaluations that arise from close collaboration between experienced researchers and farmers and that "take into account relationships between the ecological and technical environments, between techniques and farming systems, and between techniques and societies." The second is experiments that do not rely on research station methodology, but develop techniques and statistical tools for farmer-managed tests. "Some researchers consider farmer-managed tests an extension of experiments started on the station; others see them as the beginning of experiments — the true framework for dialogue with the farmer. The tests...provide information about actual production and consumption at the level of the plot, the farm, the rural community, and the country." The third category of methods, "adoption, extension, and adaptation," involves the precise adaptation of innovations developed both on the farm and in controlled environments to other localities and types of production (Matlon et al. 1984:12–13).

In this example, the proposed codification of principles for research and policy would take the three method categories and create generalizations that could be applied in other contexts. For example, agricultural programs that focused specifically on women farmers could include in the first category of methods an evaluation of the knowledge about techniques, soil conditions, etc., that is specific to women as well as an assessment of how this gender-specific knowledge may be integrated with techniques proposed by aid experts. With regard to the second category of methods, farmer-managed tests could be specifically designed to account for the opportunities and limitations presented by the female farmers' multiple responsibilities and daily schedule. With regard to the third category, research could be designed to ensure the collection of data on the implications of a particular innovation for the farming activities of women.

Beyond the agricultural setting, the RDP approach could be assessed for its adaptability to the health technology field. The emphasis on participation, dialogue, and recipient-centred testing and evaluation would provide a beneficial shift away from the treatment of health care recipients as passive, individual objects of research and service delivery. This task is likely to be difficult, given the much less obvious "expertise" of the health-care recipient in comparison to the farmer and the specialized nature of medical knowledge. Regarding research methodology, as a parallel to the farmer-managed tests, medical research methodology could be weaned from a hospital orientation and adapted to rural clinics and the abilities and know-how of paramedics, traditional healers, and midwives.

The discourse of development underlying selected projects, with the projects being viewed as "local centres" of power knowledge, need critical examination.

Much is made of the importance of identifying and replicating success, and rightly so; however, no attention is paid to the instructive value of poor policy and research. Feminist and other critics of aid projects tend to make general condemnations and not to explore in detail how and why a particular aid policy is poor and implicated in an inappropriate exercise of power over the recipients (whether by the foreign aid experts or the recipients' government). A critical examination should attempt to link project failures and the framework of knowledge in which the project was initially embedded. This task is not as eccentric as it may seem: the mistakes in development research and aid policy, so often repeated, are destined to further repetition unless a clearer and more systematized understanding of the mistakes is created. Ultimately, this task could yield a document cataloguing and explaining problems in approaches to development aid.

Alternative conceptions of the aid expert – aid recipient relationship could be formulated through a survey and analysis of research projects that are based on local empowerment. African women's research/action loci would appear to be the best candidates for such research. WRDP, for example, might serve as a model. Begun as a small study group of academic and nonacademic women in 1978, WRDP was made part of the University of Dar es Salaam's Institute for Development Studies (IDS) in 1980. "Fundamental differences over principles of organization" between the group members and the male majority of IDS, as well as efforts "to hijack the funds and equipment which the group had succeeded in acquiring," led to departure from IDS and the formal establishment of WRDP in 1982 (Mbilinyi 1985b:75–76). Now an affiliate of the International Council of Adult Education Women's Programme and the African Adult Education Association, WRDP exemplifies the lessons to be learned about the struggle to establish women-directed and women-centred development research. Priority is currently being given to a life history project that relates the experience of social change and development problems to personal lives. WRDP has as a central tenet of its research and action the involvement of ordinary Tanzanian women in the research and development process (see CWS/cf 1986:67–68).

The recovery of women's knowledge is an urgent research task for the development effort. The WRDP history project is one excellent method. Other types of fieldwork should also be called upon: contemporary African history and sociology should be explored for useful methodology. Feminist scholars, in particular, have developed field techniques useful for researching women's knowledge. As well as new fieldwork, the task should encompass a thorough survey of published ethnologies to extract information regarding individual societies, systems of male and female knowledge, and the actual content of women's knowledge. The recovery of material from past fieldwork need not stop at published documents; living ethnologists may be solicited for relevant material in their unpublished research notes.

A model for the research task suggested here is Molnos' (1972–1973) four-volume document on population in East Africa. The first volume reviews sociocultural research between 1952 and 1972. Volume II deals with innovations in East African societies, in particular with regard to family planning; the second part volume II surveys these themes in 28 East African ethnic groups. Volume III deals with the traditional beliefs and practices of these groups, the survey of the groups forms the empirical core of the study. The fourth volume is a bibliography arranged by ethnic group. In addition to reviewing published texts, Molnos solicited contributions from 37 social scientists. Many were the original ethnographers of the 28 groups (e.g., Philip Gulliver for the Turkana of Kenya and Monica Wilson for the Nyakyusa of Tanzania); however, they had not written about fertility, attitudes to children, and other factors specifically relevant to population planning. Indeed, as a consequence of Molnos's solicitation, there is now a unique body of comparative material focused on gender relations that would otherwise have been lost in the heads and unpublished notes of major anthropologists.

A central element in the success of Molnos (1972–1973) was the careful selection of anthropological contributors. Molnos sought those whose fullness of fieldwork and interest in the issues of social process in the family would render them most likely to have answers to her questions in their raw data. Another aspect of this publication's success was the meticulous methodology she devised for ensuring an enthusiastic and systematic response from the contributors. Molnos' effort, sponsored by the University of Nairobi's Institute of African Studies and funded by the Ford Foundation, ranks as one of the brilliant, unsung efforts in applied social science.

Conclusion

A central dilemma lies at the heart of efforts to transform the aid expert – aid recipient relationship. By the very nature of aid, there is a giver and a receiver. Yet, the preceding exercise — and the book as a whole — has shown that the constitution of African people as recipients by the aid process has entailed conceptualizing them as passive targets, obstacles, or beneficiaries who are receiving a handout for which they have not worked. How can aid agencies continue giving while rethinking the way the gift is given and while turning the receiver into a genuine partner in the transaction? With regard to women and technology transfer in Africa, a solution may only be found through the insights of those African women and men who have struggled with the question themselves.

References

AAWORD (Association of African Women for Research and Development). 1982. The experience of the Association of African Women for Research and Development. *In* Another development with women. Proceedings of a seminar held in Dakar, Senegal, June 1982. Development Dialogue, 1(2), 101–113.

_____1983. A statement on genital mutilation. *In* Davies, M., compiler, Third World — second sex: women's struggles and national liberation, Third World women speak out. Zed Press Ltd, London, UK.

_____1985. AAWORD Newsletter, 1985. AAWORD, Nairobi, Kenya.

Achebe, C. 1983. The trouble with Nigeria. William Heinemann, Ltd, London, UK. p. 19.

Afonja, S. 1986a. Changing modes of production and the sexual division of labor among the Yoruba. *In* Leacock, E., Safa, H., ed., Women's work: development and the division of labour by gender. J.F. Bergin, Publishers, Inc., South Hadley, MA, USA.

_____1986b. Land control: a critical factor in Yoruba gender stratification. *In* Robertson, C., Berger, I., ed., Women and class in Africa. Holmes & Meier Publishers, Inc., New York, NY, USA.

Afshar, H., ed. 1985. Women, work, and ideology in the Third World. Tavistock Publications Ltd, London, UK.

_____1987. Women, state, and ideology: studies from Africa and Asia. State University of New York Press, Albany, NY, USA.

Agarwal, A. 1984. Beyond pretty trees and tigers: the role of ecological destruction in the emerging patterns of poverty and people's protests. Fifth Vikram Sarabhai Memorial Lecture. Indian Council of Social Science Research, New Delhi, India.

Agarwal, B. 1985. Women and technological change in agriculture: the Asian and African experience. *In* Ahmed, E., ed., Technology and rural women: conceptual and empirical issues. George Allen & Unwin (Publishers) Ltd, London, UK.

_____1986. Cold hearths and barren slopes: the woodfuel crisis in the Third World. Allied Publishers Pvt Ltd, New Delhi, India.

Ahmed, E., ed. 1985. Technology and rural women: conceptual and empirical issues. George Allen & Unwin (Publishers) Ltd, London, UK.

Almond, G., Coleman, J., ed. 1960. The politics of developing areas. Princeton University Press, Princeton, NJ, USA.

Althusser, L. 1971. Ideology and ideological state apparatuses. *In* Lenin and philosophy. New Left Books, London, UK.

_____1977. For Marx. New Left Books, London, UK.

Althusser, L., Balibar, E. 1970. Reading capital. New Left Books, London, UK.

Amadiume, I. 1987. Male daughters, female husbands: gender and sex in an African society. Zed Press Ltd, London, UK.

Amin, S. 1972. Underdevelopment and dependency in Black Africa — origins and contemporary forms. Journal of Modern African Studies, 10(4), 503–524.

Anderson, M. 1985. Technology implications for women. *In* Overholt, C., Anderson, M., Cloud, K., Austin, J., ed., Gender roles in development projects: a case book. Kumarian Press, West Hartford, CT, USA.

Ardener, S., ed. 1975. Perceiving women. Benjamin Dent Publications Ltd, London, UK.

Armstrong, K. 1978. Rural Scottish women: politics without power. Ethnos (Stockholm), 43, 51–72.

ATAC (Appropriate Technology Advisory Committee). 1985. Tech & tools: an appropriate technology event for women at Forum '85. *In* Program of events: 9–19 July 1985, Nairobi, Kenya. World YWCA/International Women's Tribune Centre/ATAC, Nairobi, Kenya.

ATRCW (African Training and Research Centre for Women). 1985a. Women and development planning: an African regional perspective. *In* Were, G.S., ed., Women and development in Africa. Gideon S. Were Press, Nairobi, Kenya.

_____1985b. Women and the mass media in Africa: case studies from Sierra Leone, The Niger, and Egypt. *In* Were, G.S., ed., Women and development in Africa. Gideon S. Were Press, Nairobi, Kenya.

Badri, B. 1986. Women, land ownership, and development in the Sudan. Canadian Woman Studies/les Cahiers de la femme, 7(1/2), 89–92.

Baran, P. 1968. The political economy of growth. Monthly Review Press, New York, NY, USA.

Barrett, M. 1980. Women's oppression today: problems in Marxist feminist analysis. Verso Editions, London, UK.

Barrett, M., McIntosh, M. 1982. The anti-social family. Verso Editions, London, UK.

Baudrillard, J. 1975. The mirror of production. Telos Press, St Louis, MO, USA.

Baxter, D., ed. 1987a. Women and the environment in the Sudan. University of Toronto, Toronto, Ont., Canada. Project Ecoville, Working Paper, 42.

_____1987b. Women and the environment: a downward spiral. *In* Baxter, D., ed., Women and the environment in the Sudan. University of Toronto, Toronto, Ont., Canada. Project Ecoville, Working Paper, 42.

Bay, E., ed. 1982. Women and work in Africa. Westview Press, Boulder, CO, USA.

Bay, E., Hafkin, N., ed. 1975. Women in Africa. African Studies Review, 18(3).

Beneriá, L., Sen, G. 1986. Accumulation, reproduction, and women's role in economic development: Boserup revisited. *In* Leacock, E., Safa, H., ed., Women's work: development and the division of labour by gender. J.F. Bergin, Publishers, Inc., South Hadley, MA, USA.

Bennett, F.J. 1981. Editorial. Social Science and Medicine, 16(3), 233–234.

Berg, R.J., Whitaker, J.S., ed. 1986. Strategies for African development. A study for the Committee on African Development Strategies sponsored by the Council on Foreign Relations and the Overseas Development Council. University of California Press, Berkeley, CA, USA. 603 pp.

Bernstein, H. 1977. Notes on capital and peasantry. Review of African Political Economy, 10, 60–73.

Blair, P., ed. 1981. Health needs of the World's poor women. Equity Policy Centre, Washington, DC, USA.

Boserup, E. 1970. Women's role in economic development. George Allen & Unwin (Publishers) Ltd, London, UK.

Brett, E.A. 1973. Colonialism and underdevelopment in East Africa: the politics of economic change 1919–39. William Heinemann, Ltd, London, UK.

Brink, P. 1982. Traditional birth attendants among the Annang of Nigeria: current preactices and proposed programs. Social Science and Medicine, 16(21), 1883–1892.

Briskin, L. 1985. Theorizing the capitalistm family/household system: a Marxist–feminist contribution. York University, Toronto, Ont., Canada. PhD dissertation.

Brownmiller, S. 1976. Against our will: men, women, and rape. Bantam Books Inc., New York, NY, USA.

Bryceson, D. 1980. The proletarianization of women in Tanzania. Review of African Political Economy, 17, 4–27.

_____1985. Women and technology in developing countries: technological change and women's capabilities and bargaining positions. United Nations International Research and Training Institute for the Advancement of Women, Santo Domingo, Dominican Republic.

Bryson, J. 1981. Women and agriculture in sub-Saharan Africa: implications for development (an exploratory study). Journal of Development Studies, 17(3), 29–46.

Buvinic, M., Lycette, M., McGreevey, W., ed. 1983. Women and poverty in the Third World. Johns Hopkins University Press, Baltimore, MD, USA.

CAAS (Canadian Association of African Studies). 1972. The roles of women: past, present and future. Canadian Journal of African Studies, 6.

_____1985. Mode of production: the challenge of Africa. Canadian Journal of African Studies, 19(1), 258 pp.

Cain, M. 1981. Overview: women and technology — resources for our future. In Dauber, R., Cain, M.L., ed. Women and technological change in developing countries. American Association for the Advancement of Science, Washington, DC, USA. Selected Symposium, 53.

Callaway, B. 1984. Ambiguous consequences of the socialisation and seclusion of Hausa women. Journal of Modern African Studies, 22(3), 429–450.

Caplan, P. 1981. Development policies in Tanzania — some implications for women. In Nelson, N., ed., African women in the development process. Frank Cass & Co. Ltd, London, UK.

_____ed. 1987. The cultural construction of sexuality. Tavistock Publications Ltd, London, UK.

Carr, M. 1981. Technologies appropriate for women: theory, practice, and policy. In Dauber, R., Cain, M.L., ed., Women and technological change in developing countries. American Association for the Advancement of Science, Washington, DC, USA. Selected Symposium, 53.

Carr, M., Sandhu, R. 1987. Women, technology, and rural productivity: an analysis of the impact of time and energy-saving technologies on women. Intermediate Technology Consultants Ltd, Rugby, UK.

CDPA (Centre for Development and Population Activities). n.d. A manual on planning, implementation, and management of development projects. CDPA, Washington, DC, USA.

Cecelski, E. 1987. Energy and rural women's work: crisis, response, and policy alternatives. International Labour Review, 126(1), 41–64.

Chambers, R. 1983. Rural development: putting the last first. Longman Group Ltd, London, UK.

Charlton, S.E. 1984. Women in Third World development. Westview Press, Boulder, CO, USA.

Chege, R.N. 1986. Communal food production: the Mukuru–Kaiyaba women's group in Nairobi. Canadian Woman Studies/les Cahiers de la femme, 7(1/2), 76–77.

Cherian, A. 1981. Attitudes and practices of infant feeding in Zaria, Nigeria. Ecology of Food and Nutrition, 11(2), 75–80.

Chintu-Tembo, S. 1985. Women and health. In Women's rights in Zambia: Proceedings of the Second National Women's Rights Conference held at Mindolo Ecumenical Foundation, Kitwe, Zambia, 22–24 March 1985. Zambia Association for Research and Development, Lusaka, Zambia.

Chipande, G.H.R. 1987. Innovation adoption among female-headed households: the case of Malawi. Development and Change, 18(2), 315–328.

Ciancanelli, P. 1980. Exchange, reproduction, and sex subordination among the Kikuyu of East Africa. Review of Radical Political Economy, 12(2), 25–36.

CIDA (Canadian International Development Agency). 1987. Sharing our future: Canadian international development assistance. CIDA, Hull, Que., Canada.

Clark, C.M. 1980. Land and food, women, and power in nineteenth century Kikuyu. Africa, 50(4), 357–369.

Cohen, A. 1969. The migratory process: prostitutes and housewives. In Custom and politics in urban Africa. University of California Press, Berkeley, CA, USA.

Collier, J., Rosaldo, M. 1981. Politics and gender in simple societies. In Ortner, S., Whitehead, H., ed., Sexual meanings: the cultural construction of gender and sexuality. Cambridge University Press, Cambridge, UK.

Collier, J., Rosaldo, M., Yanagisako, S. 1982. Is there a family? New anthropological views. In Thorne, B., Yalom, M., ed., Rethinking the family: some feminist questions. Longman Goup Ltd, New York, NY, USA.

Commonwealth Secretariat. 1984. Working into the system: a calendar for the integration of women's issues into international development dialogue. Commonwealth Secretariat, London, UK.

Conti, A. 1979. Capitalist organization of production through non-capitalist relations: women's role in a pilot resettlement in Upper Volta. Review of African Political Economy, 15/16, 75–92.

Coquery-Vidrovitch, C. 1977. Research on an African mode of production. In Gutkind, P., Waterman, P., ed., African social studies: a radical reader. Monthly Review Press, New York, NY, USA.

Cousins, M., Hussain, A. 1984. Michel Foucault. Macmillan Publishers Ltd, London, UK.

Coward, R. 1983. Patriarchal precedents: sexuality and social relations. Routledge & Kegan Paul Ltd, London, UK.

Coward, R., Ellis, J. 1977. Language and materialism: developments in semiology and the theory of the subject. Routledge & Kegan Paul Ltd, London, UK.

Crummey, D., Stewart, C.C., ed. 1981. Modes of production in Africa. Sage Publications, Inc., Beverly Hills, CA, USA.

162

Cutrufelli, M.R. 1983. Women of Africa: roots of oppression. Zed Press Ltd, London, UK.

CWS/cf (Canadian Woman Studies/les Cahiers de la femme). 1986. Post Nairobi. Canadian Woman Studies/les Cahiers de la femme, 7(1/2).

Dahl, G. 1981. Production in pastoral societies. *In* Galaty, J., Aronson, D., Salzman, P., Chouinard, A., ed., The future of pastoral peoples. Proceedings of a conference held in Nairobi, Kenya, 4–8 August 1980. International Development Research Centre, Ottawa, Ont., Canada. IDRC-175e, 200–209.

Daniels, D., Nestel, B., ed. 1981. Resource allocation to agricultural research. Proceedings of a workshop held in Singapore, 8–10 June 1981. International Development Research Centre, Ottawa, Ont., Canada. IDRC-182e, 170 pp.

Dauber, R., Cain, M.L., ed. 1981. Women and technological change in developing countries. American Association for the Advancement of Science, Washington, DC, USA. Selected Symposium, 53.

Davidson, B. 1969. The African genius: an introduction to African cultural and social history. Little, Brown and Co., Boston, MA, USA.

Davies, M., compiler. 1983. Third World — second sex: women's struggles and national liberation, Third World women speak out. Zed Press Ltd, London, UK.

DAWN (Development Alternatives with Women for a New Era). 1986. Development crisis and alternative visions: Third World women's perspectives. Canadian Woman Studies/les Cahiers de la femme, 7(1/2), 53–59.

DHF/SIDA (Dag Hammarskjöld Foundation/Swedish International Development Authority). 1982. Another development with women. Proceedings of a seminar held in Dakar, Senegal, June 1982. Development Dialogue, 1(2).

Dey, J. 1981. Gambian women: unequal partners in rice development projects? *In* Nelson, N., ed., African women in the development process. Frank Cass & Co. Ltd, London, UK.

Dickinson, J., Russell, B., ed. 1986. Family, economy, and state: the social reproduction process under capitalism. Garamond Press, Toronto, Ont., Canada.

D'Onofrio-Flores, P., Pfafflin, S., ed. 1982. Scientific–technological change and the role of women in development. United Nations Institute for Training and Research, New York, NY, USA.

Douglas, M. 1963. The Lele of Kasai. Oxford University Press, London, UK.

Doyal, L. 1981. The political economy of health. Pluto Press Ltd, London, UK.

Dreyfus, H., Rabinow, P. 1983. Michel Foucault: beyond structuralism and hermeneutics (2nd ed.). University of Chicago Press, Chicago, IL, USA.

Duley, M., Edwards, M., ed. 1986. The cross-cultural study of women: a comprehensive guide. The Feminist Press, Old Westbury, NY, USA.

Dwyer, D.H. 1978. Images and self-images: male and female in Morocco. Columbia University Press, New York, NY USA.

Eastman, P. 1980. An end to pounding: a new mechanical flour milling system in use in Africa. International Development Research Centre, Ottawa, Ont., Canada. IDRC-152e, 62 pp.

ECA (Economic Commission for Africa). 1977. Origin and growth of the African Research and Training Centre for Women of the Economic Commission for Africa. Proceedings of a Regional Conference on the Implementation of National, Regional, and World Plans of Action for the Integration of Women in Development, Nouakchott,

163

Mauritania, 27 September 2 to October 1977. ECA, Addis Ababa, Ethiopia. E/CN.14/ACTRW/BD.7

Elling, R. 1981. The capitalist world-system and international health. International Journal of Health Services, 11(1), 21–51.

Elliott, C. 1977. Theories of development: an assessment. Signs, 3(1), 1–8.

El Naiem, A.A. 1984. A modern approach to human rights in Islam: foundations and implications for Africa. In Welch, C., Jr., Meltzer, R., ed., Human rights and development in Africa. State University of New York Press, Albany, NY, USA.

Elson, D. 1987. The impact of structural adjustment on women: concepts and issues. Paper presented at the Institute for African Alternatives Conference on the Impact of International Monetary Fund and World Bank Policies on the People of Africa, City University, London, UK, September 1987. Commonwealth Secretariat, London, UK.

Engels, F. 1884. The origin of the family, private property, and the state. International Publishers Company, Inc., New York, NY, USA. (1970 edition)

Etienne, M. 1980. Women and men, cloth and colonization: the transformation of production–distribution relations among the Baule (Ivory Coast). In Etienne, M., Leacock, E., ed., Women and colonization: anthropological perspectives. Praeger Publishers, Inc., New York, NY, USA.

Etienne, M., Leacock, E., ed. 1980. Women and colonization: anthropological perspectives. Praeger Publishers, Inc., New York, NY, USA.

Evans, P. 1979. Dependent development: the alliance of multinational, state, and local capital in Brazil. Princeton University Press, Princeton, NJ, USA.

Feldman, R. 1981. Employment problems of rural women in Kenya. ILO-JASPA, Addis Ababa, Ethiopia.

_____1984. Womens groups and women's subordination: an analysis of policies towards rural women in Kenya. Review of African Political Economy, 27/28, 67–85.

Feuerstein, M.T. 1976. Rural health problems in developing countries: the need for a comprehensive community approach. Community Development Journal, 11(3), 38–52.

Firestone, S. 1970. The dialectic of sex: the case for feminist revolution. William Morrow & Co., Inc., New York, NY, USA.

Flora, C.B. 1982. Incorporating women into international development programs: the political phenomenology of a private foundation. Women's Politics, 2(4), 89–107.

Fortmann, L. 1981. The plight of the invisible farmer: the effect of national agricultural development policy on women. In Dauber, R., Cain, M.L., ed., Women and technological change in developing countries. American Association for the Advancement of Science, Washington, DC, USA. Selected Symposium, 53.

Foucault, M. 1973. Madness and civilization: a history of insanity in the age of reason. Random House, Inc., New York, NY, USA.

_____1979. Discipline and punish: the birth of the prison. Random House, Inc., New York, NY, USA.

_____1980a. The history of sexuality. Volume I. An introduction. Random House, Inc., New York, NY, USA.

_____1980b. Power/knowledge: selected interviews and other writings 1972–1977. Pantheon Books, Inc., New York, NY, USA.

_____1983. Afterword. In Dreyfus, H., Rabinow, P., Michel Foucault: beyond structuralism and hermeneutics (2nd ed.). University of Chicago Press, Chicago, IL, USA.

Frank, A.G. 1967. Capitalism and underdevelopment in Latin America. Monthly Review Press, New York, NY, USA.

Galaty, J., Aronson, D., Salzman, P., Chouinard, A., ed. 1981. The future of pastoral peoples. Proceedings of a conference held in Nairobi, Kenya, 4–8 August 1980. International Development Research Centre, Ottawa, Ont., Canada. IDRC-175e, 396 pp.

Gascon, G. 1986. Les femmes et la production alimentaire. Canadian Woman Studies/les Cahiers de la femme, 7(1/2), 28–30.

Geertz, C. 1983. Local knowledge: further essays in interpretive anthropology. Basic Books, Inc., New York, NY, USA.

George, S. 1977. How the other half dies: the real reasons for world hunger. Penguin Books, New York, NY, USA.

_____1979. Feeding the few: corporate control of food. Institute for Policy Studies, Washington, DC, USA.

Getechah, W. 1981. The role of women in rural water development in Kenya. In Rural water supply in developing countries. Proceedings of a workshop on training held in Zomba, Malawi, 5–12 August 1980. International Development Research Centre, Ottawa, Ont., Canada. IDRC-167e, 85–88.

Ghai, Y.P., McAuslan, J.P.W.B. 1970. Public law and political change in Kenya. Oxford University Press, Nairobi, Kenya.

Glazier, J. 1985. Land and the uses of tradition among the Mbeere of Kenya. University Press of America, Lanham, MD, USA.

Gordon, J. 1984. Important issues for feminist nutrition research a case study from the savanna of West Africa. In Research on rural women: feminist methodological questions. Institute of Development Studies, Sussex, UK, Bulletin, 15(1), 38–42.

Gramsci, A. 1971. Selections from the prison notebooks. Lawrence & Wishart Ltd, London, UK.

Group for the Critical Study of Colonial Discourse. 1985. Inscriptions. University of California, Santa Cruz, CA, USA. Bulletin, 1.

Gulliver, P.H. 1955. The family herds: a study of two pastoral tribes in East Africa, the Jie and the Turkana. Routledge & Kegan Paul Ltd, London, UK.

Gumede, M.V. 1978. Traditional Zulu practitioners and obstetric medicine. South African Medical Journal, 53(21), 823–825.

Guyer, J.I. 1986. Women's role in development. In Berg, R., Whitaker, J.S., ed., Strategies for African development. University of California Press, Berkeley, CA, USA.

Guyer, J.I., Peters, P.E., ed. 1987. Conceptualizing the household: issues of theory and policy in Africa. Development and Change, 18(2), 368 pp.

Hafkin, N., Bay, E., ed. 1976. Women in Africa: studies in social and economic change. Stanford University Press, Stanford, CA, USA.

Hanger, J., Morris, J. 1973. Women and the household economy. In Chambers, R., Morris, J., ed., Mwea: an irrigated rice settlement in Kenya. Welforum Verlag, Munich, FRG.

Hanna, W., Hanna, J. 1971. Urban dynamics in Black Africa. Aldine Publishing Company, Chicago, IL, USA.

Hartmann, H. 1981. The unhappy marriage of Marxism and feminism: towards a more progressive union. In Sargent, L., ed., Women and revolution. South End Press, Boston, MA, USA.

Hay, M.J., Stichter, S., ed. 1984. African women south of the Sahara. Longman Group Ltd, London, UK.

Henn, J.K. 1983 Feeding the cities and feeding the peasants: what role for Africas women farmers? World Development, 11(12), 1043–1055.

Hobley, C.W. 1922. Bantu beliefs and magic. Frank Cass & Co. Ltd, London, UK (1983 edition)

Hoskyns, M., Weber, F. 1985. Why appropriate technology projects for women fail? Environment Liaison Centre, Nairobi, Kenya. Ecoforum, 10(2), 6–8.

Howard, R. 1984. Women's rights in English-speaking sub-Saharan Africa. *In* Welch, C., Jr., Meltzer, R., ed., Human rights and development in Africa. State University of New York Press, Albany, NY, USA.

Hyden, G. 1986. African social structure and economic development. *In* Berg, R., Whitaker, J.S., ed., Strategies for African development. University of California Press, Berkeley, CA, USA.

IBRD (International Bank for Reconstruction and Development). 1979. Recognizing the "invisible" woman in development: the World Bank's experience. IBRD, Washington, DC, USA.

_____1981. Accelerated development in sub-Saharan Africa: an agenda for action. IBRD, Washington, DC, USA.

_____1983. World development report 1983. Oxford University Press, New York, NY, USA.

_____1986. Financing adjustment with growth in sub-Saharan Africa, 1986–90. IBRD, Washington, DC, USA.

IDRC (International Development Research Centre). 1981. Rural water supply in developing countries. Proceedings of a workshop on training held in Zomba, Malawi, 5–12 August 1980. IDRC, Ottawa, Ont., Canada. IDRC-167e, 144 pp.

Igun, U.A. 1982. Child-feeding habits in a situation of social change: the case of Maiduguri, Nigeria. Social Science and Medicine, 16(7), 769–781.

ILO (International Labour Office). 1977. Employment, growth, and basic needs: a one-world problem. Praeger Publishers, Inc., New York, NY, USA.

_____1980. Women in rural development: critical issues. ILO, Geneva, Switzerland.

_____1984. Rural development and women in Africa. Proceedings of the ILO Tripartite African Regional Seminar on Rural Development and Women, and Case Studies. ILO, Geneva, Switzerland.

_____1985. Resources, power, and women. Proceedings of the African and Asian Inter-regional Workshop on Strategies for Improving the Employment Conditions of Rural Women, Arusha, Tanzania, 20–25 August 1984. ILO, Geneva, Switzerland.

ILO/INSTRAW (International Labour Office/United Nations International Research and Training Institute for the Advancement of Women). 1985. Women in economic activity: a global statistical survey (1950–2000). ILO, Geneva, Switzerland.

INSTRAW/UNICEF (United Nations International Research and Training Institute for the Advancement of Women/United Nations Children's Fund). 1985. Women and the International Drinking Water Supply and Sanitation Decade. Paper submitted to the World Conference to Review and Appraise the Achievements of the United Nations Decade for Women. INSTRAW, Santo Domingo, Dominican Republic.

Isely, R. 1984. Rural development strategies and their health and nutrition-mediated effects on fertility: a review of the literature. Social Science and Medicine, 18(7), 581–587.

Isis International. 1983. Women in development: a resource guide for organization and action. Isis International, Geneva, Switzerland.

Jackson, C. 1978. Hausa women on strike. Review of African Political Economy, 13, 21–36.

_____1985. The Kano River Irrigation Project. *In* Women's roles and gender differences in development — case study series. Kumarian Press, West Hartford, CT, USA.

Jaggar, A. 1977. Political philosophies of women's liberation. *In* Vetterling-Braggin, M., ed., Feminism and philosophy. Littlefield, Adams & Co., Totawa, NJ, USA.

_____1983. Feminist politics and human nature. Harvester Press, Ltd, Brighton, UK.

Jaggar, A., Rothenberg, P. 1984. Feminist frameworks: alternative theoretical accounts of the relations between women and men (2nd ed.). McGraw-Hill Co., New York, USA.

Janelid, I. 1975. The role of women in Nigerian agriculture. Food and Agriculture Organization of the United Nations, Rome, Italy.

Kaplinsky, R., Henley, J.S., Leys, C. 1980. Debate on "dependency" in Kenya. Review of African Political Economy, 17, 83–113.

Katz, S. 1980. Marxism, Africa, and social class: a critique of relevant theories. Centre for Developing-Area Studies, Montreal, Que., Canada. Occasional Monograph Series, 14.

_____1985. The succession to power and the power of succession: Nyayoism in Kenya. Journal of African Studies, 12(3), 155–161.

_____1989. The problems of Europocentrism and evolutionism in Marx's writing on colonialism. Journal of Political Science, in press.

Kazembe, J., Mol, M. 1986. The changing legal status of women in Zimbabwe since independence. Canadian Woman Studies/les Cahiers de la femme, 7(1/2), 53–59.

Keller, E.F. 1985. Reflections on gender and science. Yale University Press, New Haven, CT, USA.

Kenya, Government of. 1983. Development plan, 1984–1988. Government Printer, Nairobi, Kenya.

Kenyatta, J. 1938. Facing Mount Kenya. Vintage Books, New York, NY, USA.

Kershaw, G. 1973. The Kikuyu of central Kenya. *In* Molnos, A., ed., Cultural source materials for population planning in East Africa. Volume 3. Beliefs and practices. East African Publishing House, Nairobi, Kenya.

Kertzer, D., Madison, O.B.B. 1981. Women's age-set systems in Africa: the Latuka of southern Sudan. *In* Fry, C., ed., Dimensions: aging, culture, and health. Praeger Publishers, Inc., New York, NY, USA.

Kettel, B. 1986. The commoditization of women in Tugen (Kenya) social organization. *In* Robertson, C., Berger, I., ed., Women and class in Africa. Holmes & Meier Publishers, Inc., New York, NY, USA.

Keyi, V. 1986. Women's collective action as a manifestation of female solidarity from pre-colonial Zimbabwe to present. York University, Toronto, Ont., Canada.

Kimati, V. 1986. Who is ignorant? Rural mothers who feed their well-nourished children or the nutrition experts? The Tanzania story. Journal of Tropical Pediatrics, 32, 130–136.

King, K. 1986. Manpower, technology, and employment in Africa: internal and external policy agendas. *In* Berg, R., Whitaker, J.S., ed., Strategies for African development. University of California Press, Berkeley, CA, USA.

King, M. 1966. Medical care in developing countries. A primer on the medicine of poverty and a symposium from Makerere. Oxford University Press, Nairobi, Kenya.

Kirby, V. 1987. On the cutting edge: feminism and cliteridectomy. Australian Feminist Studies, 5(Summer), 35–55.

Kitching, G. 1980. Class and economic change in Kenya: the making of an African petite-bourgeoisie. Yale University Press, New Haven, CT, USA.

Kneerim, J. 1980. Village women organize: the Mraru bus service. Carnegie Corporation of New York, Ford Foundation, and The Population Council, New York, NY, USA. SEEDS (Sarvodaya Economic Enterprises Development Services) Pamphlet Series.

Koeune, E. 1952. The African housewife and her home. Kenya Literature Bureau, Nairobi, Kenya. (1983 edition)

Kutzner, P. 1982. Women and the problem of hunger. World Hunger Education Service, Washington, DC, USA. Hunger Notes, 7(8), 1–6.

_____1986a. Women farmers of Kenya. World Hunger Education Service, Washington, DC, USA. Hunger Notes, 11(9/10), 1–25.

_____1986b. Policy reforms and poverty in Africa: comparative views. World Hunger Education Service, Washington, DC, USA. Hunger Notes, 12(1), 1–23.

Laclau, E. 1977. Politics and ideology in Marxist theory. New Left Books, London, UK.

Laclau, E., Mouffe, C. 1985. Hegemony and socialist strategy: towards a radical democratic politics. Verso Editions, London, UK.

Ladipo, P. 1981. Developing women's cooperatives: an experiment in rural Nigeria. In Nelson, N., ed., African women in the development process. Frank Cass & Co. Ltd, London, UK. pp. 123–136.

Lambert, H.E. 1956. Kikuyu social and political institutions. Oxford University Press, London, UK.

Lappé, F.M., Beccar-Varela, A. 1980. Mozambique and Tanzania: asking the big questions. Institute for Food and Development Policy, San Francisco, CA, USA.

Lappé, F.M., Collins, J. 1978. Food first: beyond the myth of scarcity. Ballantine Books, Inc., New York, NY, USA.

Lawrence, P., ed. 1986. World recession and the food crisis in Africa. Review of African Political Economy/James Curry Ltd, London, UK.

Leacock, E. 1981. Myths of male dominance. Monthly Review Press, New York, NY, USA.

Leacock, E., Safa, H., ed. 1986. Women's work: development and the division of labour by gender. J.F. Bergin, Publishers, Inc., South Hadley, MA, USA.

Leakey, L.S.B. 1933. The southern Kikuyu peoples before 1903. Volumes 1–3. Academic Press Inc. (London) Ltd, London, UK. (1977 edition)

Leonard, D. 1986. Putting the farmer in control: building agricultural institutions. In Berg, R., Whitaker, J.S., ed., Strategies for African development. University of California Press, Berkeley, CA, USA.

Lévi-Strauss, C. 1969. The elementary structures of kinship. Beacon Press, Boston, MA, USA.

Lewis, B. 1984. The impact of development policies on women. In Hay, M.J., Stichter, S., ed., African women south of the Sahara. Longman Group Ltd, London, UK.

Leys, C. 1975. Underdevelopment in Kenya. William Heinemann, Ltd, London, UK.

Liddle, J., Joshi, R. 1986. Daughters of independence: gender, caste, and class in India. Zed Press Ltd, London, UK.

Llewelyn-Davies, M. 1979. Two contexts of solidarity among pastoral Masai women. In

Caplan, P., Bujra, J., ed., Women united, women divided: comparative studies of ten contemporary cultures. Indiana University Press, Bloomington, IN, USA.

Mackenzie, F. 1986. Land and labour: women and men in agricultural change, Murang'a District, Kenya, 1880–1984. University of Ottawa, Ottawa, Ont., Canada. PhD dissertation.

_____1988. Perspectives on land tenure: social relations and the definition of territory in a smallholding district, Kenya. Paper presented at the Symposium on Land in African Agrarian Systems, University of Illinois, Urbana-Champaign, IL, USA, April 1988.

Mahler, H. 1974. The health of the family. Keynote address to the International Health Conference of the National Council for International Health (NCIH), 16 October 1974. NCIH, Washington, DC, USA

Mamdani, M. 1976. Politics and class formation in Uganda. Monthly Review Press, New York, NY, USA.

March, K., Taqqu, R. 1986. Women's informal associations in developing countries. Westview Press, Boulder, CO, USA.

Marris, P., Somerset, A. 1971. African businessmen: a study of entrepreneurship and development in Kenya. East African Publishing House, Nairobi, Kenya.

Mascarenhas, O., Mbilinyi, M. 1980. Women and development in Tanzania, an annotated bibliography. African Training and Research Centre for Women, Addis Ababa, Ethiopia.

_____1983. Women in Tanzania: an analytical bibliography. Scandinavian Institute of African Studies, Uppsala, Sweden.

Matlon, P., Cantrell, R., King, D., Benoit-Cattin, M., ed. 1984. Coming full circle: farmers' participation in the development of technology. International Development Research Centre, Ottawa, Ont., Canada. IDRC-189e, 176 pp.

Mazingira Institute. 1985. A guide to women's organizations and agencies serving women in Kenya. Mazingira Institute, Nairobi, Kenya.

Mbilinyi, M. 1984. Research priorities in women's studies in Eastern Africa. Women's Studies International Forum, 7(4), 289–300.

_____1985a. "City" and "countryside" in colonial Tanganyika. Economic and Political Weekly, XX(43), 88–96.

_____1985b. Women's studies and the crisis in Africa. Social Scientist (Dar es Salaam), 13(10/11), 72–85.

_____1986. The participation of women in Tanganyikan anti-colonial struggles. Paper presented at the Biennial Conference of the Review of African Political Economy, University of Liverpool, Liverpool, UK, September 1986.

Meillassoux, C. 1972. From reproduction to production: a Marxist approach to economic anthropology. Economy and Society, 1(1), 93–105.

Mickelwait, D., Riegelman, M.A., Sweet, C. 1976. Women in rural development: a survey of the roles of women in Ghana, Lesotho, Kenya, Nigeria, Bolivia, Paraguay, and Peru. Westview Press, Boulder, CO, USA.

Middleton, J., Kershaw, G. 1965. The central tribes of the north-eastern Bantu. International African Institute, London, UK.

Mill, J.S., Taylor, H. 1851. The subjection of women. Virago Press Ltd, London, UK. (1983 edition)

Miller, C. 1985. Blank darkness. University of Chicago Press, Chicago, IL, USA.

Millett, K. 1970. Sexual politics. Doubleday & Co., Inc., New York, USA.

Minson, J. 1985. Genealogies of morals: Neitzsche, Foucault, Donzelot, and the eccentricity of ethics. St Martin's Press, New York, NY, USA.

Mohammadi, P. 1984. Women and national planning: false expectations. Development: Seeds of Change, 4, 80–81.

Molnos, A. 1972–1973. Cultural source materials for population planning in East Africa. Volumes I–IV. East African Publishing House, Nairobi, Kenya.

Momsen, J., Townsend, J., ed. 1987. Geography of gender in the Third World. Hutchinson Publishing Group Ltd, London, UK.

Monson, J., Kalb, M., ed. 1985. Women and food producers in developing countries. Crossroads Press, Inc., Los Angeles, CA, USA.

Morgan, R., ed. 1970. Sisterhood is powerful. Vintage Books, New York, NY, USA.

_____ed. 1984. Sisterhood is global. Anchor Books, New York, NY, USA.

Mosley, P. 1986. The politics of economic liberalization: USAID and the World Bank in Kenya, 1980–1984. African Affairs, 85(338), 107–119.

Mueller, A. 1987. Peasants and professionals: the social organization of women in development knowledge. University of Toronto, Toronto, Ont., Canada. PhD dissertation.

Mullings, L. 1976. Women and economic change in Africa. In Hafkin, N., Bay, E., ed., Women in Africa: studies in social and economic change. Stanford University Press, Stanford, CA, USA.

Muntemba, M.S. 1982a. Women and agricultural change in the Railway Region of Zambia: dispossession and counterstrategies, 1930–1970. In Bay, E., ed. Women and work in Africa. Westview Press, Boulder, CO, USA.

_____1982b. Women as food producers and suppliers in the twentieth century: the case of Zambia. In Another development with women. Proceedings of a seminar held in Dakar, Senegal, June 1982. Development Dialogue, 1(2).

Muriuki, G. 1974. A history of the Kikuyu 1500–1900. Oxford University Press, Nairobi, Kenya.

Navarro, V., ed. 1981. Imperialism, health, and medicine. Baywood Publishing Company, Farmingdale, NY, USA.

Nelson, N., ed. 1981. African women in the development process. Frank Cass & Co. Ltd, London, UK.

Newman, K. 1981. Women and law: land tenure in Africa. In Black, N., Cottrell, A.B., ed., Women and world change: equity issues in development. Sage Publications, Inc., Beverly Hills, CA, USA.

OAU (Organization of African Unity). 1980. Lagos Plan of Action for the economic development of Africa, 1980–2000. OAU, Addis Ababa, Ethiopia.

_____1982. Progress report of the Secretary-General of the Organization of African Unity and the Executive Secretary of the United Nations Economic Commission for Africa on the implementation of the Lagos Plan of Action and the Final Act of Lagos. OAU, Addis Ababa, Ethiopia.

O'Barr, J., ed. 1982. Perspectives on power: women in Africa, Asia, and Latin America. Center for International Studies, Duke University, Durham, NC, USA.

_____1984. African women in politics. In Hay, M.J., Stichter, S., ed., African women south of the Sahara. Longman Group Ltd, London, UK.

Obbo, C. 1980. African women: their struggle for economic independence. Zed Press Ltd, London, UK.

_____1986. Stratification and the lives of women in Uganda. *In* Robertson, C., Berger, I., ed. Women and class in Africa. Holmes & Meier Publishers, Inc., New York, NY, USA.

Oboler, R.S. 1985. Women, power, and economic change: the Nandi of Kenya. Stanford University Press, Stanford, CA, USA.

Odumosu, M.O. 1982. Mass media and immunization awareness of pregnant women in a Nigerian community. Canadian Journal of Public Health, 73(2), 105–108.

Ogunmekan, D.A. 1977. Protecting the Nigerian child against the common communicable diseases. Tropical and Geographical Medicine, 29(4), 389–392.

Ojofeitimi, E.O., Tanimowo, C.M. 1980. Nutritional beliefs among pregnant Nigerian women. International Journal of Gynaecology and Obstetrics, 18(1), 66–69.

Okafor, F.C. 1984. Accessibility to general hospitals in rural Bendel State, Nigeria. Social Science and Medicine, 18(8), 661–666.

O'Kelly, E. 1973. Aid and self help. Longman Group Ltd, London, UK.

Okeyo, A.P. 1980. Daughters of the lakes and rivers: colonization and the land rights of Luo women. *In* Etienne, M., Leacock, E., ed., Women and colonization: anthropological perspectives. Praeger Publishers, Inc., New York, NY, USA.

Oleru, U.G., Kolawole, O.O.J. 1983. Factors influencing primary health care: a look at a pediatric emergency unit. Journal of Tropical Pediatrics, 29, 319–325.

O'Neil, M. 1986. Forward-looking strategies: the UN World Conference on women. Canadian Woman Studies/les Cahiers de la femme, 7(1/2), 19–21.

Onokerhoraye, A. 1984. Social services in Nigeria: an introduction. Routledge & Kegan Paul Ltd, London, UK.

Ortner, S. 1974. Is female to male as nature is to culture? *In* Rosaldo, M.Z., Lamphere, L., ed., Women, culture, and society. Stanford University Press, Stanford, CA, USA.

Ortner, S., Whitehead, H., ed. 1981. Sexual meanings: the cultural construction of gender and sexuality. Cambridge University Press, Cambridge, UK.

Orubuloye, I.O., Oyenye, O.Y. 1982. Primary health care in developing countries: the case of Nigeria, Sri Lanka, and Tanzania. Social Science and Medicine, 16(6), 675–686.

Osuala, J. 1987. Extending appropriate technology to rural African women. Women's Studies International Forum, 10(5), 481–487.

Overholt, C., Anderson, M., Cloud, K., Austin, J., ed. 1985. Gender roles in development projects: a case book. Kumarian Press, West Hartford, CT, USA.

Palmer, I. 1978. Women and green revolutions. Paper presented at the Conference on the Continuing Subordination of Women and the Development Process. Institute of Development Studies, Sussex, UK.

_____1985. The impact of agrarian reform on women. *In* Women's roles and gender differences in development — case study series. Kumarian Press, West Hartford, CT, USA.

Parkin, D. 1972. Palms, wine, and witnesses: public spirit and private gain in an African farming community. Chandler Publishing Co., San Francisco, CA, USA.

Paulme, D., ed. 1971. Women of tropical Africa. University of California Press, Berkeley, CA, USA.

Payer, C. 1982. The World Bank: a critical analysis. Monthly Review Press, New York, NY, USA.

Poewe, K. 1981. Matrilineal ideology, male–female dynamics in Luapula, Zambia. Academic Press Inc. (London) Ltd, London, UK.

Poulantzas, N. 1973. Political power and social classes. New Left Books, London, UK.

_____1978. State, power, socialism. New Left Books, London, UK.

Rabinow, P., Sullivan, W., ed. 1979. Interpretive social science: a reader. University of California Press, Berkeley, CA, USA.

Rachlan. 1986. The Citanduy River Basin Management Project: from grass-roots experiments to full scale implementation. Institut Teknologi Bandung, Bandung, Indonesia.

Rehan, N. 1984. Knowledge, attitude, and practice of family planning in Hausa women. Social Science and Medicine, 18(10), 839–844.

RFR/DRF (Resources for Feminist Research Documentation/Documentation sur la recherche féministe). 1982. Women and agricultural production. RFR/DRF, II(1).

ROAPE (Review of African Political Economy). 1984. Women, oppression and liberation. Review of African Political Economy, 27/28, 236 pp.

_____1986. Africa — the health issue. Review of African Political Economy, 36, 120 pp.

Robertson, C. 1987. Developing economic awareness: changing perspectives in studies on African women, 1976–1985. Feminist Studies, 13(1), 97–135.

Robertson, C., Berger, I., ed. 1986. Women and class in Africa. Holmes & Meier Publishers, Inc., New York, NY, USA.

Rodney, W. 1972. How Europe underdeveloped Africa. Bogle-L'Ouverture Publications Ltd, London, UK.

Rogers, B. 1980. The domestication of women: discrimination in developing societies. Tavistock Publications, London, UK.

Rosaldo, M.Z. 1974. Woman, culture, and society: a theoretical overview. *In* Rosaldo, M.Z., Lamphere, L., ed., Woman, culture, and society. Stanford University Press, Stanford, CA, USA.

_____1983. Moral/analytic dilemmas posed by the intersection of feminism and social science. *In* Haan, N., Bellah, R., Rabinow, P., Sullivan, W., ed., Social science as moral inquiry. Columbia University Press, New York, NY, USA.

Rosaldo, M.Z., Lamphere, L., ed. 1974. Woman, culture, and society. Stanford University Press, Stanford, CA, USA.

Rostow, W.W. 1971. Stages of economic growth (2nd ed.). Cambridge University Press, New York, NY, USA.

Routledge, W.S., Routledge, K.. 1910. With a prehistoric people: the Akikuyu of British East Africa. Frank Cass & Co. Ltd, London, UK.

Rubin, G. 1975. The traffic in women: notes on the "political economy" of sex. *In* Reiter, R., ed., Toward an anthropology of women. Monthly Review Press, New York, NY, USA.

Sacks, K. 1979. Sisters and wives: the past and future of sexual inequality. Greenwood Press, Westport, CT, USA.

_____1982. An overview of women and power in Africa. *In* O'Barr, J., ed., Perspectives on power: women in Africa, Asia, and Latin America. Center for International Studies, Duke University, Durham, NC, USA.

Sai, F. 1986. Population and health: Africa's most basic resource and development problem. *In* Berg, R., Whitaker, J.S., ed., Strategies for African development. University of California Press, Berkeley, CA, USA.

Said, E. 1979. Orientalism. Vintage Books, New York, NY, USA.

Sanday, P.R. 1981. Female power and male dominance: on the origins of sexual inequality. Cambridge University Press, Cambridge, UK.

Sandbrook, R. 1985. The politics of Africa's economic stagnation. Cambridge University Press, London, UK.

Saul, J. 1979. The state and revolution in Eastern Africa. William Heinemann, Ltd, London, UK.

Savané, M.-A. 1982. Introduction. *In* Another development with women. Proceedings of a seminar held in Dakar, Senegal, June 1982. Development Dialogue, 1(2), 3–9.

Schlegel, A., ed. 1977. Sexual stratification: a cross-cultural view. Columbia University Press, New York, NY, USA.

Schuster, I. 1981. Perspectives in development: the proplem of nurses and nursing in Zambia. *In* Nelson, N., ed. African women in the development process. Frank Cass & Co. Ltd, London, UK.

Seager, J., Olson, A. 1986. Women in the world: an international atlas. Pan Books Ltd, London, UK.

Seidman, A. 1981. Women and the development of "underdevelopment": the African experience. *In* Dauber, R., Cain, M.L. ed., Women and technological change in developing countries. American Association for the Advancement of Science, Washington, DC, USA. Selected Symposium, 53.

Sender, J., Smith, S. 1986. The development of capitalism in Africa. Methuen & Co. Ltd, London, UK.

Sharma, H. 1973. The green revolution in India: prelude to a red one? *In* Gough, K., Sharma, H., ed., Imperialism and revolution in South Asia. Monthly Review Press, New York, NY, USA.

Shikwe, R.C. 1981. The planning and organization of training for water development in Kenya. *In* Rural water supply in developing countries. Proceedings of a workshop on training held in Zomba, Malawi, 5–12 August 1980. International Development Research Centre, Ottawa, Ont., Canada. IDRC-167e, 110–116.

Shivji, I. 1976. Class struggles in Tanzania. Monthly Review Press, New York, NY, USA.

SID (Society for International Development). 1984. Women: protagonists of change. Development: Seeds of Change, 4, 116 pp.

Sivard, R.L. 1985. Women...a world survey. World Priorities, Washington, DC, USA.

Slocum, S. 1975. Woman the gatherer: male bias in anthropology. *In* Reiter, R., ed. Toward an anthropology of women. Monthly Review Press, New York, NY, USA. pp. 36–50.

Solanas, V. 1968. S.C.U.M. (Society for Cutting Up Men) Manifesto. Olympia Press, New York, NY, USA.

Spender, D. 1980. Man made language. Routledge & Kegan Paul Ltd, London, UK.

Spivak, G.C. 1985. Three women's texts and a critique of imperialism. Critical Inquiry, 12(Autumn), 243–261.

Stamp, P. 1975–1976. Perceptions of change and economic strategy among Kikuyu women of Mitero, Kenya. Rural Africana, 29, 19–44.

_____1981. Governing Thika: dilemmas of municipal politics in Kenya. London University, London, UK. PhD dissertation.

_____1986. Kikuyu women's self help groups: towards an understanding of the relation between sex-gender system and mode of production in Africa. *In* Robertson, C., Berger, I., ed., Women and class in Africa. Holmes & Meier Publishers, Inc., New York, NY, USA.

_____1987. Matega: manipulating women's cooperative traditions for material and social gain in Kenya. Paper presented at the Third International Interdisciplinary Congress on Women, Dublin, Ireland, July 1987.

Stamp, P., Chege, R.N. 1984. Ngwatio: a story of cooperative research on African women. Canadian Woman Studies/les Cahiers de la femme, 6(1), 5–9.

Staudt, K. 1975–1976. Women farmers and inequities in agricultural wervices. Rural Africana, 29, 81–94.

_____1978. Agricultural productivity gaps: a case study in male preference in government policy implementation. Development and Change, 9(3), 439–457.

_____1985a. Women, foreign assistance, and advocacy administration. Praeger Publishers, Inc., New York, NY, USA.

_____1985b. Agricultural policy implementation: a case study from western Kenya. *In* Women's roles and gender differences in development — case study series. Kumarian Press, West Hartford, CT, USA.

Strobel, M. 1982. African women. Signs, 8(1), 109–131.

Subulola, G., Johnson, E.J. 1977. Benin City mothers: their beliefs concerning infant feeding and child care. Tropical and Geographical Medicine, 29(1), 103–108.

Sudaraska, N. 1973. Where women work: a study of Yoruba women in the market place and in the home. Museum of Anthropology, University of Michigan, Ann Arbor, MI, USA. Anthropological Papers, 53.

Swantz, M.-L. 1985. Women in development: a creative role denied? The case of Tanzania. C. Hurst & Co. (Publishers) Ltd, London, UK.

Taylor, J. 1979. From modernization to modes of production: a critique of the sociologies of development and underdevelopment. Macmillan Publishers Ltd, London, UK.

Terray, E. 1972. Marxism and primitive societies. Monthly Review Press, New York, NY, USA.

Thorne, B., Yalom, M., ed. 1982. Rethinking the family: some feminist questions. Longman Group Ltd, New York, NY, USA.

Tilly, L., Scott, J. 1978. Women, work, and family. Holt, Rinehart & Winston, New York, NY, USA.

Tinker, I. 1981. New technologies for food-related activities: an equity strategy. *In* Dauber, R., Cain, M.L., ed. Women and technological change in developing countries. American Association for the Advancement of Science, Washington, DC, USA. Selected Symposium, 53, 51–88.

Tinsley, S. 1985. Foreword. *In* Overholt, C., Anderson, M., Cloud, K., Austin, J., ed., Gender roles in development projects: a case book. Kumarian Press, West Hartford, CT, USA.

UNDP (United Nations Development Programme). 1982. Integration of women in development. UNDP, New York, NY, USA.

UNICEF (United Nations Children Fund). 1980. Appropriate technology for basic services.

Report of an inter-regional workshop held in Nairobi, Kenya, 19–26 March 1980. UNICEF, New York, NY, USA.

Urdang, S. 1979. Fighting two colonialisms: women in Guinea-Bissau. Monthly Review Press, New York, NY, USA.

_____1985. The last transition? Women and development. *In* Saul, J., ed., A difficult road: the transition to socialism in Mozambique. Monthly Review Press, New York, NY, USA.

USDA (United States Department of Agriculture). 1981. Food problems and prospects in sub-Saharan Africa. USDA, Washington, DC, USA.

Van Allen, J. 1972. "Sitting on a man": colonialism and the lost political institutions of Igbo women. Canadian Journal of African Studies, 6(2), 165–182.

_____1976. "Aba riots" or Igbo "women's war"? Ideology, stratification, and the invisibility of women. *In* Hafkin, N., Bay, E., ed., Women in Africa: studies in social and economic change. Stanford University Press, Stanford, CA, USA.

Van Onselen, C. 1976. Chibaro: African mine labour in Southern Rhodesia, 1900–1933. Pluto Press Ltd, London, UK.

Ventura-Dias, V. 1985. Modernisation, production organisation, and rural women in Kenya. *In* Ahmed, I., ed. Technology and rural women: conceptual and empirical issues. George Allen & Unwin (Publishers) Ltd, London, UK. pp. 157–210.

wa Karanja, W. 1981. Women and work: a study of female and male attitudes in the modern sector of an African metropolis. *In* Ware, H., ed., Women, education, and modernization of the family in West Africa. Department of Demography, Australian National University, Canberra, Australia. Changing African Family Project Series, Monograph, 7.

Weedon, C. 1987. Feminist practice and poststructuralist theory. Basil Blackwell, Oxford, UK.

Were, G.S., ed. 1985. Women and development in Africa. Journal of Eastern African Research and Development, 15.

Were, M.K. 1977. Rural women's perceptions and community-based health care. East African Medical Journal, 54(10), 524–530.

Western, D., Dunne, T. 1979. Environmental aspects of settlement site decisions among pastoral Masai. Human Ecology, 7(1), 75–98.

WHES (World Hunger Education Service). 1985. Africa. WHES, Washington, DC, USA. Hunger Notes, 10(7/8).

Whitehead, A. 1985. Effects of technological change on rural women: a review of analyses and concepts. *In* Ahmed, I., ed. Technology and rural women: conceptual and empirical issues. George Allen & Unwin (Publishers) Ltd, London, UK.

Wicker, A.W. 1969. Attitudes versus actions: the relationship of verbal and overt behavioural response to attitude objects. Journal of Social Science, 25(41).

Wilkinson, C. 1987. Women, migration, and work in Lesotho. *In* Momsen, J., Townsend, J., ed., Geography of gender in the Third World. Hutchinson Publishing Group Ltd, London, UK.

Wilson, E.O. 1975. Sociobiology. Harvard University Press, Cambridge, MA, USA.

Wilson, F.R. 1982. Reinventing the past and circumscribing the future: authenticity and the negative image of women's work in Zaire. *In* Bay, E., ed., Women and work in Africa. Westview Press, Boulder, CO, USA.

Wily, L. 1981. Women and development: a case study of ten Tanzanian villages. Regional Commissioner's Office, Arusha, Tanzania.

WIN (Women in Nigeria). 1985a. The WIN document: conditions of women in Nigeria and policy recommendations to 2000 AD. Samaru, Zaria, Nigeria.

_____1985b. Women in Nigeria today. Proceedings of the First Seminar on Women in Nigeria, Ahmadu Bellow University, Zaria, Nigeria, 1982. Zed Press Ltd, London, UK.

Wipper, A. 1975. The Maendelao ya Wanawake organization: the co-optation of leadership. African Studies Review, 18(3), 99–120.

_____1982. Riot and rebellion among African women: three examples of women's political clout. In O'Barr, J., ed., Perspectives on power: women in Africa, Asia, and Latin America. Center for International Studies, Duke University, Durham, NC, USA.

_____1984. Women's voluntary associations. In Hay, M.J., Stichter, S., ed., African women south of the Sahara. Longman Group Ltd, London, UK.

Wisner, B. 1982. Mwea Irrigation Scheme, Kenya: a success story for whom? Anthropological Research Council, Boston, MA, USA. Newsletter.

Wollstonecraft, M. 1792. A vindication of the rights of women. Penguin Books Ltd, Harmondsworth, Middlesex, UK (1975 edition)

Wood, E.M. 1986. The retreat from class: a new "true" socialism. Verso Editions, London, UK.

Youssef, N., Hetler, C. 1983. Establishing the economic condition of woman-headed households in the Third World: a new approach. In Buvinic, M., Lycette, M., McGreevey, W., ed., Women and poverty in the Third World. Johns Hopkins University Press, Baltimore, MD, USA.

ZARD (Zambia Association for Research and Development). 1985. Women's rights in Zambia. Proceedings of the Second National Women's Rights Conference held at Mindolo Ecumenical Foundation, Kitwe, Zambia, 22–24 March 1985. ZARD, Lusaka, Zambia.

_____1986. Rural women and agricultural production in Zambia: the importance of research on development issues. Canadian Woman Studies/les Cahiers de la femme, 7 (1/2), 78–84.

Acronyms and Abbreviations

AAWORD	Association of African Women for Research and Development
AIDS	acquired immune deficiency syndrome
ATRCW	African Training and Research Centre for Women
BHSS	Nigerian Basic Health Services Scheme
CAAS	Canadian Association of African Studies
CCIC	Canadian Council for International Cooperation
CDPA	Centre for Development and Population Activities
CDR	Centre for Development Research (Denmark)
CIDA	Canadian International Development Agency
CWS/cf	Canadian Woman Studies/les Cahiers de la femme
DANIDA	Danish International Development Agency
DAWN group	Development Alternatives with Women for a New Era
DHF	Dag Hammarskjöld Foundation
ECA	Economic Commission for Africa
FAO	Food and Agriculture Organization of the United Nations
HUP	household unit of production
IBRD	International Bank for Reconstruction and Development (World Bank)
IDRC	International Development Research Centre
IDWSSD	International Drinking Water Supply and Sanitation Decade
IFAA	Institute for African Alternatives
IFAD	International Fund for Agricultural Development
ILO	International Labour Organisation
IMF	International Monetary Fund
INSTRAW	International Research and Training Institute for the Advancement of Women

KAP	knowledge, attitude, and practice (a survey methodology)
KES	Kenyan shilling
KRP	Kano River Irrigation Project
NGO	nongovernmental organization
OAU	Organization of African Unity
RCCDC	Research Centre for Cooperation with Developing Countries (Yugoslavia)
RFR/DRF	Resources for Feminist Research/Documentation sur la recherche féministe
ROAPE	Review of African Political Economy
SEEDS	Sarvodaya Economic Enterprises Development Services
SID	Society for International Development
SIDA	Swedish International Development Agency
SLL	Sierra Leone leone
UN	United Nations
UNDP	United Nations Development Programme
Unesco	United Nations Educational, Scientific and Cultural Organisation
UNFPA	United Nations Fund for Population Activities
UNICEF	United Nations Children's Fund
UNIFEM	United Nations Development Fund for Women
UNITAR	United Nations Institute for Training and Research
USAID	United States Agency for International Development
USD	United States dollar
USDA	United States Department of Agriculture
WAG	Women's Action Group (Zimbabwe)
WHES	World Hunger Education Service
WHO	World Health Organization
WID	women in development
WIN	Women in Nigeria
WRDP	Women's Research and Documentation Project (Tanzania)
YWCA	World Alliance of Young Women's Christian Associations
ZARD	Zambia Association for Research and Development

Subject and Author Index

179

Geertz, C.   132, 133
gender, invisibility of   26 ff.
gender relations   2, 4, 5, 10–26, 29, 31,
    36, 37, 40, 46, 49–52, 63–65, 67–69,
    74 ff., 88, 94, 103, 114, 117–121, 129,
    133, 136–138, 150, 157
George, S.   9, 62
Getechah, W.   30, 152, 153
Ghai, Y.P.   39, 81
Glazier, J.   81, 103, 121
Gordon, J.   33, 34
Gramsci, A.   21
Gulliver, P.H.   127, 157
Gumede, M.V.   30
Guyer, J.I.   26, 27, 38, 103, 104, 116

– H –

Hafkin, N.   11
Hanger, J.   64
Hanna, W.   12
Hartmann, H.   17
Hausa   31, 32, 67–70, 78, 83, 101, 104,
    114
Hay, M.J.   49
health   ix, 2, 3, 5, 8, 27, 30 ff., 42, 47,
    51, 56–58, 63, 66, 71, 73, 94–99,
    103–107, 119, 120, 128, 131, 136–138,
    143, 150–155
Henn, J.K.   29, 48, 54
Hetler, C.   118
Hobley, C.W.   78
hoe   23, 28, 75, 76, 82, 108
Hoskyns, M.   57–59
household   19, 20, 27, 55–70, 77, 80–88,
    91, 94, 99–102, 116–120, 125, 136, 137,
    144
Howard, R.   103
Hussain, A.   21
Hyden, G.   27, 50

– I –

Ibo   77, 116, 134
Igun, U.A.   33
income generation   42, 50, 61–62, 113
indigenous technology   107–108
inheritance   87, 89, 90, 117, 118, 136,
    137
Institute for African Alternatives (IFAA)
    28
International Bank for Reconstruction and
    Development (IBRD) (see also World
    Bank)   8, 27, 28, 61, 147, 152, 153

International Development Research
    Centre (IDRC)   vii, ix, x, 6, 9, 25, 26,
    29, 30, 154
International Drinking Water Supply and
    Sanitation Decade (IDWSSD)   142,
    143
International Fund for Agricultural
    Development (IFAD)   8
International Labour Organisation (ILO)
    8, 25, 39, 40, 46, 48, 57, 60, 63, 72, 88,
    119, 140
International Monetary Fund (IMF)   8, 9,
    27, 29
International Research and Training
    Institute for the Advancement of Women
    (INSTRAW)   8, 48, 119, 142, 143, 154
inventory   29, 134, 140–146
irrigation   64–69
Isely, R.   38
Isis International   9, 42, 43
Islam   5, 67, 69, 101, 104

– J –

Jackson, C.   67–70, 72, 101, 114, 119
Jaggar, A.   14, 15, 17, 18, 22, 113
Janelid, I.   59
Johnson, E.J.   106
Joshi, R.   77

– K –

Kalb, M.   47, 49
Kano River Irrigation Project (KRP)
    67 ff., 78, 83, 101, 104, 119
Kaplinsky, R.   12, 112
Katz, S.   x, 12, 121, 150
Kazembe, J.   23
Keller, E.F.   126
Kenya   4, 5, 9, 15, 25, 29, 30, 33, 41, 46,
    55–58, 61–66, 69–71, 73–75, 79, 81, 85,
    88, 89, 103, 105, 128, 134, 141, 142,
    152, 157
Kenyatta, J.   78, 82
Kershaw, G.   78
Kertzer, D.   79
Kettel, B.   75, 97, 128
Keyi, V.   x, 73
Kikuyu   64, 65, 73 ff., 90, 101, 102, 108,
    135, 153
Kimati, V.   34, 124
King, K.   27, 56
kinship   19, 22, 75, 77, 79, 80, 82, 136,
    149

About the Institution

The International Development Research Centre (IDRC) is a public corporation created by the Parliament of Canada in 1970 to support technical and policy research to help meet the needs of developing countries. The Centre is active in the fields of environment and natural resources, social sciences, health sciences, and information sciences and systems. Regional offices are located in Africa, Asia, Latin America, and the Middle East.

About the Publisher

IDRC Books publishes research results and scholarly studies on global and regional issues related to sustainable and equitable development. As a specialist in development literature, IDRC Books contributes to the body of knowledge on these issues to further the cause of global understanding and equity. IDRC publications are sold through its head office in Ottawa, Canada, as well as by IDRC's agents and distributors around the world.